Case Studies in Community Policing

Dennis J. Stevens
University of Massachusetts-Boston

Prentice
Hall

Upper Saddle River, New Jersey 07458

Library of Congress Cataloging-in-Publication Data

Stevens, Dennis J.
   Case studies in community policing / Dennis J. Stevens.
      p. cm.
   Includes bibliographical references and index.
   ISBN 0-13-087174-5
      1. Community policing—United States—Case studies.   I. Title.

HV7936.C83 S738 2001
363.2′3—dc21
                                                                    00-061976

Publisher: *Dave Garza*
Senior Acquisitions Editor: *Kim Davies*
Production Editor: *Lori Dalberg, Carlisle Publishers Services*
Production Liaison: *Barbara Marttine Cappuccio*
Director of Manufacturing & Production: *Bruce Johnson*
Managing Editor: *Mary Carnis*
Manufacturing Buyer: *Cathleen Petersen*
Art Director: *Marianne Frasco*
Cover Design Coordinator: *Miguel Ortiz*
Cover Designer: *Joe Sengotta*
Cover Image: *AP/Wide World Photos*
Marketing Manager: *Chris Ruel*
Editorial Assistant: *Sarah Holle*
Interior Design and Composition: *Carlisle Communications, Ltd.*
Printing and Binding: *R. R. Donnelley & Sons*

Prentice-Hall International (UK) Limited, *London*
Prentice-Hall of Australia Pty. Limited, *Sydney*
Prentice-Hall of Canada Inc., *Toronto*
Prentice-Hall Hispanoamericana, S.A., *Mexico*
Prentice-Hall of India Private Limited, *New Delhi*
Prentice-Hall of Japan, Inc., *Tokyo*
Prentice-Hall Singapore Pte. Ltd.
Editora Prentice-Hall do Brasil, Ltda., *Rio de Janeiro*

10 9 8 7 6 5 4 3 2 1
ISBN 0-13-087174-5

DEDICATED

To My Children Who Inspire My Success
David D. Stevens
Mark A. Stevens
Alyssa P. Stevens

CONTENTS

FOREWORD   xiii

ACKNOWLEDGMENTS   xv

ABOUT THE AUTHOR   xv

CHAPTER ONE: Case Studies in Community Policing:
Failures and Successful Strategies   1

INTRODUCTION   1

CHAPTER OUTLINE   2

AIMS AND ISSUES EMPHASIZED   2

OBSTACLES   3

LIMITATIONS   5

AGENCIES REPRESENTED   6

DATA COLLECTION   6

COMMUNITY POLICING DEFINED   7

COMMUNITY POLICING RATIONALE AND PHILOSOPHY   8

MOTIVATORS LEADING TO COMMUNITY POLICING COMMITMENTS   9

COMMUNITY POLICING PERSPECTIVES   12

OBJECTIVES OF COMMUNITY POLICING   15

PROBLEMS OF COMMUNITY POLICING   16

TEXT FORMAT   17

EXPECTATIONS   17

DO YOU KNOW?   17

RECOMMENDED READING   18

WEB SITES   19

APPENDIX 1 POLICE AGENCIES IN STUDY   20

APPENDIX 2 AGENCY CONTRIBUTORS   20

APPENDIX 3 DATA COLLECTION   21

APPENDIX 4 JURISDICTION DEMOGRAPHICS   23

APPENDIX 5 GETTING COMMITMENTS   24

CHAPTER TWO: Broken Arrow Police Department,
Broken Arrow, Oklahoma   26

INTRODUCTION   26

CHAPTER OUTLINE   27

PART 1: COMMUNITY POLICING RATIONALE   27

PROVIDING LEADERSHIP   27

EVENTS THAT LED TO COMMUNITY POLICING COMMITMENTS   29

COMMUNITY-BASED PROGRAMS   31

RESHAPING THE PROGRAMS   32

THE PLAN   33

THE SCHEDULE   34

RESISTANCE TO CHANGE   35

SOLIDIFICATION OF THE COMMITMENT   36

PART 2: HOW THE CITY GOT ITS NAME   36

THE DEPARTMENT   37

BROKEN ARROW POLICE PROGRAMS   37

CRIME STATISTICS   39

1998 CITIZEN SURVEY SUMMARY   39

NINE HARD QUESTIONS ANSWERED ABOUT COMMUNITY
    POLICING INITIATIVES   45

MAKING THE PHILOSOPHY WORK   53

COMMENTS MADE BY BROKEN ARROW POLICE OFFICERS   56

COMMUNITY MEMBERS WRITE ABOUT BAPD'S COMMUNITY POLICING   57

SUMMARY   59

CONCLUSION   59

DO YOU KNOW?   59

CHAPTER THREE: Metropolitan-Nashville Police Department, Nashville, Tennessee   61

INTRODUCTION   61

CHAPTER OUTLINE   62

CRIME RATES AND EXPERIENCES   62

DEPARTMENTAL OBJECTIVES   63

SIGNIFICANCE OF THE PROJECT   64

THE PLAN   64

DEFINITION OF TERMS   65

COMMUNITY POLICING GUIDE   66

PHILOSOPHY   66

"WHO ARE YOU GOING TO CALL?"   67

COMMUNITY SUPPORT   67

COMMUNITY MEETINGS   68

COMMUNICATION   69

STREET OFFICERS IMPLEMENTING COMMUNITY POLICING INITIATIVES   70

SIMPLE STEPS FOR BUILDING RELATIONSHIPS   70

COMMUNITY MEMBER OFFICER EXPECTATIONS   72

IDENTIFYING AND UTILIZING RESOURCES   73

MANAGING ENVIRONMENTAL ISSUES   74

PROACTIVE STRATEGIES WITH JUVENILES   78

PROACTIVE ENFORCEMENT STRATEGIES   82

SUCCESS STORIES   87

SUMMARY   88

CONCLUSION   88

DO YOU KNOW?   89

CHAPTER FOUR: Columbus Division of Police, Columbus, Ohio   91

INTRODUCTION   91

CHAPTER OUTLINE   92

OBSTACLES ENCOUNTERED BY THE CDP   92

OVERVIEW OF CHANGE   94

STRATEGIC RESPONSE BUREAU   97

MAPPSTAT CRIME STRATEGY MEETINGS   103

NINE HARD QUESTIONS ANSWERED ABOUT COMMUNITY
  POLICING INITIATIVES   105

TRAINING ISSUES FOR COMMUNITY-ORIENTED POLICING/
  PROBLEM-ORIENTED POLICING   107

AN EVALUATION OF CDP'S COP/POP EFFORTS   110

SURVEY CONCLUSION   114

SUMMARY   114

CONCLUSION   115

DO YOU KNOW?   115

REFERENCES   116

APPENDIX 1: ORGANIZATIONAL STRUCTURE   116

APPENDIX 2: PROGRAM HIGHLIGHTS OF THE CDP   118

APPENDIX 3: UNIFORM CRIME INDEX OFFENSES, NINE-YEAR COMPARISON   119

APPENDIX 4: CRIME REPORTS 1999–2000   120

CHAPTER FIVE: Lansing Police Department, Lansing, Michigan   121

INTRODUCTION   121

CHAPTER OUTLINE   121

COMMUNITY POLICING OBSERVATIONS AND DEPARTMENTAL INFLUENCES   122

COMMUNITY SERVICES   124

NORTH PRECINCT   125

SOUTH PRECINCT   127

EIGHT HARD QUESTIONS ANSWERED ABOUT COMMUNITY
  POLICING INITIATIVES   129

A COMMUNITY OFFICER'S ACTIVITIES   131

COMMUNITY POLICING TRAINING   132

COMMUNITY POLICING STRATEGIES   132

A COMMUNITY PRESIDENT ADDRESSES COMMUNITY POLICING   140

COLLABORATION WITH LANSING PAROLE OFFICERS   141

CITIZEN SURVEY   142

SUMMARY   144

CONCLUSION   144

DO YOU KNOW?   145

APPENDIX 1: LANSING FIVE-YEAR ARREST RECORD   146

CHAPTER SIX: Harris County Precinct 4 Constable's Office
Harris County, Texas   147

CHAPTER OUTLINE   147

FUNCTIONS OF A CONSTABLE   147

DEMOGRAPHICS OF PRECINCT 4   148

MISSION STATEMENT   148

EVENTS LEADING TO COMMUNITY POLICING   149

PROGRAM RATIONALE   149

PRECINCT 4 PROGRAMS   150

HISTORY OF PRECINCT 4'S HIRING-OUT PRACTICES   151

CONTRACT DEPUTY PROGRAM   152

TEXAS LAW ENFORCEMENT   154

PROFILE OF THE PRECINCT   155

RESPONSES TO CRIME   155

PRECINCT UNITS   156

CONSTABLE DICK MOORE— "A LIFETIME IN PUBLIC SERVICE"   158

DEPUTY CHIEF RON HICKMAN   160

TRAINING AND HOW IT RELATES TO COMMUNITY POLICING   160

ASSESSMENT OF PROGRAMS   161

SUMMARY   164

CONCLUSION   164

DO YOU KNOW?   165

CHAPTER SEVEN: Sacramento Police Department,
Sacramento, California   166

    INTRODUCTION   166

    CHAPTER OUTLINE   167

    PROFILE OF THE DEPARTMENT   167

    COMMUNITY POLICING   171

    THE COMMITMENT TO PARTNERSHIPS   177

    CRIME RATES   178

    SUMMARY   179

    CONCLUSION   179

    DO YOU KNOW?   181

CHAPTER EIGHT: Fayetteville Police Department,
Fayetteville, North Carolina   182

    INTRODUCTION   182

    CHAPTER OUTLINE   183

    DEPARTMENT PROFILE   183

    DESCRIPTION   184

    BRIEF HISTORY OF THE COMMUNITY POLICING EFFORTS   184

    PROGRAMS   188

    THE CHIEF   193

    DEPARTMENT ATTORNEY   196

    TRAINING   197

    CRIME STATISTICS   198

    A FEW QUESTIONS ANSWERED ABOUT COMMUNITY
       POLICING INITIATIVES   198

    A FORMER OFFICER TALKS ABOUT FPD   200

    SUMMARY   202

    CONCLUSION   202

    DO YOU KNOW?   203

CHAPTER NINE: St. Petersburg Police Department,
St. Petersburg, Florida   204

    INTRODUCTION   204

    CHAPTER OUTLINE   204

    REPORTS   205

    THE PRESS   205

    BLOCK ORGANIZING   207

    COMMUNITY POLICING HISTORY   207

    SHIFTS TO PROBLEM-ORIENTED POLICING   210

    NATIONAL RECOGNITION   210

    WHAT WENT WRONG?   211

    LESSONS LEARNED   211

    INITIAL POLICE AND COMMUNITY RETREAT   213

    REORGANIZATION   214

    COMMUNITY OVERSIGHT   215

    PARTNERSHIPS   216

    EVALUATION   217

    FOLLOW-UP RETREAT II   217

    COMMUNITY POLICING TODAY   218

    INITIATIVES   219

    DECENTRALIZATION   220

    COMMUNITY INVOLVEMENT   220

    TRAINING   221

    FUNDING   223

    SUMMARY   225

    CONCLUSION   225

    DO YOU KNOW?   226

    REFERENCES   227

CHAPTER TEN: Camden Police Department, Camden, New Jersey   228

INTRODUCTION   228

CHAPTER OUTLINE   229

THE PROBLEM   229

HISTORY AND DEMOGRAPHICS   230

DEPARTMENT PROFILE   231

COMMUNITY POLICING   232

COMMUNITY POLICING IN THE YEAR 2000   240

PROBLEM-ORIENTED POLICING AND PARTNERSHIPS: THE CAMDEN PLAN   240

COMMENTS FROM CAMDEN COMMANDERS AND OFFICERS   245

SUMMARY   249

CONCLUSION   249

DO YOU KNOW?   250

CHAPTER ELEVEN: Conclusion   252

CHAPTER OUTLINE   252

NEGLECTED AREAS OF COMMUNITY POLICING   252

IMPRESSIONS   253

DOES COMMUNITY POLICING EXIST?   253

POLICE THEORY   255

AN OPERATIONAL DEFINITION: NINE EXPERIENCES   257

GENERAL OBSERVATIONS   268

IN CLOSING   271

DO YOU KNOW?   271

REFERENCES   273

INDEX   277

FOREWORD

In the mid-1970s my late colleague, Robert Trojanowicz, worked with the Flint (Michigan) Police Department to experiment with a new method of deploying police officers by having them perform their responsibilities in a manner emphasizing service and customer orientation. He felt that officers should, first, "get the predators off the street" and, second, eliminate disorder in the neighborhoods. With funding from the Mott Foundation, Bob tested this concept, which was initially called Neighborhood Foot Patrol and later community policing. At the same time, Herman Goldstein was building on his idea of problem solving to emphasize that officer behavior should be proactive, rather than reactive. Such an approach, Professor Goldstein argued, would not simply have temporary preventive effects nor would it just displace crime. Rather, it would substantively alter the environment in the community which contributed to criminality, thus having long-term preventive effects.

It was becoming increasingly clear: Policing was on the verge of a significant paradigm shift. There was an intuitive understanding of the need to change both the operational and management styles of the police service. The private sector was increasingly adopting the principles of total quality management (TQM), which had important tenets of being customer driven, emphasizing quality of work, and performing responsibilities in a manner that prevented future problems. These elements resonated well with the principles of community policing, thus the informal conceptual merger of management philosophy (total quality management) and police operations (community policing).

During the ensuing years experimentation with community policing models emerged. Conceptually, many police agencies had difficulty with the concept because it was philosophical, rather than programmatic. As such, there was no "recipe" for its implementation, but the need to develop a creative plan for deployment and operational strategies to accomplish goals that were community specific. Some agencies could not resolve operational and philosophical conflicts in making this change, thus essentially abandoning the idea. Others forged on, doggedly experimenting with service delivery methods and trying to change their organizations. With support from professional police organizations—such as the Police Executive Research Forum, International Association of Chiefs of Police, National Organization for Black Law Enforcement Executives, and National Sheriffs' Association—and research funded by the National Institute of Justice, the vision of community policing was gaining increased clarity. With the creation of the Office of Community Oriented Policing Services (COPS), there were new incentives—employment funds and cost-free training opportunities—for police agencies to adopt the community policing philosophy. The momentum was pushing the concept forward.

Changes continue with new iterations of community policing emerging. The use of crime analysis, applications of crime mapping, and new accountability initiatives such as the COMPSTAT (COMPuterized STATistics) program in New York and MAP (Management Accountability Program) in San Antonio are focusing police resources with greater specificity to not only solve problems but also ensure the efficacious use of police personnel and the wise expenditure of funds. The adoption of technologies for police records' management systems and the use of Internet web pages to better connect the police and community serve as further illustrations that the community policing concept embraces change if it will help facilitate the accomplishment of goals.

Throughout these developments, it is important to document the experiences of what works—and what doesn't—in order to continually refine the philosophy and practice of community policing. This book is an important contribution in this regard. Examining agencies of various sizes and looking at their programs and experiences serves as a laboratory from which others may learn. Practitioners can extract policy issues that may serve them while the academic and research communities can identify important issues for which empirical assessment is needed.

Dennis J. Stevens has put together an eclectic group of agencies differing in size, type of jurisdiction, and approaches to implementation. As such, *Case Studies in Community Policing* provides important insights for ongoing development and a glimpse inside the debates and challenges that lie ahead.

David L. Carter, Director
National Center for Community Policing
Michigan State University
East Lansing, Michigan

ACKNOWLEDGMENTS

There are always numerous individuals who deserve acknowledgment when work of this variety is conducted. Those individuals include each of the contributors to this work: Broken Arrow Police Chief Carolyn M. Kusler, Camden Police Captain Charles J. Kocher, Columbus Division of Police Commander Kent Shafer, Fayetteville Chief of Police Ron Hansen, Harris County Precinct 4 Assistant Chief of Police Ron Hickman, Lansing Police Department Chief Mark Alley, Metropolitan-Nashville Police Department Lt. Ben Dickie, Sacramento Police Department Captain Steve Segura, and St. Petersburg Police Department Sargent Gary Dukema. Special acknowledgment goes to Fayetteville Police Attorney Carl Milazzo who spent extra time in reviewing much of this work. I also thank reviewer Will Oliver, Department of Criminal Justice, Radford University and David L. Carter, Carl B. Klockars, Herman Goldstein, Frank Schmalleger and Lawrence W. Sherman for their personal insights.

ABOUT THE AUTHOR

Dennis J. Stevens holds a Ph.D. from Loyola University of Chicago. He is currently an associate professor in the College of Public and Community Service at the University of Massachusetts in Boston. In addition to teaching traditional students in the university classroom, he has taught and counseled law enforcement officers at police academies such as the North Carolina Justice Academy and felons at maximum custody penitentiaries such as Attica in New York, Eastern Corrections and Women's Prison in North Carolina, Stateville and Joliet near Chicago, and CCI in Columbia. On behalf of Boston University, he currently works at MCI Framingham for Women and Bay State, and Norfolk Corrections.

CHAPTER ONE

CASE STUDIES IN COMMUNITY POLICING: FAILURES AND SUCCESSFUL STRATEGIES

INTRODUCTION

This book examines the ongoing experiences of nine diverse police agencies as they develop, implement, and maintain a community policing approach to public safety. It is a collection of policing failures and success stories, strategies, and recommendations from the agencies and their personnel who are on the front lines of policing (see Appendixes 1 and 2). Two goals of this book are to help the experienced practitioner form an operational definition of community policing initiatives and to provide a method to measure a professional policing approach that addresses organizational strategies intended to reduce the fear of crime and social disorder through collaborative problem-solving partnerships.[1]

It is also hoped that this work will help bridge the primary social constructs of community policing strategies for concerned students who may be curious as to how a revitalization of the policing enterprise fits into the new millennium. This work validates its claims through various, diverse police agency accounts that also helped guide this work. It can be viewed as a "how-to" manual validating how community policing initiatives were experienced as a collaboration between police agencies and community members with the intention of enhancing the quality of life and promoting public safety through those partnerships. However, the concept referred to as *community policing* has resulted in many idealized versions but few accounts of automatic success. In fact, of the nine agencies studied, most of them failed at both their earlier and recent

---

[1]In 1999, nearly 41 percent of American police agencies serving populations of 50,000 or more were employing a community policing agenda. Another 19 percent planned on developing community policing policies within the year (Carter & Radelet, 1999).

attempts to implement what they thought were solid police strategies guided by idealized versions of community policing prerogatives that allegedly worked in other departments.

CHAPTER OUTLINE

This chapter offers a brief introduction to community policing along with a description of aims and issues and a discussion of obstacles to community policing initiatives. Community policing limitations and how this text can help overcome those limitations are discussed. A generic definition of community policing is provided along with a general rationale and philosophy. This chapter highlights some of the motivators, perspectives, and objectives that have shaped other strategies used by other agencies. Differences between community policing and problem-oriented strategies are reviewed along with a brief discussion about SARA. The nine law enforcement agencies studied are identified, as are common problems experienced by other agencies in pursuit of community policing strategies. The chapter indicates how *Case Studies in Community Policing* can address those problems. One of the primary points that emerges within these pages is that community policing is not a pipe dream.

AIMS AND ISSUES EMPHASIZED

One aim of this work is to develop an operationalized definition of community policing by examining the experiences of police agencies and permitting rationale or theory, if you will, to flow from those experiences as opposed to the other way around. This thought is in agreement with Chief Dennis Nowicki of the Charlotte, North Carolina Police Department (1998), Professor David Bayley (1998), and my own research (Stevens, 1999b, 1999c), which shows experience to be the centerpiece of quality policing and community police initiatives.

However, an equally important perspective to be shared is that, contrary to some observations, a police agency does not operate in a world of its own. Many influences are brought to bear on police service and on implementation efforts of new strategies. Often, those influences can have a greater impact on the final outcome of a police effort than all the plans, pain, and/or perseverance of the most virtuous of police professionals, as will become evident in the chapters ahead.

For the most part, four issues are emphasized in this work:

1. Both past and present events that led an agency to community policing initiatives. This issue is consistent with priorities outlined by the Police Executive Research Forum's (PERF, 1996) evaluation of police agencies.
2. The policies, officer responses, and reactions of community and civic leaders shaping community policing implementation initiatives that led to the success and/or the failure of police strategies.
3. An understanding of those elements and conditions that support the active involvement of residents in community policing prerogatives whose focus is on proactive police service through implementation of

problem-solving strategies. This thought is consistent with researchers who see community issues as the core of community policing endeavors. Both of these latter issues are also concerns of writers who ask if the public acclamations of community policing by police officials are more rhetoric than reality.[2]

4. Concerns related to community policing assessment and methods of change.

OBSTACLES

Although perspectives about community policing vary widely, one point that all of the practitioners who guided this work agreed on is that there are always obstacles originating inside and outside of the department that need to be overcome when developing, implementing, maintaining, and evaluating police services. Obstacles occurring inside an agency can include officer resistance and police management objection to a facilitative role for policing, and obstacles outside an agency might include political intervention and suspect agendas held by community members.

In keeping with these thoughts, a set of 10 questions was developed to help guide the investigation of the 9 agencies (see Appendix 3). That is, three questions solicited responses about community recruitment and decision making, three questions related to community policing assessment, and one question each asked about funding alternatives, officer training, events leading to community policing commitments, and changes in the organizational structure of the department.

Other hurdles relate to the gathering of appropriate and applicable information to structure a community policing strategy. Because police agencies are largely as different from each other as are the communities they serve, every strategy reflects those differences. Also, despite the fact that there is a host of information available from a huge selection of sources, deciding which one is more appropriate in itself creates its own set of problems as experienced in this study by the police departments in St. Petersburg, Florida, and Columbus, Ohio.

Second, traditional measurements of officer productivity through stops, calls, response time, officer complaints, and arrests are inadequate when measuring community policing advances. However, to get a sense of the agencies studied, their jurisdiction demographics are reported in Appendix 4. Community policing efforts are hard pressed to be found among incident-driven data such as arrest rates. Nonetheless, patrol officers, policy makers, and community members might seek undeveloped or unrealistic outcomes to appease

---

[2]For a brief description see Cardarelli, McDevitt, and Baum (1998). For an in-depth study of the Chicago PD and its community policing progress, see Skogan et al., (1999). These writers reported on how community policing really works on the streets of Chicago and their book describes the five-step problem-solving model that the city developed for tackling neighborhood problems that ranged from graffiti to gang violence.

themselves or their mentors that their philosophy is or is not working, depending on which side of the political triangle they reside. A police agency must adopt a realistic method of evaluating community policing initiatives.

Third, one reason police managers become concerned about community policing productivity is because this strategy mandates a vesting of decision-making prerogatives among line officers and their supervisors (and community members) in order to expedite the problem-solving initiatives at the community level. This simple element in effect changes the lines of organizational command by changing authority from a top-down hierarchical command to across an agency. Some individuals might refer to this process as empowerment, which is also a product of decentralization. Often, this strategy sets precedents in an agency and could expose those top officers to the threat of litigation. Consequently, some managers might feel uncomfortable and other officers might resent this new organizational structure for a host of reasons including the provision to younger, less experienced officers of certain decision-making prerogatives. However, a police agency should consider adapting a democratic organizational style of management if community policing strategies are to be effectively implemented and maintained. Skogan and Hartnett (1997) say it this way: Community policing "relies upon organizational decentralization and a reorientation of patrol to facilitate the two-way communication between police and the public" (p. 5).

Fourth, the intentions of many agencies might be highly subject to controversy because their organizational motives in developing and implementing community policing strategies often relate more to opportunities for the agency as opposed to opportunities for the community. The mission of community policing is to control crime including the fear of crime through a partnership with the community and the various institutions of the community. Some of those institutions can include its corporate and retail members, and human resources such as schools, social services, and churches. The police cannot control crime themselves, nor should they. However, there is often more rhetoric than reality among community policing agendas because there are few collaborative partnerships at work and those that are might not embrace community recruitment and tactics such as citizen discipline boards to encourage community decision-making input into police strategy. Community members are, like line officers, in a decision-making role and, therefore, within limitations are also empowered within the partnership.

However, simply because an agency falls short of some idealistic theoretical component of community policing does not mean that community policing is pure rhetoric. It could mean that the tools to measure community policing were inappropriate or that researchers were measuring something different than what they thought was measured.

Insofar as community policing shapes discretion of rank-and-file officers, the themes that a department emphasizes can determine how officers spend their time and with whom (Parks, Mastrofski, Dejong , & Gray, 1999). Yet, this shaping of rank-and-file discretion might have a downside. That is, adapting of community policing practices could lead to an increase in lawsuits through the following three avenues: the resuscitation of state tort actions and negligence claims; through Title 42 of the United States Code, Section 1983 suits as the threshold of the "color of law" becomes clouded (Stevens, 2000); and through ambiguities in the notion of "legal duty" (Worrall & Marenin, 1998).

LIMITATIONS

Initially, two issues require attention: First, community policing is a contemporary policing concept believed by some to be a modern cure-all that can solve all of the problems a police department encounters. Unwisely, it is sometimes seen as the "best" strategy to the exclusion of others. But it has yet to be reliably supported that community policing initiatives are advantageous for all communities and/or can be implemented and operated by all police agencies. Community policing is a different strategy depending on a number of variables. Some of those variables include why it was developed, where it was developed, resources of the agency, community resources, and responses of the community. Some writers take this thought further and suggest that police rank-and-file leadership, even under the same command, can account for a variation in community policing outcomes (Skogan et al., 1999). For example, in Chicago, beat team sergeants answering to the same lieutenant seemed to have a greater impact on community policing performance in their patrol areas than their supervisor (Skogan et al., 1999). What's more, a reality that should be understood by every community policing planner is that every police agency has its own unique features, due in part to its history, location, tax base, officer demographics, prior experiences and memories of agency and community members, police management and policy makers, and intervention experiences by other private and public institutions in the jurisdiction. Therefore, it is unlikely that any single model of community policing or policing strategy—no matter how eloquent the model—can be promoted as "best" for every agency. If we accept this idea, then it follows that we should also realize that some agencies are unsuited for community policing prerogatives. One analogy might be that of trying to push a Buick through the eye of a needle.

Second, while there are few precise case studies of community policing for both the typical practitioner and the college student, many texts on community policing are largely academic in their orientation. Although these academic texts may represent an excellent resource, they focus on generic theoretical perspectives as compared to the daily experiences of individual agencies. Conversely, the few texts produced by practitioners, although excellent resources, are more likely to utilize mega-metropolises such as Chicago, New York, and Los Angeles as models. Those huge agencies possess diverse resources, populations, and conditions that are unique only to those individual cities. Therefore, it can be argued that their community policing strategies are not typical of the 18,000 other agencies in the United States. Nonetheless, huge agencies, while excellent role models, are collectively less similar to other agencies than similar.

One aim of this book is to report on how community policing experiences are doing in nine medium-sized police agencies (100 to 2,000 officers) without all of the academic icons or police imagery usually associated with most works on the subject. Consistent with these thoughts, the U.S. Department of Justice argues that "to date, no succinct overview of community policing exists for practitioners who want to learn to use this wide-ranging approach to address the problems of crime and disorder in their communities" (Bureau of Justice Assistance [BJA], 1994).

AGENCIES REPRESENTED

The agencies represented in this book were selected based on their jurisdictional populations, their self-described agency-wide participation in community policing, their variation of community policing strategies, and their geographically diverse jurisdictions. These law enforcement communities are represented:

- Broken Arrow, Oklahoma
- Camden, New Jersey
- Columbus, Ohio
- Fayetteville, North Carolina
- Harris County Precinct 4 Constable's Office, Spring, Texas
- Lansing, Michigan
- Nashville, Tennessee
- Sacramento, California
- St. Petersburg, Florida

DATA COLLECTION

Data for this study were collected during the winter of 1999 and the spring of 2000. The principal researcher (Dennis J. Stevens) established contact with various departments that demonstrated an interest in pursuing this project (see Appendix 5, Getting Commitments). A sworn officer involved with community policing prerogatives was assigned as a liaison from each department to help gather information. Of course, other resources were utilized such as media (newspaper/magazine) accounts, personal visits and observations, web sites, and colleagues in other agencies and at other universities. Chat rooms were visited by the writer and when information could be documented, it was used in the context of this work. Nonetheless, each chapter was developed largely through collaboration with specific individuals in each agency.

The principal researcher constructed the introductory chapter (Chapter 1), the conclusion chapter (Chapter 11), and a brief conclusion at the end of each chapter. The researcher is the only individual responsible for the content of this text. The information provided in the case studies that follow was deemed accurate up to the completion of the data collection period. Many conditions in these organizations are likely to have changed since the data were originally collected. No effort has been made to make the cases unconditionally current, a status that can be achieved once but never maintained due to the limitations of publication. These inherent limitations are an important part of understanding this work and their contributions to policing.

Moreover, the researcher recognizes that many influences shape community policing prerogatives and quality police service, some of which are beyond the scope of this work. Therefore, this work is not intended to be a final or last word on the subject. That is, this work should be considered a working study toward a discovery of links between police service and community policing initiatives.

COMMUNITY POLICING DEFINED

The "broken windows" theory of crime describes urban deterioration as fostering an environment conducive to criminal behavior. This perspective provided a basis for the adoption of community-oriented policing programs and the establishment of various strategic and neighborhood-oriented policing methods (Oliver, 2000; Wilson & Kelling, 1982). One assumption centered in this perspective is that criminals require an opportunity to commit a crime, and opportunity is perceived in a neighborhood where no one cares if homes have broken windows, cars are abandoned, and scattered trash is everywhere. The community and the police can take preventive measures against crime and repair the "broken windows" in the neighborhood together, thereby reducing the window of opportunity for the criminal. The aim of community policing is to promote public safety and enhance the quality of life through a partnership of police and community. Thus, community policing expands the responsibility for crime control to the community at large.

The focal point of community policing is on proactive (prevention) strategies and can be defined as "a collaboration between the police and the community that identifies and solves community problems" (BJA, 1994). The collaboration, however, is not necessarily an equal relationship, rather the police must play the role of a facilitator in a two-way relationship with the public in order to address and solve public problems. However, the mission of recent community policing projects is primarily to enhance the quality of police service, whereas older community policing projects used community policing as a means of giving the community more direct control over police operations (Goldstein, 1987). Nonetheless, the Community Policing Consortium (CPC, 2000),[3] argues that at the core of community policing, there are essential and complementary components. Largely, community policing programs as described by the CPC (2000),

---

[3]The Community Policing Consortium is a partnership of five of the leading police organizations in the United States: International Association of Chiefs of Police (IACP), National Organization of Black Law Enforcement Executives (NOBLE), National Sheriffs' Association (NSA), Police Executive Research Forum (PERF), and Police Foundation. These five organizations play a principal role in the development of community policing research, training, and technical assistance, and each is firmly committed to the advancement of this policing philosophy. The Community Policing Consortium is administered and funded by the U.S. Department of Justice, Office of Community Oriented Policing Services (COPS).

Goldstein (1987), Manning (1997), DuBois and Hartnett (2002), and Stevens (2002) are characterized by the following:

- Permanent assignment of officers to specific duty assignments and often geographical areas,
- Significant decentralization of authority and responsibility,
- Empowering of officers and community members with decision-making authority although limited,
- Community member participation in decision-making processes that can include identification and prioritizing of social issues that impact their community,
- Partnerships with public and private institutions and agencies, and
- Adoption of a problem-solving approach to the daily work of the agency.

That is, community policing is a fundamental shift in authority, obligations, and decision-making expectations and responsibilities from the traditional chain-of-command organizational type of control (top-to-bottom) to a contemporary method of control that fits a community policing philosophy (bottom up; that is, turning an organization upside down) (Wycoff & Skogan, 1998). Expressed another way, a community policing strategy is the community's obligation and responsibility in a partnership with police efforts to control crime.

COMMUNITY POLICING RATIONALE AND PHILOSOPHY

Community policing must be both a philosophy and a practical approach or working strategy if it is to succeed in offering quality police service. Commander Michael Nila of Aurora, Illinois, says it is a "customized" approach to law enforcement based on the needs of the people it seeks to protect and serve" (CPC, 1996). Chief Ronald Hansen of Fayetteville, North Carolina, adds that "community policing is not a single program, nor is it a group of programs lumped together; it's a departmental wide commitment to serving the client" (personal communication with the researcher).

Policing has attempted to change from a closed, incident-driven and reactive bureaucracy to a more open, dynamic, quality-oriented partnership with the community to safeguard basic human and constitutional rights (Taylor, Fritsch, & Caeti, 1998). More succinctly, Captain Linda Frost (1998) says, "Departments must make the transition to facilitator of community needs and through a positive relationship, work to achieve a desirable community." Community members have resources and skills that can, once facilitated into community action, enhance their community and help the police keep them safe. In a sense, people governing themselves might be one way to describe community policing as a strategy. Government, business, and community leaders are aware that they, too, should share in crime control by keeping their neighborhoods safe (BJA, 1994).

Community policing can be conceptualized as democracy in action. But it requires active participation, responsibility, and decision-making prerogatives by public and business leaders, residents, and church, school, and hospital leaders. The decision-making processes can include input into a host of police activities (without compromising public safety) such as these:

- Police deployment strategies relevant to activities such as foot patrols, mini stations, K9 units, water patrol, and bike units;
- Crime-targeted strategies such as neighborhood crime watches, owner notification, hot-spot identification, and criminal trespass;
- Policing response policies such as use of force, tactical unit response, road blocks, saturation operations, stinks, reverse stinks, and narcotic surveillance; and
- Collaborative strategies such as advisory councils, crime prevention councils, and police disciplinary committees.

In essence, community policing offers a way for the police and the community to bond in a common goal—to raise the quality of life for everyone in that jurisdiction. Ideally, contemporary community policing is centered on the notion that all residents within a specific jurisdiction should be empowered to enhance their quality of life and prevent or eliminate crime and problems that lead to crime (Carter & Radelet, 1999). But, these ideals do not necessarily mold themselves into working models anymore than a model works because someone commands it to work.

MOTIVATORS LEADING TO COMMUNITY POLICING COMMITMENTS

There are a number of influences or motivators that have set the stage for the emergence of community policing concepts, and those motivators often help shape the community policing agenda of a police agency (Peak & Glensor, 1999; PERF, 1996). For every community, a different set of variables interacts to produce a community policing initiative decision. The following is a list of the variables, created by Peak and Glensor (1999) and the Community Policing Consortium (2000), that may have prompted an agency to make a decision to pursue partnership strategies:

- Narrowing of police mission,
- Increased cultural diversity,
- Increased violence,
- Scientific view of management,
- Downturn in the economy,
- Increased dependence on high-technological equipment,
- Emphasis on organizational change,
- Isolation of police administration,
- Concern with police,
- Personalization of governmental services,
- Attempts to reach the community,
- Changing character of American communities,
- Changing level and nature of crime,

- Changing social fabric (fewer stable families and more working parents), and
- Smaller amounts of government money to allocate for these increasing needs.

Many of these issues work together; in fact, it is unlikely that any one alone would bring about a community policing commitment. This represents in part an academic perspective.

The PERF (1996) study on community policing, consisting of six jurisdictions (Santa Barbara, Las Vegas, Edmonton, Savannah, Newport News, and Philadelphia), is consistent with the principles offered by Peak and Glensor (1999), but not necessarily the reasons. The PERF study suggests that troubled race relations, particularly between police and minority communities, rising crime problems, and difficulty in handling workload demands were the primary motivators toward community policing commitments.

A few more motivators that need to be added to the list include these:

- Cultural diversity has intensified among different groups.
- Community policing strategies are methods of eliminating "old guard" idealists.
- Hate crimes are on the rise.
- Terrorism and violence from outside a jurisdiction are on the rise.
- Liability questions inhibit officer conduct.
- Specific group strategies are required for people with physical or mental challenges.
- And, of greatest concern, police officers cannot and should not do the job of crime control alone.

We can see how different the views are between academics and practitioners. Nonetheless, it is curious that none of the agencies visited by the PERF research team reported "old guard" elimination, federal grant opportunities, and/or liability issues as contributors to community policing programs. Old guard elimination suggests community policing can provide a vehicle for some younger, less experienced commanders to advance faster to top command over traditional experienced officers. Conversely, some civic leaders might use a community policing excuse to unseat a current police chief whose policies tend to interfere with civic leader agendas. Therefore, despite the fact that few individuals really understand community policing, it can be utilized as a tool of mobility and/or a tool to eliminate a top commander whose party line is different than that of policy makers.

The federal government has issued millions of dollars to police departments to create community policing programs.[4] Recently, for example, Vice President

---

[4]During his 1994 State of the Union address, President Clinton pledged to put 100,000 additional police officers on America's neighborhood streets. On September 13, 1994, with bipartisan support, President Clinton signed into law the Violent Crime Control and Law Enforcement Act of 1994—popularly known as the "Crime Act"—which authorized $8.8 billion over six years for grants to local policing agencies to add 100,000 officers and promote community policing in innovative ways.

Gore announced that 45 communities in 23 states nationwide will receive $12 million to add an additional 170 community policing officers (COPS, 1999). These grants will provide funding for 75 percent of the total salary and benefits of each officer hired for three years, up to a maximum of $75,000 per officer. The remainder is paid with state or local funds. Nonetheless, federal money tends to be temporary and often requires participation in dollars or services.

Then, too, American police agencies have paid millions in liability cases (*Liability Reporter*, 1999). One example comes from the Los Angeles Police Department (LAPD) who reports that litigation against police officers has cost the city more than $322 million dollars since 1992 (Barrett, 1998). It was expected that Los Angeles would pay out $42 million in 1999 alone. The suits range from police shootings to civil rights violations. Of course, Los Angeles is not a typical city, yet it is one of the leading cities arguing that community policing works for them. The LAPD has accepted millions of federal dollars to further community policing efforts and have liability exposures suggesting an immediate response—a community policing response fits the bill.

Two other issues require some attention before we continue. Is community policing really a new innovation—a new strategy of policing—and will it solve some criminal activity? Utilizing Elliott Currie (1999) as a guide, there is a sense that community policing strategies possess some kind of secret know-how to fight crime, and that everyone else in the world ought to learn to do things the way American police do. When it comes to the economy, American know-how's secret, Currie says, "is usually said to be things like a 'flexible' labor market, a minimal welfare state, a willingness to deregulate economic life whenever and wherever we can" (p. 1). But when it comes to crime, "the secret of our supposed success is variously said to be our "tough policing strategies—zero tolerance, quality of life—and/or that our enormous investment in incarceration is finally paying off in a big way" (p. 3).

Community policing may not be the answer to controlling crime, which, of course, is one primary function of police agencies. If we can accept the recent declines in violence in the United States in the proper perspective, and realize that community policing is relatively new to policing agendas, can it be argued that, if an agenda were to move more concretely toward community policing, crime can be more controlled or less controlled? It doesn't make us any less glad that those declines have happened, but it does serve as a check against going overboard when interpreting them. A second issue is whether community policing may exist more in rhetoric than in reality (Eck & Rosenbaum, 1994; Kraska & Kappeler, 1997; Maguire, 1997; Moore, 1994). Clearly, observational case studies, including the ones you are about to read, describe the struggle to introduce changes in police organizations and its bureaucracies (Greene, Bergman, & McLaughlin, 1994). And, despite success stories such as those described in this book at Broken Arrow, Fayetteville, and Sacramento, other researchers, including the case studies here on Camden, Columbus, and St. Petersburg, report widespread resistance to change from the police culture, numerous organizational barriers, and a desire by stubborn personnel to "weather the storm" (i.e., outlast the current administration) (DuBois & Hartnett, 2002).

COMMUNITY POLICING PERSPECTIVES

For the most part, five distinctive community policing perspectives are held by various law enforcement policy makers as outlined by PERF (1996). These perspectives are idealized examinations of community policing. Caution is advised, suggests PERF, when evaluating a specific perspective for three reasons:

1. Strategies of community policing programs often overlap among programs and agencies.
2. Assessment of a community policing program tends to focus on a specific perspective.
3. Official rhetoric and actual strategies might be two different things.

These are the five distinctive community policing designs:

1. *Deployment* is a perspective held about community policing that can be understood from the idea of a regular "beat officer" working in a specific neighborhood (PERF, 1996). There is evidence both supporting and not supporting this method of policing, assuming the goal is to reduce crime. Some studies suggest that foot patrols had little impact on crime, fear of crime, or disorder (Bowers & Hirsch, 1987; Pate, 1989).
2. The *community revitalization perspective* focuses on prevention by reducing the social indicators of criminal activities. Perhaps the most well-known reference to this perspective is James Q. Wilson and George Kelling's (1982) "broken windows" analogy.[5] That is, a home or a community with many broken windows might be a signal to criminals that a home or the community is a safe target for criminal activities. Neighborhood disorder including drunkards, gangs, panhandlers, prostitutes, and other urban incivilities can further citizen fear and criminal conduct leading to more serious disorder and crime. Therefore, effectively addressing the signals of neighborhood decay might prevent crime and enhance community pride. The "broken windows" theory of crime provided a basis for the adoption of community-oriented policing programs. Yet, there is evidence on both sides of the debate concerning this issue, some supporting revitalization and other bits of evidence not supporting it (Champion & Rush, 1997; Skogan, 1990).
3. A third perspective to community policing can be found in Goldstein's (1979, 1990) *problem-solving perspective* (PERF, 1996).[6] Goldstein ar-

---

[5]See the Recommended Reading section at the end of this chapter to find most of the classical and contemporary works on community policing issues. "This article became the basis for the police and community movement toward developing partnerships and the establishment of various strategic and neighborhood-oriented policing methods" writes Oliver (2000, p. 1).

[6]Goldstein applied basic problem-solving methods of decision making to the police because he felt these methods would prove far more successful than the confrontational, win–lose style of decision making the police most often employed (Oliver, 2000, p. 2). Goldstein is considered the "father of problem-oriented policing."

gues that the police are concerned with a "means over ends" syndrome, which translates to concerns about improvement efforts in organizational and operating methods rather than on substantive outcomes of their work. He maintains that police should move from a reactive, incident orientation toward identifying and addressing crime and disorder issues that continue to drain police resources. That is, law enforcement agencies are immersed in administrative and management concerns, resulting in difficulty meeting their departmental missions. An implication from this study was the need to develop formal call-screening procedures to accurately discriminate between emergency and nonemergency calls for service. Consistent with that thought, research has suggested that police officers who score low on job satisfaction tests provide poor levels of police service. Those officers said that their dissatisfaction was largely due to a distrust of management, redundant reform policy that had little to do with law enforcement, and mountains of paperwork that made them less effective (Stevens, 1998e, 1999a). Then, too, although many occupations share stress-related problems similar to those found in policing, officer stress is enhanced by unpredictable situations, periods of work that ranges from inactivity to extremely stressful activity, instantaneous decision making, the court system, and the use of force (Dantzker, 2000). Therefore, it is no surprise when officers concern themselves more often with administrative matters and personal health than matters of police service. Goldstein's perspective is that the mission of policing is to address the vast variety of problems of concern to citizens and that through problem-oriented sessions, the focus of officers will be on police service to the community (PERF, 1996).

4. A fourth view of community policing is the *customer or client perspective*. This perspective focuses on developing proactive mechanisms such as routine citizen surveys and citizen advisory groups for determining the needs of the public concerning police service. Chief Ronald Hansen from the Fayetteville PD takes this perspective in part. He says, "One way to listen to the community is for officers and officials to attend community meetings and to listen to what community members have to say about their lives. After all, we work for them and if our clients express a problem with something then we must find the appropriate response bringing them closer to their goals without sacrificing safety or bending the laws." (Personal communications with the researcher).

5. *Legitimacy* is the fifth perspective offered by the PERF (1996). From this perspective, community policing is an attempt by the police to be equitable and to be seen as equitable. This perspective draws attention to the fact that minority group members, particularly racial minorities, have historically been subject to more law enforcement activities than members of majority groups. Commonly cited evidence of this disparity is the disproportionate number of blacks and Hispanics arrested. The rise

of an increasingly powerful minority group political voice might have motivated this perspective's utilization. Critics of community policing suggest that this approach is more "window dressing than substance," arguing that the police are trying to make themselves look good in order to placate dissatisfied citizens without making any real fundamental changes (Klockars, 1988). However, it might be closer to reality to suggest that some agencies utilize the principles of this perspective to avoid or neutralize liability issues among minority groups and special groups such as gays.

As noted earlier, these five community policing perspectives are seldom, if ever, found in their pure form within any police agency. Instead, departments mix these perspectives to varying degrees. However, community policing and problem-solving perspectives can be different perspectives. Probably the most common combination is the community revitalization and problem-solving perspectives as evidenced by some of the agencies in these case studies. Yet, some agencies use one perspective in one specific section of the city and another in another section of the city.

Differences Between Community Policing and Problem Solving

Community policing initiatives are characterized by the many variables outlined earlier in the chapter and relate primarily to (not necessarily in this order) empowerment, partnerships, solutions, and evaluations (Skogan et al., 1999). Each of these components is essential to a community policing strategy. However, it can be argued that community policing cannot be effective if it lacks a problem-solving component. On the other hand, problem-solving strategies can be employed without many of the community policing elements (Moore & Trojanowicz, 2000). Although both concepts reach out to community members, one notable distinction between the two concepts might be the method of problem solving as guided through community member decision-making processes. When individuals say that community policing is a philosophy as opposed to a program, they mean that it is a system approach to policing. As such, community policing refers to the way the entire department conducts its business and how it interacts with the community (Oliver, 2000). More specifically, community policing has the full attention of the department, and every member of the community has an equal opportunity to become involved in its initiatives (Oliver, 2000). Problem solving can be a program and limited by its use or limited to a specific geographical area, but it is also essential to community policing initiatives. Ideally, there are three variations of problem-solving strategies (Oliver, 2000):

1. *Strategic oriented:* police-initiated activities that target specific criminal or order maintenance problems to reduce the level of crime, fear of crime, and/or disorder.

2. *Neighborhood oriented:* any type of controls that bring community and police together to address problems.
3. *Problem oriented:* a partnership between police and community whereby they work together, implement an agreed-on solution, and evaluate the success of the solution.

SARA

Regardless of which problem-solving strategy is operationalized, problem solving involves new units of work and a larger set of approaches to solve them (Moore & Trojanowitz, 1988; Skogan et al., 1999).[7] Once the decision is made to move forward, four steps can be used to help solve problems: (1) scanning stage (identifies problems), (2) analysis stage (collect and study data), (3) response stage (develop solutions), and (4) assessment stage (evaluate how well all is going), or SARA. This is a process successfully utilized by many agencies including the Chicago Police Department and Newport News PD in Virginia.

OBJECTIVES OF COMMUNITY POLICING

The objectives of an agency tend to impact the style adapted by an agency when conducting a community policing program. Eck and Rosenbaum (1994, as found in PERF's study) suggest that three idealized models underlie agency participation in community policing efforts:

1. Improving the efficient delivery of police services,
2. Achieving equitable delivery of services to all communities, and
3. Enhancing the effectiveness of police work.

As idealized models of course, they are rarely found in their pure state:

- An *efficiency-based model* of community policing tends to organize around changes in modes of policing, such as deployment methods, decentralization, telephone or walk-in reporting, foot patrol, and permanent beats. This model is most common where 911 calls are perceived as excessively burdensome and where financial resources for police personnel are in short supply (PERF, 1996).
- An *equity-based model* of community policing often evolves from demands for racial access and equity within a city. Such demands might include more personnel resources or greater access to police services (PERF, 1996). For the most part, it is the form of police service delivery designed to build trust between citizens and police or to "empower" citizens rather than the substance of delivery that is the focus of equity-based models.

---

[7]For an in-depth discussion on each step, see Skogan et al. (1999), pages 4–8.

- An *effectiveness-based model* of community policing represents a focus on substantive community problems. Although this model may use community-outreach approaches such as foot patrol or community meetings, the objective is to resolve substantive community problems.

PROBLEMS OF COMMUNITY POLICING

Problems associated with community policing are not necessarily linked to motivators, perspectives, or objectives, but rather occur in the implementation and assessment stages. This notion finds consistency with Taylor, Fritsch, and Caeti (1998) who add that community policing has been defined so many different ways that an evaluation of specific programs has been "benign." The result is that what works is "relegated to a few initiatives highlighted in a few, select cities across the country" (p. xx). Therefore, an aim of *Case Studies in Community Policing* is to help the practitioner and the student better understand "how" the often misunderstood, yet arbitrary concept of community policing is actually applied and maintained in typical agencies.

Another problematic concern relates to the flattening of the organizational pyramid through the empowerment of line officers and community members. This goal is probably one of the most difficult tasks within a community policing agenda. One ethical question here is that since the primary goal of community policing is crime control and enhancement of the quality of life through partnerships, and if community members have different perspectives of order than that of law enforcement officers, whose perspective of order will prevail? Then, too, empowering community policing officers or other officers involved in the process with authority or decision-making potentials different than other officers might detach those officers from patrol officers. This could produce a negative reaction among uniformed officers similar to an alienation effect and possibly impair any unity established among the officers of a department or a division.

Professionals across the country say that the greatest challenge to community policing is yet to come (Community Policing Pages [CPP], 2000). Though an important component in the criminal justice policy of both Presidents Bush and Clinton, its future is uncertain. What will happen to community policing when federal funding expires? Is community policing sufficiently entrenched to sustain itself? When funding is gone, will the concept be cast aside for something new and stylish (CPP, 2000)?

An interesting observation can be made from the perspective held by many police experts that traditional police approaches have not succeeded (Carter & Radelet, 1999). One general implication from those thoughts is that quality law enforcement services can only be provided through community policing strategies. However, this implication raises two issues: first, community policing has yet to be crowned the cure-all to police services; and second, law enforcement has performed above and beyond its expectations but of late, the expectations of the police, civil liabilities through the courts, and the sophistication of crime and criminals have all submerged law enforcement in an entirely new set of responsibilities.

Many of the current programs called community policing do not possess important elements of the philosophy, reports one professional agency (CPP, 2000). They suggest that some of these initiatives stray far from the principles and objectives of community policing. To call these programs community policing is inappropriate. Unfortunately, these mislabeled initiatives may influence the perceptions of community policing. To accurately evaluate community policing, an agency must distinguish between legitimate implementation and misdirected efforts (CPP, 2000).

Some evidence has been seen that when a community policing effort is under way, other departments within government might want to make use of those networks for other purposes, argues Chief Ron Hansen of the Fayetteville PD in North Carolina.

TEXT FORMAT

Case Studies in Community Policing consists of three parts: We start with a single chapter that highlights general community policing principles and discoveries and offers some insight into the findings of this study. The next nine chapters describe the experiences of nine police agencies. The last chapter represents a conclusion centered on a compare-and-contrast exercise.

EXPECTATIONS

It is expected that on successful completion of this text, a practitioner should have a better picture of how the nine police agencies examined moved closer to developing, implementing, and maintaining quality police services through community partnerships. When a student completes this work, she or he can expect to better understand the major concepts and issues of community policing and expect to have a stronger sense of community policing models in order to see how police services might fit in the real world. Readers in general will see the real-life drama played out in police agencies and have a better sense of the obstacles that hinder quality police service.

DO YOU KNOW?

1. *Case Studies in Community Policing* offers a decisive overview for practitioners who want to see how other agencies experienced implementation of community policing initiatives. Describe what you think you will find on the following pages relative to implementing community policing prerogatives in any one of the nine cities identified in this case study.
2. The author argues that community policing as outlined by the "book" does not exist. Explain what you think the author means by that statement. In what way might you agree or disagree with it?

3. Many influences are brought to bear on police service and implementation efforts of new strategies, the author says. Describe some of the influences that might impact community policing implementations. What other obstacles can you think of that might also hinder police service?
4. According to the author, what are the aims of community policing and how might they differ from traditional strategies?
5. Define community policy initiatives and a problem-solving strategy. Compare and contrast the two strategies. Under what conditions might community policing be impractical, giving way to the utilization of a problem-solving strategy?
6. What activities are generally used to measure the productivity of traditional patrol officers? In what way might those measurements be inappropriate when evaluating the productivity of community police officers?
7. In what way might the decision-making processes or authority of a community policing officer differ from that of a patrol officer? How would those differences of authority impact the task of community policing initiatives? How might patrol officers perceive the authority of community policing officers?
8. Describe SARA and discuss its advantages and disadvantages as a problem-solving strategy for one of the cities highlighted in this book.
9. Explain why you think the problems associated with community policing are not necessarily with the motivators or objectives but rather with implementation and assessment.
10. In what way might community policing be perceived as a crime fighting cure-all in policing? What are your thoughts about that perspective?
11. Identify the events leading an agency to a community policing decision from the perspective of academics and the perspective of practitioners. Why are they different views?

RECOMMENDED READING

Oliver, W. M. (2000). *Community policing: Classical readings.* Upper Saddle River, NJ: Prentice Hall. This work contains a classical and a contemporary collection of articles that helped shape community policing initiatives more than any other articles. The writers are on the "must read" list and include James Q. Wilson, George L. Kelling, Herman Goldstein, Mark H. Moore, Robert C. Trojanowicz, and Lawrence W. Sherman.

Police Executive Research Forum. (1996). *Themes and variations in community policing: Case studies in community policing.* Washington, DC: Police Foundation. Probably one of the best accounts of community policing implementation and maintenance from an applied perspective offered through policing manager practitioners.

Skogan, W. G., Hartnett, S. M., DuBois, J., Comey, J. T., Kaiser, M. & Lovig, J. H. (1999). *On the beat: Police and community problem solving.* Boulder, CO: Westview Press. This work contains a detailed method of recruiting and maintaining community members to advance community policing initiatives. It also contains a detailed account of how the Chicago Police utilizes SARA's problem-solving skills to help solve social issues that lend themselves to quality of life matters.

WEB SITES

Community Policing Consortium (CPC)

http://www.communitypolicing.org/

The CPC is a partnership of five of the leading police organizations in the United States:

- International Association of Chiefs of Police (IACP)
- National Organization of Black Law Enforcement Executives (NOBLE)
- National Sheriffs' Association (NSA)
- Police Executive Research Forum (PERF)
- Police Foundation

These five organizations play a principal role in the development of community policing research, training and technical assistance, and each is firmly committed to the advancement of this policing philosophy. At this site you can research publications and access a chat room, training information, bulletins, discussions, and other material related to community policing.

Community Policing Pages

http://msnhomepages.talkcity.com/LibraryLawn/devere_woods/

Dedicated to continuing the work of Robert C. Trojanowicz. This site publishes pages to stimulate research and decisions on policing issues. There are papers on community policing, an extensive bibliography, and a forum for comments.

Federal Bureau of Investigation

http://www.fbi.gov

Contains links, crime statistics, job opportunities, most wanted list, and major investigations.

Police Executive Research Forum (PERF)

http://www.policeforum.org/

The PERF is a national membership organization of progressive police executives from the largest city, county, and state law enforcement agencies. PERF is dedicated to improving policing and advancing professionalism through research and involvement in public policy debate. Incorporated in 1977, PERF's primary sources of operating revenues are government grants and contracts, and partnerships with private foundations and other organizations. Contains research, resources, a bulletin board, and more.

National Criminal Justice Reference Service

http://www.ncjrs.org

Information, statistics, links, and publications on corrections, courts, and police are available online at this site.

APPENDIX 1   Police Agencies in Study

1. Broken Arrow PD, Broken Arrow, Oklahoma, http://www.city.broken-arrow.ok.us/
2. Camden PD, Camden, New Jersey, http://www.camdenpd.com
3. Columbus Division of Police, Columbus, Ohio, http://www.police.ci.columbus.oh.us/
4. Fayetteville PD, Fayetteville, North Carolina, http://www.fayettevillenc.com/citygov/
5. Harris County Precinct 4 Constable's Office, Spring, Texas, http://www.co.harris.tx.us/pct4/
6. Lansing PD, Lansing, Michigan, http://www.lansingpolice.com/
7. Metro-Nashville PD, Nashville, Tennessee, http://www.nashville.net/~police/index.htm
8. Sacramento PD, Sacramento, California, http://www.sacpd.org
9. St. Petersburg PD, St. Petersburg, Florida, http://www.stpete.org/sppd.htm

APPENDIX 2   Agency Contributors

Chief Carolyn M. Kusler
ckusler@baliving.com
Broken Arrow Police Department
Broken Arrow, OK

Captain Charles J. Kocher, Ph.D.
kocher@voicenet.com
Camden Police Department
Camden, NJ

Commander Kent Shafer, MA
kshafer@cmhmetro.net
Columbus Division of Police Commander
Columbus, OH

Carl Milazzo, JD
cmilazzo@ci.fay.nc.us
PD Attorney and Trainer
Fayetteville Police Department
Fayetteville, NC

Asst. Chief Ron Hickman, MA
hickman@co.harris.tx.us
Harris County Precinct 4 Constable's Office
Spring, TX

Captain Mark Alley, MA
Malley@voyager.net
Chief
Lansing Police Department
Lansing, MI

Lt. Ben Dickie
nashcop1@aol.com
Metro-Nashville Police Department
Nashville, TN

Captain Steve Seguar
ssegu@aol.com
Commander Patrol Division
Sacramento Police Department
Sacramento, CA

Sgt. Gary Dukema
gldukema@stpete.org
Community Policing Coordinator
St. Petersburg PD
St. Petersburg, FL

APPENDIX 3   Data Collection

A list of questions follows that helped guide data collection. There were many other questions, observations, and material but these 10 questions were emphasized as a starting point. Of course, not every agency responded to all of these questions, and they were not necessarily answered in order, nor were the questions emphasized in every chapter, but these ten guided my investigation.

1. What methods were employed to insure that typical members of the community were represented in the community policing process?
2. In what way are community residents included in the decision-making processes associated with community policing? Explain the feedback and/or the decision levels of community members in:
   • Deployment strategies relevant to activities such as foot patrols, mini stations, bike patrols;
   • Crime-targeted strategies and activities such as neighborhood crime watches, owner notification, criminal trespass; and
   • Collaborative strategies such as advisory councils, crime prevention councils, and police disciplinary committees.
3. What are the elements and/or conditions that will sustain the active involvement of residents in the community?

4. How will your organization pick up the slack from federal funding money when it runs out, assuming some part of your community policing program is being funded or subsidized?

5. What were the historical events that influenced organizational decisions to establish a community policing agenda at your agency?

6. What are the methods used to assess and/or evaluate the progress of the community policing effort?

7. How does your agency determine the success or failure of your community policing effort?

8. In what way have any community policing programs been changed or altered as a result of community policing assessments?

9. In what way has the training differed as compared to precommunity policing efforts?

10. In what way has decentralization been accomplished in keeping with community policing efforts? In what way have assignments changed, chain-of-command been altered, and use of equipment been shifted?

Appendix 4 Jurisdiction Demographics

	Broken Arrow, OK	Camden, NJ	Columbus, OH	Fayetteville, NC	Harris County, TX*	Lansing, MI	Nashville, TN	St. Petersburg, FL	Sacramento, CA
Population, 1999	81,000	83,546	641,338	113,561	750,000	123,086	531,908	250,572	383,921
Sworn officers, 1999	87	386	1,770	317	376	373	1,500	520	642
One officer to population, 1999	930	216	362	358		330	355	482	598
Robbery, 1997	26	1,110	3,104	653	87	265	2,583	1,255	1,851
Rape, 1997	18	96	696	84		154	550	201	161
Homicide, 1997	0	42	84	11		16	112	21	41
Aggravated assault, 1997	77	1,164	2,103	359	66	1,086	6,046	3,781	1,664
Motor vehicle theft, 1997	145	1,492	7,618	796	733	506	8,173	1,774	6,260
Total crime index, 1997	690	3,904	13,605	1,903		2,027	17,464	7,032	9,970
Violent crime per 100,000	0.008	46.7	21.2	16.7		16.4	32.8	28.0	25.9

*Since Harris County has more than Precinct 4 personnel serving the country, any calculations would be misleading.

APPENDIX 5   Getting Commitments

There are many unspoken experiences in the pages of this work that merit attention. The likelihood exists that those experiences influenced the conclusions of the principal researcher. When soliciting police agency participation early in the project through e-mail, telephone, and personal interviews, 22 police chiefs initially committed their support, although in the final analysis, the experiences of only 9 agencies are described in this work.

Three of the 22 chiefs, after many conversations with the researcher, apparently changed their minds about participating. Their decision not to participate was presented through lower level personnel. The reason for their change of mind can be found in the following typical statement made by a captain from a large agency in Florida: "We've been burnt by academics in the past. We're still trying to regain some of our lost ground as a result of that relationship."

Five other agencies backed out once their midmanagers learned of the scope of the commitment: interviews, visits, and documented information. One of these agencies indicated that they were "over researched" (which they were). The remaining four led the researcher on a chase through months of promises and transfers from division to division, and person to person, seeking a point person who would guide the discovery process of the agency. Yet, almost all of those interactions ended with individuals who knew little about the community policing initiative in their departments, but most of them demonstrated through their earnest efforts that they wanted to help.

Four agencies through their point person, up to the final draft deadline of this work, continued to make assurances that they had a community policing agenda, but failed to produce sufficient evidence that a community policing initiative existed other than on their web site or in their brochures. In one case, a local television network provided information about the city's community policing effort which read "Contact Lt. So and So at such and such phone number to discuss the department's community policing program." The researcher called the officer in charge and met with him and his assistant. Both were very agreeable to an examination of their program, yet when it came time to meet with the first community group, that group could not be found. Each of these four agencies was unable to provide times of community meetings, names or phone numbers of participates, or even letters of introduction to meet with members of those groups.

Finally, one agency that had been supplying information—although hesitantly—asked that their chapter not be included since they were currently involved in litigation.

Of course, that is not to say that working with the nine agencies who did end up in this work was without incident. In fact, two of the agencies were so unorganized about community policing initiatives that the researcher often thought about asking them not to participate. However, seven of the agencies within these pages were professional, efficient, and a positive energy within their communities as evidenced by responses the researcher received from individuals who helped supply information from outside the respective police agencies. All information, interviews, and supporting materials were documented. Indeed, each interaction with the personnel, community leaders, and other individuals in those jurisdictions was rewarding and professional. I learned a great deal from them about policing, management, and honor.

CHAPTER TWO

BROKEN ARROW POLICE DEPARTMENT

Broken Arrow, Oklahoma

INTRODUCTION

This chapter was primarily prepared by Chief Car-olyn M. Kusler[1] who believes that community polic-ing is a mind-set, a way of thinking about the busi-ness of policing. It takes us back to Sir Robert Peel's comment that "the police are the public and the pub-lic are the police, the police being only full-time in-dividuals charged with the duties that are incumbent on all of the citizens." While not Sir Robert's inten-tions, human nature is such that once a group is cre-ated to deal with an issue, it suddenly becomes that group's problem and everyone else is happy to stand back and let the specialized group deal with it. When the public lose their perception of responsibility for

Chief Carolyn M. Kusler

crime, they place that responsibility totally on the police who then become the "thin blue line." Community policing causes us to rethink the compartmental-ization of responsibility for law and order. If we are to keep our organizations from becoming compartmentalized as well—between those who fight crime and those who involve the community—it appears that this type of philosophy ought to be implemented department wide.

---

[1]Chief Carolyn M. Kusler can be reached at ckusler@baliving.com.

CHAPTER OUTLINE

This chapter has two parts: The first part focuses on conceptual perspectives of community policing, and Part 2 emphasizes outcomes. Specifically, in Part 1 the rationale behind the community policing initiatives of the Broken Arrow Police Department is described followed by the department's challenges to provide appropriate leadership to its officers and the communities they serve. Those challenges are centered in a modeling perspective, developing a successful work environment, and integrating a community policing philosophy department wide. The events leading to community policing commitments in Broken Arrow are highlighted, leading to an evaluation of police service profiles and community program leader resistance to new management. The plan to implement community policing initiatives is revealed including partnership arrangements with public and private organizations. Resistance to change by various organizations including the FOB takes center stage followed by a solidification of the community policing commitment.

Part 2 explains how Broken Arrow got its name and describes the department. It describes the department's programs, crime rates, and trends, and also volunteers results from a citizen survey. Nine questions about community policing are answered by an official of the Broken Arrow Police Department. The chapter includes an example of community policing initiatives taken by the department. Finally, Broken Arrow police officers present their point of view about community policing followed by comments from community members.

PART 1: COMMUNITY POLICING RATIONALE

We view with nostalgia the beat officer of days gone by and laud the fact that all good police officers engaged the community, even if the engagement was unrecognized by the organization. But in spite of the claims that "we have always done it," community policing is always discussed in the context of change for present-day law enforcement. Creating the atmosphere for change is the challenge for the leadership. And the challenge can be met by modeling the precepts of community policing, developing a work environment facilitating success toward the mission of the department, and integrating the philosophy of community policing in every activity.

PROVIDING LEADERSHIP

How does an agency model community policing? The philosophy is difficult for some officers to grasp. The problem-oriented approach to policing, however, is a framework that provides a concrete format in which to lead the Citizen Police Academy, Neighborhood Watch, Citizens on Patrol, volunteers, and other similar programs that, in effect, are avenues to educate the community about police work. They create strong relationships between community and police and provide vital support when an incident occurs. However, problem solving involves the community where the rubber meets the road—where the community's responsibility and law enforcement's endeavors come together to create safe communities. Management must not stop at the feel-good approaches. They must encourage patrol officers to seek community involvement in discovering root causes and meaningful solutions where possible. In this sense, programs become tools to aid in the prevention of crime.

As police leadership models the problem-solving process, beat officers follow. When a police managerial issue surfaces, leadership takes the initiative in the analysis of the issue by communicating with everyone concerned prior to reaching a solution. Likewise, beat officers who identify a problem in their beats are encouraged to obtain as much data as possible by communicating with those affected by the events. As management involves those affected in developing responses to management issues, so the officers will involve those affected in developing responses to crime problems. As with managerial issues, common sense and professionalism frequently influence ultimate recommendations. So it is with officers, who communicate the constraints of the law and personal responsibility to those who are creating or being affected by the problem. The problem-solving process forces the officers into communications with the community and other governmental entities. Once a success is realized and appreciation received from outside the department, then reluctance to engage the community is diminished.

It is important for management to model problem-solving processes, but it is also important for management to ensure the organizational structure is there to support problem solving at the beat officer level. During the regular workday when the beat officer is responding to calls for service, is it fair to expect him or her to utilize the unassigned time in working on problem solving? Although the unassigned time may seem to be there, it may need to be used for regrouping mentally after an intense encounter or for tending to administrative matters. Managers should look at alternative ways to provide large blocks of time set aside specifically for problem solving. In Broken Arrow, we have two squads of officers per shift on four 10-hour-per-day schedules who share the same days off with their supervisors and who have one overlap day per week. On this overlap day, the squads alternate taking calls and working on problem-solving projects free from the constraints of the radio. Providing this kind of time is essential to developing the problem-solving, community policing mindset. Once it is engrained, officers will find creative ways to conduct problem-solving activities during their unassigned time while they are responding to calls for service. Multitasking is not easy for everyone, and it is particularly difficult if you are not sure about the task of problem solving. Providing a block of uninterrupted time allows the officers the opportunity to adjust to the water before they take the plunge.

Stating and modeling values is also important. As a society we have become used to the quick fix—create a new stand to address a moral dilemma. However, even as far back as biblical times we can find the truth that the law will not make people law abiding; only character accomplishes that—the Old

Testament "do not kill" became the New Testament "do not hate." This concept was recognized by our forefathers as they framed the Constitution. John Adams stated:

> *"We have no government armed with power capable of contending with human passions unbridled by Morality and religion. Avarice, ambition, revenge, or gallantry would break the strongest cords of our Constitution as a whale goes through a net. Our Constitution was made only for a moral and religious people. It is wholly inadequate to the government of any other."*

> —*John Adams,* The Works of John Adams—Second President of the United States *(Boston: Little, Brown, 1854) Vol. IX, p. 229.*

As we experience more and more acts of senseless, random violence perpetrated by people who show no regret or remorse for their actions, community policing and the problem-solving approach show great promise for bringing our society back to center by reminding us that values are important, that character does count, and that we all must be held accountable.

In like manner, the leadership of law enforcement agencies not only must have stated values, the values must permeate the structure, the operations, and the decisions of the department. If we are committed to justice, valuing people regardless of ethnicity or status in life, and professionalism in all we do, then we in leadership must seek ways to build trust within the department as well as without. Our values must permeate disciplinary actions where we also look for root causes and fix faulty processes and then educate in the proper manner of doing business. Our values must be reflected in our policies, in promotional processes, in recruiting and hiring practices, and in our methods of dealing with each other. We must illustrate that "commitment and character" rather than "rules and regulations" govern our agencies if we expect our officers to model character in exercising their discretion with the public rather than the letter of the law.

The philosophy of community policing and the problem-solving approach has permeated many aspects of government to the betterment of our communities. As citizens assume the responsibilities they have abdicated to government, as the police become reconnected to the communities they serve, and as management practices model the values of their organizations, perhaps we will continue to diminish the violence within our homes, our neighborhoods, and our communities. No other approach fosters such hope for our future.

EVENTS THAT LED TO COMMUNITY POLICING COMMITMENTS

The Broken Arrow Police Department[2] suffered several episodes of being placed in a holding pattern over a two-year period. The January 1996 retirement of the chief who had served the department for 18 years was quickly followed by the

---

[2]See Broken Arrow Police Department's web site at http://www.city.broken-arrow.ok.us/bapd/police.htm.

city manager's leave of absence to attend to a major illness. During this time the search for a new chief was suspended until the city manager could return to assume his duties. A new chief was finally appointed on May 29, 1997. However, his tenure was short lived. He quit after two days as chief, leaving behind a bewildered department. A new search was undertaken and ultimately Carolyn Kusler was hired to come on board September 22, 1997.

Chief Kusler is a 23-year veteran of the Tulsa (Oklahoma) Police Department and became committed to community policing and the problem-solving approach during her involvement with the Problem Oriented Approach to Drug Enforcement grant awarded to the Tulsa Police Department in 1988. She continued to apply the philosophy and practice of problem solving throughout her career and had a ready mind-set to implement the philosophy and practice of problem-solving department wide when she accepted the position of chief of the Broken Arrow Police Department. At her swearing-in ceremony, she espoused the philosophy that would guide the department under her leadership:

> . . . *Achieving this position is not the culmination of a lifelong dream, but is an opportunity to meet the challenges of policing as the profession transitions into a community-minded model. As I have thought about this opportunity during my own transition from the Tulsa Police Department to BAPD, my vision evolved into four characteristics that I believe are foundational for twenty-first century policing. . . .*

> ". . . *professionalism, in appearance, for facilities and equipment as well as officers; in attitudes towards each other as well as towards the public; in work ethic and work product for every level within the organization; an interest in continuing education and training and the development of relationships with our peers not only locally, but throughout the nation to remain current on crime trends and resources, programs and techniques to address them before they have a major impact on our city.*

> . . . *people-oriented. Valuing human worth and dignity as the first criteria of our response to those not only within our organization, but also with those we work with within city government and the criminal justice system, as well as with community groups and individual citizens, whether they be victims, witnesses, suspects, or someone simply just concerned about crime. A willingness to help regardless of whether the request falls within a job description or not and regardless of the attributes of the person requesting.*

> . . . *purpose-focused. The concept of justice must drive our every action—justice that is community based and constitutionally sound, rather than based on dollar value or social standing.*

> . . . *problem solving. We don't just react to crime, we proactively seek to link incidents and events and discover underlying causes which can be addressed. We will be tough on crime because we are alert to the precursors*

of criminal activity identified through aggressive use of analytical tech-nologies. We won't just rely on our own talents and abilities, but will seek partnerships in the community that can bring their resources to bear on the particular manifestations of crime that are evident in our community.

The problems presented to Kusler at the onset were allegations of sexism arising from the firing of a female officer and a "good old boy" system in oper-ation. Previous to her tenure, an outside investigator had been hired to look into these allegations and his report revealed that while the action against the officer was not based on gender, there was a perception within the department that female officers are singled out as "female" officers and not just as officers. He also found that decisions relating to promotions, assignments, and disci-plinary matters, while not based on gender or race, were based on friendships and favoritism. From written responses to a survey and personal interviews conducted after she came on board, Chief Kusler found that these perceptions were still prevalent within the department. Out of 81 authorized positions, only 6 were held by females and minorities.

Other issues consuming the department were a lawsuit over an officer-involved shooting and the firing of an officer who, while off duty, had been drinking and driving in uniform and in a city vehicle and was subsequently in-volved in an injury accident. There was a great divide between the FOP and the administration of the police department and a general feeling that "they" had no care or concern for the officers or the department. "They" included City Hall. Broken Arrow, Oklahoma, now had two city managers who shared simi-lar perspectives about community policing perspectives.

COMMUNITY-BASED PROGRAMS

The department had several programs in place that were community oriented prior to Chief Kusler's arrival. Two school resource officers were assigned to the six middle schools within the city. The department abandoned the DARE pro-gram in August 1995, but maintained their presence in the schools with the SRO program. Additionally, the department was in the process of initiating the COP (Citizens on Patrol) program. The Alert Neighbors program was operat-ing in the department through the efforts of volunteers. The department was represented on the SALT Council (Seniors and Lawmen Together) and worked with the Senior Center director on issues of mutual concern.

Most of these programs were successful in their own right; however, they were primarily identified with one individual and hardly considered a department-wide commitment to community policing. Making the programs city wide in scope was one of the first priorities for the new chief who recog-nized that community policing was a departmental philology as opposed to several independent programs.

RESHAPING THE PROGRAMS

Through the individualized programs scattered throughout the city of Broken Arrow, it was clear that a concentrated consistency might serve the department and the community more advantageously at the time. However, the new administration felt the pull-and-tug of individual leaders who might have felt threatened by a city-wide effort to incorporate those individual programs into departmental leadership. The administration followed this principle: If you want to get people to support your priorities, you must first address theirs. Thus, Chief Kusler's administration sought to correct the perceptions of favoritism produced by individual leaders through a revamping of the promotional process to include an assessment center by outside evaluators and through the establishment of a participatory decision-making process. As expected, professional perspectives met more residence than expected from several leaders who then felt under personal attack and responded accordingly.

Lack of manpower was a major concern and budget preparation was fast approaching, so the chief commissioned an evaluation of the manpower needs of the department along with an aggressive recruitment campaign to bring the department from 74 sworn officers to its authorized strength of 81. One area of concern was the number of calls for service the department received, which in 1998 totaled 25,067, and another 41,812, which were initiated by the department, for a total of 66,879 calls for one year. Additionally there were 665 domestic violence reports, 9,807 citations, 1,470 arrests, 555 arrest warrants served, and 36 problem-solving projects completed. Nonetheless, the chief was successful in increasing the strength of the department by 6 officer positions, after the budget process, to a total of 87. Civilian increases were also achieved. Further manpower increases were approved in the 1999–2000 budget moving the authorized strength of sworn personnel to 98 with an additional two officers pending approval of an SRO grant, and two additional civilian positions allowing the creation of a fully functional Records Division as well as the ability to provide an animal control officer on duty during evening hours to relieve patrol officers of those types of calls.

To further remove bias and favoritism and enhance the standards of the department, a Professional Standards Division was created to handle internal affairs investigations, policy development, grant management, and training. This new division, which reports directly to the chief, never existed prior to her administration. In fact, in 1998, one unit within this division, Internal Affairs, examined 12 pursuits and 10 use-of-force reports and conducted 51 internal investigations; 19 were determined unfounded, 21 unsubstantiated, 3 exonerated, and 8 were substantiated. Problems discovered through Internal Affairs investigations were addressed through the training curriculum. The department launched the Oklahoma Chiefs Association accreditation process as a means to review all governing documents in light of accepted standards for law enforcement. Increases in personnel, improvements in the facility, involvement of personnel in decision making, and movement toward improving the technological capabilities of the department paved the way for the changes that were in the making.

THE PLAN

The Broken Arrow Police Department (BAPD) held a retreat for its police manager and supervisors. The morning was spent in a facilitated discussion about community policing. The afternoon was spent reviewing the outline of a strategic plan based on the values and concerns expressed by the participants. Mission and vision statements were developed, restructuring concerns resolved, and new visions were adopted department wide. The new mission statement for the BAPD is to protect and serve the community with integrity. This is their new vision statement:

> *The Broken Arrow Police Department is committed to enhancing the quality of life for its citizens through the creation of safe neighborhoods. We partner with the community to address crime problems in an environment of trust, professional pride, personal responsibility, integrity and service.*

Many of the questions about community policing were determined as a result of that meeting which included answers to these questions:

- What is community policing? (*Answer:* Partnership, problem solving, organization change, and prevention.)
- Why? (*Answer:* Because crime does not flourish in strong self-sufficient communities who work with and trust the police.)
- What are the primary components of community policing for the BAPD? (*Answer:* (1) Community partnership recognizes the value of bringing people back into the public process. (2) Problem solving identifies concerns community members feel are most threatening to their safety and well-being. (3) Change management recognizes that a police department will have to change its organizational structure to forge partnerships and implement problem-solving efforts.)
- What is the focus of community policing for the BAPD? (*Answer:* In community-based policing, officers still maintain law and order, but they move beyond just "catching the bad guys" to examining specific conditions, including problems of disorder and neglect, that breed both minor and serious crimes. People talk about their concerns, which range from burglary to speed bumps, with community-based policing officers—who are familiar faces in the neighborhood—and ask for help. Many programs that support community-based policing are old news to crime prevention specialists—Neighborhood Watch, citizen police academies, school resource officers, Citizens on Patrol.)
- What does it take to build trust? (*Answer:* Community-based policing cannot work without trust. Residents who trust the police provide valuable information that can lead to the prevention and solution of crimes. Mutual trust leads to advocacy for police activities and productive partnerships that find solutions to community problems. A police officer studies and listens to the community and respects residents' instincts and concerns. On the other hand, residents need to learn how the police

department works and what it can and cannot do. Then we need to work together to reach our ultimate objective: safe neighborhoods.)

THE SCHEDULE

The four-ten schedule for patrol was eventually adopted as a further result of the retreat. The schedule allowed for two squads per shift to split the weekend for days off and to have an overlap day on Wednesday. The two squads would alternate working the field on Wednesdays. The other squad would be free to work on problem-solving activities and/or to engage in training. The overlap Wednesday enabled the development of partnerships within the department—between patrol officers and detectives, patrol officers and Special Operations Team (SOT), patrol officers and the narcotics unit, as well as patrol officers and their beat partners on the same and different shifts. Officers were being cross-trained in all areas of the department, which increased communications and camaraderie. The overlap between shifts enabled uninterrupted squad meeting times as well as an increased presence in the field during the busy times.

Involvement within the community was also emphasized through the development of "beat books," which included intelligence information as well as information about businesses, schools, hazards, and so on, that are prevalent in a particular beat. The officers conducted surveys of all businesses in the community to gather emergency notification information as well as hazard data for easy access should an emergency occur. Beat officers would have responsibility for the schools in their areas to develop relationships with the staff and the students so that should an emergency occur, there was familiarity with the location and avenues for increased intelligence developed.

The problem-solving approach was taught to all officers so that they would be familiar with the terminology and the underlying assumptions about its effectiveness in creating safe neighborhoods.

Domestic violence was the leading offense in the city of Broken Arrow, so a grant to fund a domestic violence counselor during the evening hours was developed and eventually awarded. Counseling was available during the day, but for those victims who worked during that time, the closest services were in Tulsa, Oklahoma. The counselor recruited volunteers to be a part of the DiVert team, someone who could be called if services were needed on scene at a domestic dispute (i.e., child care, transportation, procurement of a protective order, etc.). The officers were reluctant to call on the counselor at first, but eventually they developed problem-solving activities that included a domestic violence response unit on problem-solving Wednesdays. Counselors were commonplace ride-alongs after a while.

A committee was formed to revamp the personnel evaluation form to include community policing, problem-solving activities. A problem-solving project request and tracking form was developed to assist officers with their activities. The first problem to be addressed was generated by a community complaint about skateboarders vandalizing the downtown area. After the analysis phase, the officers discovered that the underlying cause was that there was no place for the skateboarders to practice. The final outcome was that the Parks Department secured funding to build a skateboard park, designed and governed by a board of officers, skateboarders, parents, and Parks Department employees. Other successes have included resolution of a neighborhood dispute that involved allegations of racism by the sole African-American family living in the neighborhood.

Partnerships have been formed with the Broken Arrow Public School system, primarily initiated by our being awarded a School Based Partnership Grant. The partnership was among the school administration, a student group, and the police department. We facilitated the students leading the problem-solving approach and applying it to the problem of violence in the schools. Involvement of patrol officers as mentors to the student groups increased the understanding and commitment to community policing by all involved. We also partner with the Metropolitan Citizens Crime Commission to increase Broken Arrow residents' involvement in the Alert Neighbors program, participate in the Human Resources Council, and are active members of the SALT Council to address concerns of senior citizens and of the Safe Place Coalition, which is seeking to build a teen center in the city so that teens will have "safe" alternatives to idle time after school. Partnerships with other city government functions such as Public Works, Parks and Recreation, and Code Enforcement have eased the tensions between the rank and file and the "they" perceived to live at City Hall.

We have encouraged community involvement in the police department by asking about their priorities for the police in a citizen survey, following up on police response with random surveys of callers to 911, hosting a Citizens Police Academy, participating in National Night Out, and creating community focus groups to address specific problems such as truancy and animal control issues.

We have undertaken an aggressive training program to acquaint officers with not only the processes but also the real-life experiences of other agencies involved in problem solving. Lack of crime analysis information has hampered the identification/analysis of problems. However, we now have a crime analyst on board and are moving toward our own version of the COMSTAT process to hold managers accountable for controlling crime.

RESISTANCE TO CHANGE

Initially, officers were reluctant to offer input into the direction of the department. They had never been involved before and were suspicious of the new style. Additionally, the FOP was in the forefront of challenging the changes and decisions that were being made. The old style of policing was prevalent and the community expressed concerns that officers were "heavy-handed." Grievances were filed on every decision made. In the meantime, new officers were being hired who supported the community policing philosophy and the problem-solving approach. An unbiased promotional process was held and newly promoted captains, lieutenants, and sergeants embraced the participatory model as well as the direction of the department. Other timely events led to the reassessment of the stance of the FOP and ultimately a realization that management and the

FOP want many of the same things and that good things are happening. While not always seeing eye to eye, the FOP, management, and personnel are now moving in the same direction on many of the issues that are of concern to both: personnel increases, promotional opportunities, and input in decision making.

SOLIDIFICATION OF THE COMMITMENT

The city manager who had hired Chief Kusler succumbed to his illness in the spring of 1998. A nationwide search began for his replacement. In September 1998, Michael D. Kadlecik, former city manager for Palentine, Illinois, joined the city of Broken Arrow as the new city manager. He brought with him a customer service orientation and a commitment to community policing and involvement in the community. His positive attitude and disposition toward the police department and his commitment to training, professionalism, and customer service have been the icing on the cake. Community policing is not just a movement or a program within the police department, but a way of thinking about the way we conduct the business of keeping the streets and neighborhoods safe. The problem-solving approach is the framework the department uses to involve the officers with the community and the community with the department and the officers. The community no longer views the officers as "heavy-handed," but as a helpful part of city government that is committed to a safe environment, improved quality of life, and open communications.

POLICE

We, the Broken Arrow Police Department, having been duly appointed police officers of the City of Broken Arrow, and peace officers of the State of Oklahoma, do solemnly swear (or affirm) that we will defend, enforce and obey, the Constitution and laws of the United States, the State of Oklahoma and the ordinances of the City of Broken Arrow. That we will obey the lawful orders of our superior officers and the regulations of the Broken Arrow Police Department. That We will faithfully discharge our duties and responsibilities as citizens of the United States. That we will protect the rights, lives and property of all citizens and uphold the honor of the police profession, with our lives if need be.

PART 2: HOW THE CITY GOT ITS NAME!

Anyone who knows about Oklahoma knows about Indians, and it's a safe bet that most Oklahoma towns are named by or for Indians. Broken Arrow is no exception. The name was here—in the Creek language, "Thlikatchka"—before the town was born. Early settlers simply translated the Indian syllables into a language they understood. Contrary to expectations, however, the name had nothing to do with "peace."

The Creeks lived in Alabama before they were relocated to Oklahoma. One tribe of Creeks in Alabama lived on the Broken Arrow Creek, which flowed into the Chattahoochee River. Along this creek grew canes which they would break off to make their arrows. This tribe became known as the tribe of "broken arrow" as a result of breaking off these canes rather than cutting them, as most tribes did. It was that Broken Arrow Indian community which settled north of the Arkansas River that gave the town of Broken Arrow its name.

THE DEPARTMENT

The Broken Arrow Police Department is comprised of 98 sworn and 49 nonsworn men and women who serve approximately 80,000 residents (in 1970, the population was 11,000) in the city of Broken Arrow, Oklahoma. The city has a new $27 million campus for Northeastern State University, which will be opened soon, and is a 15-minute drive to Tulsa. Its ecomony is stable and its educational centers boast that 90 percent of all high school graduates continue on to college or technical training programs. The police department contains many divisions in which various services are provided. These divisions deliver services in the areas of patrol, investigations, traffic, communications, civil defense, jail facilities, records management, animal control, and administration. The Broken Arrow Police Department is committed to delivering these services with unwavering integrity and assurance of equality to all persons who reside or travel within the jurisdiction of the city of Broken Arrow. The following information summarizes the activities and organizational changes that occurred during 1998.

The Broken Arrow Police Department

BROKEN ARROW POLICE PROGRAMS

In addition to law enforcement protection the Broken Arrow Police Department offers a number of community services to its residents, including these:

- *Alert Neighbors programs:* In conjunction with the Citizens Crime Commission to empower area residents with the knowledge of how to protect their property and that of their neighbors.
- *Domestic violence counselor:* A trained counselor to provide services to victims of domestic violence.
- *Domestic Violence Response Team:* Trained volunteers who will respond to provide services and counseling for victims of domestic violence.

- *Crime prevention for senior citizens:* Crime prevention education programs for senior citizens to provide instruction on how to avoid victimization by crimes that are typically targeted at the elderly.
- *Crime analysis services:* Information regarding crime statistics and calls for police service within the community.
- *Registered sex offender information:* Where in the city registered sex offenders reside.
- *Traffic calming and enforcement requests:* For residents who suffer from reoccurring problems regarding traffic matters.
- *Child safety programs:* Bicycle safety programs, "Stranger Danger," and other child safety instruction is provided by our Crime Prevention Unit.
- *Drug, tobacco, and gang prevention:* Provided by the police department's school resource officers in the public school system.
- *Watch orders:* To request special checks of residents' homes when they are away.
- *Citizens on Patrol program:* A program designed for area community watch and neighborhood organizations to provide necessary education and resources which allow residents to embark on crime prevention patrols of their neighborhoods.
- *Citizens Police Academy:* A "mini" police academy for citizens to provide insight into what type of training their police officers receive.
- *Broken Arrow Police Reserves:* This organization provides a number of public safety services including supplementing police staffing, disaster response, traffic control, and police services for community events.
- *Animal control services:* Animal control officers provide enforcement of local laws regarding wild and domestic animals in addition to impoundment of animals and a pet adoption program.
- *CRIMELINE:* Citizens are encouraged to call our 24-hour CRIMELINE to provide information on known or suspected criminal activity. Citizens can call to report information that will be forwarded to the appropriate division for investigation. Callers can remain anonymous.
- *National Night Out program:* The police department is proud to participate in this national crime prevention program, which is held annually to encourage community involvement to reduce crime in our neighborhoods.

Broken Arrow Canine Team

CRIME STATISTICS

In 1998 Broken Arrow, Oklahoma, experienced three homicides, 25 rapes, 24 robberies, 92 aggravated assaults, 338 burglaries, 1,281 larcenies, and 177 auto thefts for a total of 1,940 Index Crimes (see Table 1). Additionally, there were 912 nonaggravated assaults and 665 domestic violence calls.

In reviewing Index Crimes in Broken Arrow for a 10-year period, it becomes clear that Index category crime has decreased by approximately 3 percent (see Table 2). However, nonaggravated assaults and domestic violence over the same period has increased by approximately 115 percent.

When a crime comparison is made between Broken Arrow and three similar cities, it appears that Broken Arrow is a safer city to live in (see Table 3). The 1997 Crime Index figures were used for these comparisons. The cities used for comparisons were chosen because of comparable populations. Broken Arrow's crime index per 1,000 was calculated at 27 as compared to Edmond, Oklahoma, at 38, Enid at 91, and Midwest City at 65. These rates might suggest that Broken Arrow has fewer reported crimes than similar sized cities in the same geographical area.

1998 CITIZEN SURVEY SUMMARY

A survey was developed by the police department to be disseminated to residents of Broken Arrow. The intent of the survey was to find out what citizens perceived to be crime problems in their neighborhoods, the level of their fear of crime, their perception of the police services being rendered and the level of citizen involvement in neighborhood watch programs.

Approximately 30,000 citizen surveys were mailed with city water bills during the September 1998 billing cycle. Only 1,851 surveys were completed and returned by residents.

Completed surveys were forwarded to Broken Arrow High School, where Mrs. Karen Barnes' Advanced Placement Mathematics classes tabulated the results. Students prepared a report on their findings. Students organized the surveys by square mile. Several surveys did not indicate the area where the resident lived, so they could not be placed within a particular square mile of the city. The surveys that did not indicate a neighborhood were placed into an at-large category.

When the survey results were returned to the police department, data from each square mile was organized into the current patrol districts to illustrate citizen views in each district. Each district and the at-large categories were combined to represent a city-wide perspective.

TABLE 1 Index Crime Statistics Per Month, 1998

	Homicide	Rape	Robbery	Aggravated Assault	Burglary	Larceny	Auto Theft	Total Index	Nonaggravated Assault	Domestic Violence
January	1	2	3	10	19	102	15	152	83	81
February	0	1	0	9	32	75	6	123	55	48
March	0	2	1	6	29	88	14	140	75	56
April	0	2	0	8	28	110	14	162	77	56
May	0	2	3	5	37	125	15	187	87	59
June	0	1	0	6	24	99	27	157	83	58
July	0	2	2	4	31	125	10	174	95	69
August	0	2	3	12	21	126	19	183	92	54
September	0	2	3	10	39	97	15	166	93	67
October	1	3	0	4	33	132	12	185	58	35
November	0	4	4	7	24	92	10	141	60	41
December	1	2	5	11	21	110	20	170	54	41
Totals	3	25	24	92	338	1,281	177	1,940	912	665

TABLE 2 Ten Year Comparison of Index Crimes

INDEX CRIMES	1988	1989	1990	1991	1992	1993	1994	1995	1998	1997	1998
Homicide	2	0	1	0	0	0	0	0	0	0	3
Rape	12	14	13	8	14	14	17	19	12	18	25
Robbery	28	10	15	14	20	16	18	26	15	26	24
Aggravated assaults	82	70	75	72	84	88	113	112	94	77	92
Burglary	541	486	393	422	428	395	379	504	519	410	338
Larceny	1,219	1,506	1,712	1,574	1,388	1,439	1,524	1,450	1,107	1,161	1,281
Auto theft	121	171	230	174	127	114	141	201	190	145	177
TOTAL INDEX	2,005	2,257	2,439	2,264	2,061	2,066	2,192	2,312	1,937	1,837	1,940
Nonaggravated assaults	442	494	454	486	654	729	725	728	650	840	912
Domestic violence	309	315	337	333	445	433	510	559	656	734	665

TABLE 3   Comparison of Oklahoma Cities' UCR Statistics for 1997

	BROKEN ARROW	EDMOND	ENID	MIDWEST CITY
Homicide	0	0	5	3
Rape	18	18	22	17
Robbery	26	37	40	84
Aggravated assault	77	59	266	135
Burglary	410	443	924	655
Larceny	1,161	1,624	2,732	2,283
Auto theft	145	162	273	377
Total	1,837	2,343	4,262	3,554
Population	66,867	62,331	46,680	54,440
Crime index per 1,000	27	38	91	65

Citizen Survey Results

Question 1: Has the incidence of crime changed in your neighborhood over the past year?

DISTRICT	INCREASED	DECREASED	NO CHANGE	NO ANSWER	N RESPONSES
1	27%	5%	60%	6%	308
2	21%	3%	69%	5%	130
3	37%	2%	55%	4%	251
4	20%	7%	68%	4%	200
5	17%	6%	69%	6%	179
6	23%	4%	66%	4%	430
At-large	19%	5%	67%	6%	219
City-wide average	23.4%	4.5%	64.8%	5%	1,717

Question 2: What type of crime occurs most often in your neighborhood?
This question listed 12 categories and asked the resident to rank them from highest to lowest occurrence. The categories were burglary, vandalism, traffic problems, juvenile problems, gang activity, auto theft, stray animals, family fights, child abuse, drugs, assault, and trash.

Responses to this question were tabulated by the AP Mathematics students and recorded for each square mile. This information was then analyzed and totaled for each of the patrol districts. Responses that did not list the neighborhood or were outside the city fence line were placed in an at-large category.

The top four concerns of citizens regarding the highest incidents of offenses in each district are as follows:

DISTRICT	CONCERN 1	CONCERN 2	CONCERN 3	CONCERN 4
1	Traffic	Vandalism	Juveniles	Burglary
2	Traffic	Strays	Vandalism	Juveniles
3	Vandalism	Strays	Traffic	Burglary
4	Traffic	Strays	Vandalism	Juveniles
5	Traffic	Vandalism	Strays	Burglary
6	Traffic	Vandalism	Strays	Juveniles
At-large	Traffic	Vandalism	Vandalism	Burglary
City-wide average	Traffic	Vandalism	Vandalism	Burglary

City wide, the number one concern was traffic. Stray animals ranked second. Vandalism ranked third. Juvenile problems and burglary tied for fourth place.

Question 3: Do you have concerns about other types of crime? If so, what?
Fifty-three separate crime categories were noted by residents. Several of these offense categories were noted multiple times by residents. A number of the items listed were similar in nature and were grouped together, for summary purposes. The top five complaints were:

1. Speeding and traffic related problems,
2. Drugs and drug trafficking,
3. Loud car radios at night,
4. Unmonitored juveniles, possible drinking/driving juveniles and loitering, and
5. Road rage.

Question 4: Have you been a victim of a crime in the past year? If yes, crime type. Did you report it to the police?
A total of 1,844 responses were reported by the participants. Four hundred forty-eight residents or 24.3 percent indicated that they had been victimized in the last year; 1,396 residents or 75.7 percent responded no to the question. Seven surveys had no response to the question.

Property crimes appear to be the most reported type of crime indicated by respondents.

- Vandalism was noted 187 times,
- Theft 86 times, and
- Burglary 85 times.

Of the 448 respondents who reported being victimized, 295 indicated that they had made police reports, while 139 advised that they did not report the crime to police. Fourteen residents did not respond to the third part of the question.

Question 5: Have you been involved in a traffic accident in the past year?

1,649 or 89.07% responded no.

183 or 9.86% responded yes.

19 or 1.07% did not respond to the question.

Question 6: Are you afraid you may become the victim of a crime?

1,187 or 60.31 percent responded no.

540 or 32.29 percent responded yes.

124 or 7.40 percent did not respond to the question.

Question 7: Have you had contact with a Broken Arrow police officer in the past year? If yes, what type of contact? If yes, please rate your contact on the following points: knowledge, courteous, respectful, listened.

Contact?

784 citizens responded yes.

937 responded no.

130 did not respond to this question.

112 citizens had casual contact.

656 citizens had legal contact.

794 did not indicate the type of contact.

Citizens having contact with Broken Arrow police in the last year rated the officers as follows:

Knowledge:	Approximately 82 percent rated officers excellent to good.
	(56 percent excellent, 26 percent good, 9 percent average, 3 percent fair, 6 percent poor)
Courteous:	Approximately 84 percent rated officers excellent to good.
	(62 percent excellent, 22 percent good, 7 percent average, 3 percent fair, 6 percent poor)
Respectful:	Approximately 84 percent rated officers excellent to good. (62 percent excellent, 22 percent good, 7 percent average, 3 percent fair, 6 percent poor)
Listened:	Approximately 83 percent rated officers excellent to good.
	(59 percent excellent, 24 percent good, 8 percent average, 4 percent fair, 5 percent poor.)

Question 8: If the police department assisted with a crime in the last year, were you satisfied with the outcome?

359 answered yes.

302 answered no.

1,190 no response.

Question 9: Are you a member of a neighborhood watch group or citizens on patrol?

_____ yes _____ no

How often does the group meet? Weekly, monthly, semi-annually, other?

NEIGHBORHOOD WATCH/CITIZEN ON PATROL				MEETINGS			
DISTRICT	YES	NO	NO ANSWER	WEEKLY	MONTHLY	SEMI-ANNUALLY	OTHER
1	24	308	30	0	3	5	16
2	17	77	15	0	1	2	9
3	12	219	17	0	1	1	10
4	9	111	22	0	1	2	6
5	9	135	26	0	1	3	5
6	50	332	36	0	11	8	31
Total	121	1,182	146	0	18	21	77
At-large City-wide	17	362	23	0	2	0	15
Total	138	1,544	169	0	20	21	92

NINE HARD QUESTIONS ABOUT COMMUNITY POLICING INITIATIVES

Question 1: What methods are employed to ensure that typical members of the community are represented in the community policing process?

We take a problem-solving approach to community problems that requires obtaining the perspective of all who may have a point of view: suspects, citizens, witnesses, neighbors, victims, officials, etc. All officers have been trained in problem-solving methods and are encouraged to use these approaches to everyday activities. We also have a number of officers who actively participate in school safety committees and school-based partnership problem-solving projects to encourage open communication with the education community, police, and the students. These programs encourage participation from all community stakeholders through such avenues as open "town hall" meetings in which we invite the general public, parents, police, students, school officials, and all persons affected by school problems to participate and provide input. This helps to ensure the focus is maintained toward a long-term solution to problems faced by the education system.

The use of school resource officers, the presence of the beat officers in local schools on a regular basis, and regular contact between school and police representatives allows the constant flow of information between the two entities. The implementation of two school-based partnership problem-solving projects has provided the catalyst for regular contact between school and police participants.

To ensure proper quality control is maintained in regard to routine police activities, our agency conducts ongoing random sampling of 911 callers to enlist their feedback on the appropriateness of the response they received to our service. This allows the actual users of our police services to critique the response and effectiveness of the services they receive and allows the public a venue to provide input to the department in regard to the services that are provided by our agency. We promote public input and participation in all aspects of our duties, even in regard to critiquing our own performance.

To further enhance our ability to reach the public, we have established relationships with the media so that our priorities can be presented to the public and to allow for the regular publication of information for general review. This allows the community's citizens to have access to information that may affect their quality of life. The citizens are kept abreast of crime trends and policing projects through regular news releases and features. Because information is power, the citizens are able to review published information to determine what issues are important to them.

The BAPD is active in a local Community Resource Council, comprised of a number of local business leaders, social service organizations, schools, and governmental agencies. The members of the Community Resource Council meet on a monthly basis, with representatives of our agency included, in order to exchange information on various programs and community events. This Resource Council serves as an excellent avenue for our agency to receive feedback from community members, to spotlight our programs, and to network with other community groups in the exchange of ideas and resources for the betterment of the community.

The Broken Arrow Police Department recently developed a Citizen Police Academy to improve the amount of communication and interaction between the public and the police. We encourage our community residents to participate in the "mini police academy" so they can see firsthand what services we provide, to allow our officers and the public to get to know each other through direct interaction, and to provide our community members with some insight into the duties of our employees. This program results in a large amount of interest from the public by spotlighting the needs of the community.

We have established the CRIMELINE, which is a publicized number to the police department. This number is monitored 24 hours a day and allows community members to call our agency at any time to report crime information. Developed primarily for the reporting of narcotics information, we encourage community members to use the CRIMELINE to report any concerns or to pass on any information they desire to our agency. Whether it is known or suspected criminal activity or complaints, all information from the public is forwarded to the appropriate division for follow-up.

An officer was recently appointed as a full-time crime prevention officer, and we anticipate the hiring of a civilian crime prevention specialist in the near future. The Crime Prevention Unit will provide a number of opportunities to expand our community policing programs. This will result in the enhanced ability to enlist assistance from the community and also allow us to reach greater numbers of citizens through various crime prevention programs. We plan to develop a number of projects in the future to help us network in more detail with the community. These programs include the following:

- Regular communication with our neighborhood watch and homeowner organizations. This will be accomplished with regular presentations at these organizations as well as correspondence through the use of newsletters, bulletins, and the Internet.
- Expanded use of technology will provide better information exchange with the public. We plan to develop a web site that will allow citizens to obtain real-time crime statistic information. Through the Crime Analyst, citizens will be able to determine what areas of town are experiencing increases in crime or what particular occurrences are happening in their neighborhood.
- We intend to make our district officers more directly available to the public in order to allow better flow of communication. By publicizing what areas of town are in a particular district or beat, citizens will know exactly which beat officer is responsible for their neighborhood. We will then be able to publish a phone number for each beat number as a single point of contact for our citizens. This will allow the public to call the beat officer in their area of town to allow direct communication between police and the public.
- Development of a Citizen Crime Prevention Committee, comprised of representatives of Neighborhood Watch, Citizens on Patrol, and homeowners associations who can meet with police representatives on a regular basis to discuss crime trends and crime prevention methods and to exchange information regarding community activity.

Question 2: In what way are community residents included in the decision-making processes associated with community policing? Explain feedback and/or the decision levels of community members in the following areas:

Deployment strategies relevant to activities such as foot patrols, mini stations, bike patrols. The BAPD does not operate mini or substations, bike patrols, or foot patrols. We anticipate adding a bike patrol as an option for officers in our downtown business district in the future. While researching the feasibility of implementing such a program we expect to receive input from the Downtown Merchants Association as well as the various schools in the area to respond about the benefits and/or drawbacks of such a program.

Crime-targeted strategies, activities such as neighborhood crime watches, owner notification, criminal trespass. Neighborhood Watch and Citizens on Patrol are two examples of programs operated by our agency to empower the citizens to work with the police department on proactive prevention measures. Our citizens are recruited through the news media, fliers in water bills, brochures, etc., to recruit volunteers for inclusion in these activities. We work in conjunction with the Citizen Crime Commission in providing proactive crime prevention measures to local neighborhood watch groups and we provide training and solicit commercial support from businesses to fund the operation of the Citizens on Patrol program. This particular training for our citizens gives instruction on how they may conduct their own preventive patrols of their neighborhoods and provides the necessary means, such as cellular phones, for the citizens to work directly with police in reporting criminal behavior. Although we rely on the citizens to contact us, we anticipate more active recruitment in these programs with the implementation of a full-time Crime Prevention Unit. Once a year we participate in the National Night Out program by soliciting community members to take a stand against crime and we showcase our agency services and those of other community service groups at an annual Public Safety Festival. We actively recruit community members into these programs during the National Night Out program and have a number of officers available for interaction with the public and to answer their questions. In addition, we have a presence at a number of other community events, such as the local Rooster Day Festival and the Tulsa State Fair where all our programs are spotlighted.

As previously mentioned, our officers regularly make contact with local businesses in their beat to ensure regular communication and to obtain emergency contact information for local merchants. Through this avenue our beat officers are able to enlist direct input from local merchants about areas of concerns that can be addressed by the officers or other community resources. As far as specific crime problems, our officers utilize the problem-solving approach to specific problems by enlisting assistance from all stakeholders who are affected. These problem-solving activities include interviews and information collected from all neighbors or citizens who may have an understanding of the problem as well as implementing solutions to rectify the situation.

As a bedroom community, we suffer from the disproportionately large problem of domestic violence crimes. As a result, our agency has recognized the importance of intervention to solve the problem, as opposed to the typical police response of simply temporarily fixing the problem. We took the rather unusual approach of trying to solve the issues that lead to the crimes of domestic violence. The BAPD in collaboration with local domestic violence services developed a grant to fund a domestic violence counselor program for domestic abuse victims. This particular grant provides funding to allow the police department to employ a civilian domestic violence counselor who is available during the evening hours. In addition, our agency has provided training to a number of volunteer domestic violence counselors who are available to respond 24 hours a day to assist in domestic-related calls for assistance.

Collaborative strategies such as advisory councils, crime prevention councils, police disciplinary committees. All supervisors are encouraged to become involved with local civic and resource groups in which they may have an interest. The police department is actively involved in the local community resource group to ensure that networking between our agency and other agencies is established. The chief of police is active on several boards and coalitions, and command staff is represented in a number of civic organizations. These organizations are all concerned with crime prevention activities and provide a conduit for feedback to the department as to what needs exist in the community.

The police department animal control officers are in the process of forming an animal adoption program through the use of an advisory group. We are actively attempting to find alternatives to destroying animals that are impounded and unclaimed at the city animal shelter. To change this process, we have begun formulating plans to expand our agency animal adoption program. Through the use of the local media, an "Animal of the Week" spotlight on the Internet, and other public exposure, we hope to increase the number of animals who are spayed/neutered and turned over to happy homes for adoption.

As a result of the domestic violence counselor program, we have increased our interaction with domestic violence agencies to the betterment of both groups. Our officers have received more training in domestic violence issues, and we have established a great rapport and partnership with the local domestic violence service as a result of our efforts to specifically target domestic violence. The domestic violence program initiated by our agency provides the resource for our agency to interact with the servers of domestic violence to ensure that every step possible is taken to reduce the incidents of abuse. Because the domestic violence counselors respond to calls immediately and follow up on every reported case of domestic abuse, this provides the opportunity for our officers to interact directly with the domestic violence agencies to facilitate the exchange of information.

Our agency will soon employ a crime prevention specialist to focus on problem solving related to drugs and violence at the school system Alternative Academy for at-risk youth. The problem-solving strategy will involve the students who attend the school as participants in the process. The crime prevention specialist will have daily contact with students and school administrators, and will be able to facilitate regular interaction between police, the city's youth, and school staff.

Question 3: What are the elements and/or conditions that will sustain the active involvement of residents in the community?

Institutionalizing the problem-solving process in all facets of the department will ensure that the police remain active with the community and vice versa. By making the problem-solving process standard procedure, and allowing the time, resources, and encouragement for the officers to successfully complete these projects, the officers will begin to use this process routinely. The problem-solving process works. The utilization of community resources works. The gathering of information from all stakeholders works. The officers know this, have begun to put it to practical use, and are realizing the fruits of their efforts. Once the officers have realized the benefits of community interaction, the citizens will soon follow and will also be encouraged to see their police as a resource as opposed to a necessary evil. Part of the responsibility of the police is to educate the public as to what the roles of the citizens and the police are in the protection of the community. Once the community realizes that the police are limited in their abilities, and even more importantly, how important a role the citizens can play in their own proactive measures, the involvement of the community should be a normal reaction of most reasonable persons to protect that which is important to them. Although complacency can hamper any attempt to solicit public participation, it will be the job of the police department to attempt to ensure active participation through proactive crime prevention programs, public contacts, presentations, and solicitation of community involvement.

Question 4: How will your organization pick up the slack from federal money when it runs out, assuming some part of your community policing program is being funded or subsidized?

The BAPD is an aggressive grant seeking agency, which, through its current administration, has civic support to both match grant money and to continue those programs with allocated personnel when grant funding ends. Table 4 shows their efforts as of June 1999, however, seven additional grants are pending for $871,156, which would require a match of $203,767. The department has committed to the use of some federal funds, such as for school-based partnership grants and the Universal Hiring Program, and city leaders have agreed to continue funding after the completion of the grant period. The partnerships the department has developed with schools through these grants will continue long after the grants have expired. The additional officers produced by these grants will be hired eventually, but the grants allow the vehicle to achieve these goals sooner than city coffers would allow.

TABLE 4   Grant Efforts as of June 1999

GRANT AGENCY	DESCRIPTION	AMOUNT RECEIVED	MATCH AMOUNT	SOURCE OF MATCH
DAC/VOCA	DiVert* counselor	19,200*	4,800	Volunteer labor
DOJ/COPS	COPs Universal Hiring, 1999 (6 officers)	450,000	166,995	General fund
BJA	Local law enforcement block grant (LLEBG)	32,998	3,621	Federal asset forfeiture
DOC	VOI/TIS jail grant	50,000	5,556	CIP
DOJ/COPS	School-based partnership	130,692	No match required	
BJA	LLEBG	33,018	3,669	Nonprofit organization
DAC/VOCA Subgrant	DiVert counselor grant, 1999–2000	17,300	4,325	In kind, volunteer labor
	Total awarded	733,208	188,966	922,174
	*Cents not shown			

*Domestic Violence Emergency Response Team

BAPD expects the problem-solving process to become a way of life for their officers and they rely on members of the community or the schools for inter- action as a routine, regardless of the origination of funds. The community policing philosophy is an evolving process which will become standard opera- tion for every police officer employed by the BAPD. Because every police agency in the United States is different, the size of the grants is less important than the number and diversity of grant sources, suggesting that BAPD is pro- fessionally pursuing resources to enhance its residents and bring the depart- ment closer to its mission.

Question 5: What were the historical events that influenced organiza- tional decisions to establish a community policing agenda at your agency?

The primary reason for the installation of the community policing philosophy was the employment of a new chief of police who is dedicated to the philoso- phy. The new chief of police retired from an agency that practiced the com- munity policing philosophy, was educated and trained in the concept, and knew it would work for this agency. Although many officers employed by our agency had practiced many of the theories of community policing for many years, we did not recognize it as community policing.

The installation of a new chief provided the guidance and direction that al- lowed the implementation of the community policing philosophy. This went far beyond the training of officers in the concepts of community policing and problem solving. Reorganization and a commitment to allow the officers to achieve these objectives had to be made. Every employee, from the adminis- tration down to the line officers, had to recognize what resources were needed to allow the officers to be successful in the community policing philosophy. This required restructuring, reorganization, and rescheduling of personnel. This also resulted in some resentment to the initial changes, which created some tension. However, once the reality of the changes was seen, the improve- ments were realized, and the employees were empowered with the ability and responsibility for their own beats, the process began to work successfully.

Question 6: What are the methods used to assess and/or evaluate the progress of the community policing effort?

To this point, the evaluation has been primarily community feedback and re- sponse to various programs. Informal comments made to the chief indicate that the perception of the public has changed during the past two years. Two years ago, comments were made that the police were "heavy-handed," aggressive, and unfriendly. Now, the public feedback is positive; they comment that they see the police more frequently, that the police are viewed as helpful and friendly, and that relationships between the community and the police have improved. The positive steps taken by the agency in the last two years to improve communica- tion with the public and community resources has resulted in a more progres- sive stance in our ability to provide professional services to the public. Keep in mind that our progression to community policing activities is relatively new. As time progresses we will be afforded the opportunity to establish more evaluation processes for our rapidly growing system.

Part of our efforts have included the employment and training of a crime analyst and the active improvement of technology for the agency. These steps will allow our resources to be directed toward problems which are occurring, to provide information to the officers and the public regarding crime trends, and to allow the ability for crime forecasting in the future. The crime analyst will have the capability to provide our officers with the data necessary to conduct a proper problem-solving effort. The crime analyst will also provide the necessary information to allow the police department to assess our own initiatives in crime suppression by acting as a barometer to ensure that we are focusing our attentions where they should be.

Question 7: How does your agency determine the success or failure of your community policing effort?

We track problem-solving initiatives, complaints for rudeness/inappropriate conduct and perform regular performance evaluations on the officers to determine their level of activity, community involvement, and what attitudes they are exhibiting to the public. These items provide management with insight into the "personality" of the department and whether it reflects the community policing spirit. The feedback we receive from the community is a direct reflection of the type of service that is being provided to the community. We are able to gauge the performance level of our officers and employees and the level of service to the community by the amount of and type of positive or negative feedback we get from our community partners, community resources, and the citizens.

Question 8: In what way have any community policing programs been changed or altered as a result of community policing assessments?

The majority of changes in community policing programs involve growth. As the police department structure grows and changes, the BAPD has additional resources to utilize for additional community policing programs. Since the inception of the community policing philosophy, the BAPD has implemented a number of programs and assignments directly for the community in an effort to provide additional exposure and networking with the public.

Occasionally, you find yourself in the opposite position. For example, we deemphasized the Citizens on Patrol program for a while due to a group of citizens who were in conflict with a resident in their neighborhood. After determining this was an isolated incident, we asked for mediation between these particular groups and continued with the program. The biggest change in the department as a whole is that we have become more public oriented and strive to solve the problems we are faced with rather than simply trying to remedy the situation. Because the BAPD became more aware of resources such as grants through community policing initiatives, one push led to more funding for productive programs such as the Domestic Violence Response Team (DiVert) program. For instance, BAPD was recently rewarded a second grant from the Oklahoma District Attorney's Council to continue the program. The award provides funding for fiscal year 1999–2000 to continue the Domestic Violence Counseling program that was established in 1998 through the same grant. The program provides for a contract counselor through the Domestic Violence Intervention Service to provide counseling, follow-up, and response for domestic situations. This year's award also allows additional funding for travel expenses to allow the counseling staff to receive training pertinent to giving domestic counseling services. In addition to our part-time counselor, the program continues the use of DiVert volunteers to provide after-hours services to police and victims of domestic violence.

Question 9: In what way has the training differed as compared to pre-community policing efforts?
Prior to community policing efforts, most of the training focused on firearms qualifications and shooting scenarios. The training program is more balanced now by providing a variety of required and elective training courses to the officers. Officers are encouraged to seek outside training and are provided the resources to do so.

Making the Philosophy Work

The question for many police departments is the same: Can community policing work? The Broken Arrow Police Department faced this question and developed a progressive implementation plan. The plan included foundation decisions about where they were going and how to get the skills to get there. They organized themselves to provide opportunities to practice the skills, and are now thinking about celebrating their level of success.

Where Were They Going?

The BAPD command staff attended a management retreat to change the way they did business. Guidelines such as their mission statement, vision, and values were defined. Those concepts served as a catalyst for moving the department forward.

How Do They Get the Skills to Get There?

Training it was decided is the backbone of any change process and the BAPD knew that they required a commitment of time, resources, and patience. It was their perspective that:

The greater the momentum of a ship, the longer it takes to turn. One comforting observation is that a huge ship can nevertheless be turned by a small rudder. It just takes time, and it requires the rudder to be set steadfastly for the turn throughout the whole turning process.

—Malcolm K. Sparrow

Early in 1998 all department personnel including civilians were trained in the concepts of community policing (which included their new mission statement, values, and their shared new vision) and problem solving to ensure the department shifted its focus within every division at the same time. Supervisors were given training in how to manage problem-solving efforts by their officers. It was a family affair!

Organized Themselves to Provide Opportunities to Practice the Skills

The next step was to provide opportunities for the use of those new skills. The first obstacle was the traditional mind-set of "If it ain't broke, don't fix it," regarding changing the structure of the police department. Inadequate manpower levels exacerbated the problem. The BAPD's limited manpower resources were addressed before any new philosophy was implemented. They committed to an aggressive recruiting campaign to fill vacancies and lobbied for six additional personnel. In September 1998 the BAPD realigned their five-eight shifts into the four 10-hour configuration. This new shift allowed one squad at a time from each shift to work on problem-solving and/or training without depleting patrol resources. District alignments were made permanent to create "ownership" for the beats. So now twice a month officers have the opportunity to work on problem-solving projects specific to their beat. To fill in the gaps, detectives serve warrants, conduct special traffic enforcement, and address other specific concerns needing patrol attention. Individuals were cross-trained to help the department meet their mission.

An Example of Success

It is clear that the following problem might not be a big concern to some hardcore officers, but the method of solving problems and preventing crime in Broken Arrow is revealed in the following account. There was a recurring problem with skateboarders and in-line skaters in the business district. Broken Arrow residents take their business district and the skateboarding seriously. Officers researched ways in which to alleviate the problems. Under old perspectives, the skateboarders would have been involved in a situation with the police. This time, no one wanted skateboarding to get out of hand for anyone concerned.

Officers responded to location calls and ran off skateboarders at the request of shop owners. The businesses were reluctant to press trespassing charges against the skateboarders for fear of economic reprisal from angry parents. The relatively minor damage occurring to business property was due to the act of skating itself as opposed to malicious acts. The type of terrain offered by loading docks and handrails proved to be too tempting for many of the skaters.

Officers conducted written surveys of the skateboarders themselves. The businesses were surveyed in person by two officers on foot. Answers on both surveys from the businesses and kids alike were similar. The teenagers were surveyed during lunch periods at the schools and while they were skating out in public. Both surveys pointed to the obvious answer—Broken Arrow needed a skate park. Research on skateboarding and skate parks was completed via the Internet and magazines. Professional magazines associated with parks and recreation had cover stories about skate parks growing in popularity again. Research included subjects such as liability, cost, safety, usage, and management, which were important aspects of a skate park. One of the officers made sight visits to a couple of skate parks in Chicago during an unrelated business trip. Several businesses stated that they would help with partial funding if needed for a skate park. Everyone contacted agreed that the skateboarders were a problem in the business districts but they also needed a place to skate. The progress of the project continued through two city administrations. Contact was made individually with the City Council and other city officials to gain support for the project. After reviewing our data, the Parks Department came on board and is working with the BAPD to secure funding.

As soon as funding is available, a building committee will be formed to include skaters, business owners, residents near the proposed site, and parents to hammer out the rules of the park and to help with its construction and set rules for operation. The problem-solving effort seemed to come to a conclusion when a Grant for Innovative programs for youth became available and a proposal for the skate park was written. Unfortunately, the grant was not awarded, but the process continued. During the budget process for the city of Broken Arrow in 1999 the proposal was made to the City Council as part of the Parks and Recreation budget. Surprisingly the $50,000 park was approved without dissension.

The youth for the city will now get their skate park thanks to the efforts of patrol officers who gained support from citizens, businesses, civic organizations, and city government. During the remainder of 1999 the youth in Broken Arrow were part of the building process for the park, and the opening in the year 2000. During the initial stages of the research it never entered the minds of either officer that the endeavor they undertook might take three years to come to fruition.

Breakdown of Skate Boarding Problem: Evening shift calls increased in reference to skateboarders in business parking lots and walkways. Two patrol officers identified the reoccurring problem and recognized the pattern and trend. The objectives for the project were to reduce the amount of calls associated with skateboarders to allow patrol officers more time to perform other job functions. Written surveys of the skateboarders and door-to-door written surveys were conducted at the major business districts where the problems were occurring.

Meetings with school officials, city officials, civic groups, and business leaders were held and the problem was viewed from each angle. The efforts have culminated in the funding of a $50,000 skate park, which is in the development phase. The Broken Arrow Police Department is proud to say that it has added community policing as a tool to its tool belt in addressing quality of life issues for the city of Broken Arrow.

COMMENTS MADE BY BROKEN ARROW POLICE OFFICERS

I believe that community policing is the partnership between the Broken Arrow Police Department and the community to attempt to resolve any conflicts or to answer any concerns that those in the community may have. The Broken Arrow Police Department has provided its police officers with training, such as conflict resolution seminars, to help better prepare us to help citizens. The changes have not affected or improved my ability to serve the community. I have found that the majority of the concerns of the citizens can be easily solved. The residents just need someone to lead them in the proper direction and this is where the police department comes into effect. The police department has benefited through forming partnerships with the community in the way that we have received positive feedback from the citizens of Broken Arrow.

—Officer Mike Berry

My concept of community policing is the use of all community resources to solve problems. In the past, officers had more time to stay in contact with other groups and the people of the community. However, due to the increased call load, this practice has stopped. Now with the new work schedule the officer has two days per month to renew old partnerships and develop new ones. The use of community policing has given the officer the chance to solve problems instead of just responding to the same problems again and again. With theses changes it has allowed the officers to assist the public, not only in law enforcement but in other areas, which could prevent other problems from occurring.

With the training of our officers in community policing strategies, communication has improved, consequently opening doors that the officers are keeping open due to the new time allowed them. The formation of these partnerships has resulted in the police department being able to solve problems we would not have been able to solve previously. The Day Center has provided us with a place to take the homeless, Youth Service a place to take juveniles for a time out, and DVIS shelter for battered women.

I have seen these and more used time and time again, allowing us to help people in need. I personally used school administration and the PTA to solve a problem that no matter how hard we tried we could not resolve. The last day of school we had so many fights and vandalism it took two hours to get the children home. This was utilizing all the officers, leaving no one for other calls. I made arrangements with the school administrator to have teachers and members of the PTA at our trouble locations with video cameras and signs stating they were being videotaped and would be held responsible for their actions. With their help it now takes the normal amount of time to get the children home.

When the police department is faced with problems in the community we can now use the problem-solving techniques to determine the problem and get the necessary help from our partners to resolve it instead of fighting the symptoms.

—Sargent M. Martin

Sargent M. Martin

COMMUNITY MEMBERS WRITE
ABOUT BAPD'S COMMUNITY POLICING

The police department should be excited to see [so many] Broken Arrow citizens anxious to come and support its community [because of the good job they've done with community policing programs].

—Chuck Stophel, Citizens Crime Commission volunteer

Restructuring and moving an entire police force ahead with your vision is a difficult task. . . . I will do my part to help the program run smoothly. . . . I would like to be an active supporter of your vision not only in the educational arena, but also in the community.

—Michelle Warris, Broken Arrow Alternative Academy

. . . Your efforts this past year to have the police department attend regularly and participate in our BA Human Resource Council's networking and planning meetings has resulted in our agencies working with each

other in many ways and at many times to better the health and safety of our community.

—Phillip Lipscomb, Tulsa City-County Health Department

I am pleased that Broken Arrow Public Schools and the Broken Arrow Police have established an ongoing partnership . . . presentations . . . "Tools of Tomorrow" conference on Early Warning Signs of Violence and the School Resource Officer's presentation on identifying concealed weapons were well received. . . . As a coordinator of Broken Arrow Schools' Crisis Response Team, I am very pleased with the collaboration of the police in planning for any emergency. I believe the response to the bomb threat that occurred at our high school shortly after the tragedy at Columbine High School demonstrated efficiency and coordination due to previous planning. The six-hour hostage situation we staged at the senior high school using high school students and school staff was an excellent opportunity to gain valuable information for both police and school. The tabletop exercises involving crisis situations at all 24 sites which are planned for this year will certainly give us added knowledge and practice. . . . I am pleased that you have initiated another resource for our schools. Having each beat officer visit the school that is in her/his beat will afford the officer the opportunity to become acquainted with school staff and students. . . . Finally, it is my belief that by establishing this partnership we have safer schools and a safer community.

—Judy Jones, Broken Arrow Public Schools

I am writing in reference to my ride-along. It was a learning experience I will never forget. I wanted you to know that I am aware the BAPD is human and that you are understaffed. My questions were answered. . . . I am able to pass this information along. . . .

—Belinda Haney, Broken Arrow resident

Providing information, creating positive attitudes, enhancing self-esteem, infusing new ideas, and extending friendships—[BAPD] gave all of this to our teachers. Thank you for your generosity of spirit and resources. . . . From the results of the evaluations, we are counting this [community policing program] a success.

—Vicki Venable, School to Work coordinator, South Tulsa Partnership

To me, community policing is where the police department takes an active part in the life of the city and all citizens. This proactive stance gives ordinary citizens the opportunity to interact with the department in nonstressful situations. . . . This partnership with the police is very advantageous for the Optimist Club and has improved communication (and city moral). . . . One example is the formation of an Optimist Teen Center. . . . The department obtained a grant to study violence in the schools and at one of the cit-

izen input meetings we got from the teenagers a need that existed for them. In turn, this started the ball rolling and with active participation by the department, we are working toward the teen center. . . . As a citizen and public official, community policing Broken Arrow style is the way to go. Thank you, BAPD.

—Ron Whitaker, Broken Arrow Council, Optimist Club

SUMMARY

The new administration in Broken Arrow experienced resistance from individual program leaders who were threatened by a city-wide community policing philosophy effort to incorporate their programs into the department. The chief chose professional leadership techniques through modeling the precepts of community policing, developing a work environment facilitating success toward the mission of the department, and integrating the philosophy of community policing in every activity. One goal was to bring stability to a fragmented department and eventually to the community at large. All sworn officers under her command became part of the community policing team. BAPD's officers would maintain law and order, but were informed to move beyond just "catching the bad guys" to examining specific conditions, including problems of disorder and neglect that breed both minor and serious crimes. Programs are avenues to educate the community about police work in order for every officer to aid the community. To measure the success of community policing initiatives, Broken Arrow tracks complaints for rudeness/inappropriate conduct and performs regular performance evaluations on the officers to determine their level of activity, community involvement, and what attitudes they are exhibiting to the public. Their perspective is that community feedback is a direct reflection of the type of service provided to the community.

CONCLUSION

How did Broken Arrow implement a community policing initiative? By leadership modeling the precepts of community policing, developing a work environment facilitating success toward the mission of the department, and integrating the philosophy of community policing in every activity. That is, by stepping outside police traditional thinking and applying sound management concepts. The top command helped develop community partnerships with business, schools, and community groups by going out and recruiting them. Broken Arrow's best weapon? Probably an experienced officer with community policing experience who linked her office with a new city manager (her boss) who was pro-community policing. The trend of stable management (which means more than time on the job) seems to play a key role in each successful community policing implementation in this text, but rank and file officers and nonsworn personnel contribute to community policing maintenance.

DO YOU KNOW?

1. The challenge of community policing can be met by modeling the precepts of community policing, creating a work environment that facilitates success, and infusing the philosophy in every activity of the department. In what way can this perspective be met by a police department?

2. The new administration in Broken Arrow experienced the resistance of individual program leaders who were threatened by a city-wide community policing philosophy effort to incorporate those individual programs into the department. The administration followed this principle: If you want to get people to support your priorities, you must first address theirs. What priorities might the individual program leaders have and how did the administration address their priorities?

3. In community-based policing, officers continue to maintain law and order, but in what way might they move beyond just "catching bad guys"? How might they uncover specific conditions, including problems of disorder and neglect?

4. The chief of Broken Arrow created one new division within the department that answered directly to her office. In what way might that division impact community policing partnership relationships?

5. The local school system in Broken Arrow was determined to be an important partner with the police department. Their rationale was that students would provide feedback to aid the needs of the community-at-large. However, in what way might the department, in keeping with community policing initiatives, enhance its partnership relationship with school-aged individuals and thereby ultimately enhance police service to that population?

6. To measure the success of their community policing initiatives, Broken Arrow tracks complaints for rudeness/inappropriate conduct and performs regular performance evaluations on the officers to determine their level of activity, community involvement, and what attitudes they are exhibiting to the public. Their perspective is that community feedback is a direct reflection of the type of service provided to the community. How might their evaluation focus be different from other police agencies who lack a community policing spirit? That is, what might other agencies measure to determine if they are meeting their objectives? Why the difference?

7. In what way did BAPD's command staff demonstrate their clients' needs and the principles of quality police service?

CHAPTER THREE

METROPOLITAN-NASHVILLE POLICE DEPARTMENT

Nashville, Tennessee

INTRODUCTION

There are approximately 1,500 sworn officers employed by Metropolitan-Nashville Police Department (METRO)[1] who largely deliver a traditional response policing strategy to approximately 1 million people given the influx of 450,000 commuters and tourists in Davidson County, Tennessee. Nashville is the county's largest city. The department is currently instituting a community policing initiative directed by Chief of Police Emmett H. Turner who took office January 10, 1999. Lt. Ben Dickie[2] is both the major contributor to this chapter and one of the architects of METRO's community policing effort. This chapter can be considered a guide on how Davidson County initiated a community policing strategy and may render aid to other agencies that are thinking about implementing community policing initiatives.

Nashville is a growing city but has experienced a continuum of crime, despite aggressive enforcement policies and proactive programs implemented by the department. One problem is that crime, especially violent crime, occurs equally throughout every quarter of the county. As one response, METRO is a quasi-military organization in structure, with ranks of officer, sergeant, lieutenant, captain, major, assistant chief, and chief of police. For patrol purposes, the county was divided into four sections. However, in keeping with its quasi-military hierarchy model, command central directs METRO from the top

---

[1]METRO's web site is at http://www.nashville.net/~police/.
[2]Lt. Ben Dickie can be reached at nashcop1@aol.com.

61

down. Its hierarchy model of command might well remain in effect throughout the term of the current administration regardless of new initiatives. METRO is a new entity resulting from the merger of the Davidson County Sheriff and Nashville Police Department.

CHAPTER OUTLINE

There are two parts to this chapter. The first part reveals crime rates and experiences of METRO that apparently lend support to an aggressive enforcement of laws and regulations toward street crime and police officer conduct. The departmental objective to implement community policing initiatives is summarized followed by the results from an officer survey about their knowledge and application of community policing perspectives. METRO's community policing plan is revealed, including its philosophy, definition of terms, mission statement, and values.

The second part of the chapter is a community policing guide concerned with implementation of METRO's community policing project. This guide will be distributed to the personnel of METRO to familiarize them with the perspective and the process of community policing as instituted by the Metropolitan Nashville Police Department. Objectives, definitions, rationale, and philosophy are highlighted. Also addressed in this section are community support, community meetings, foundations for community policing, communication, street officer implementations, working with neighborhoods, and building relationships. Identifying and utilizing resources is discussed followed by methods of managing environmental issues. This section includes strategies on how to eliminate abandoned buildings, automobiles, and community trash.

There is also a discussion about METRO's newest programs, the Neighborhood Notifier and their bike patrols. Proactive strategies with juveniles are explained, including volunteer mentoring programs, neighborhood meeting challenges, truancy reduction programs, and child development programs in partnership with Yale University. Finally, numerous proactive enforcement strategies are highlighted that include hot-spot identification, undercover buy/bust operations, and enforcement roadblocks.

CRIME RATES AND EXPERIENCES

Motor vehicle theft, robbery, and aggravated assault are down, but murder, non-negligent manslaughter, and rape increased throughout the county by 25 percent from 1996 to 1997 (despite the high murder rate of 107 victims in 1995 of which 68 percent were black victims and 74 percent were black suspects). Burglary has increased from 8,025 in 1996 to 8,834 in 1997. For patrol purposes, Davidson County was divided into four sections: east, west, south, and central.

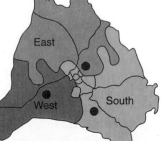

Metropolitan Nashville
Davidson County

County-wide, patrol officers answered over 6,000 shots fired calls in 1996 and made over 50,000 adult arrests in 1998.

What type of crime happens in Davidson County? A Nashville baby-sitter duct taped two children in her care and pleaded guilty to two counts of kidnapping; a Maplewood High School teacher was robbed while at work. Monica Starks, a seventh grader, was charged with two counts of aggravated assault and one count of carrying a weapon onto school property in connection with a stabbing incident inside a classroom at Wright Middle School. Homicide detectives arrested Anthony R. McGlother, 18, on a charge of assault with intent to commit murder of 16-year-old Antonio Grisham. McGlother is also under investigation for other shooting incidents. Although these crimes vary little from those of other jurisdictions its size, they give a reader an understanding of the criminal activity that exists in Davidson County, Tennessee.

Also, there are reports of continual racial and criminal misconduct by METRO officers. For example, on November 8, 1999, Detective Al Gray was placed on administrative leave with pay for violation of police department policy revealed during a random inspection process conducted by the department's Inspections Division. Gray was placed on a special police department/district attorney's office task force to investigate allegations of abuse against Hispanic citizens and other individuals, and altercations arose from that assignment. Patrol Officer Gregory Lofton was arrested and charged with one count of aggravated sexual battery and two counts of sexual battery in connection with the molestation of a teenage female on three occasions.

DEPARTMENTAL OBJECTIVES

METRO wants to return to the original concept of patrol as practiced prior to the use of the automobile as an enforcement tool. That is, the use of the automobile changed police patrol service from a daily face-to-face proactive delivery encounter to a quick-response delivery process within a large geographical area. Interaction with the public happens primarily during calls for service. When the police started to use police cars, the public became isolated from police officers resulting in public alienation. Continuing along this line of reasoning, it could also be argued that patrol officers became distant from top managers, too.

Therefore, one departmental objective of community policing practices for METRO is to eliminate the feelings of alienation produced, in part, through the use of police vehicles. Additionally, METRO recognizes that its predecessor, the Nashville Police Department, endured three decades of growing pains, which included police racism and police corruption. Therefore, public alienation linked to racism and corruption produced a deterioration of public trust. It is this lack of trust that is the driving force to return to an old concept of police delivery, now called *community-oriented policing*.

Other methods to win the trust from the community include enforcing the same laws for street officers as would be enforced in the community itself. For instance, in the fall of 1999, South Patrol Officer Brad Turner was placed on administrative assignment and was disempowered as a police offi-cer as a result of an accident while off duty. He pulled out of a parking lot into the path of a Tennessee Highway Patrol cruiser. Alcohol is believed to have been a contributing factor to the accident. Disciplinary action was also initiated against two off-duty officers who were riding with Turner. They are accused of being irresponsible for letting Turner drive a vehicle while impaired. In another typical case, one eight-year veteran, Bradley Mitchell, was terminated and two other officers, William J. Patterson and Vincent Archuleta, were both suspended as the result of disciplinary hearings in January 2000 in connection with their patronization of an adult-oriented business downtown while off duty.[3]

SIGNIFICANCE OF THE PROJECT

To measure what METRO officers understood about community policing and their level of partnership applications, a survey was conducted. Sixty officers from 20 patrol shifts participated in the survey. Once the data were collected and pooled, distinctive patterns arose. The findings showed that only about 21 percent of the respondents were familiar with METRO's community policing perspectives, and less than 20 percent of the participants applied community policing techniques to further public safety and/or reduce the fear of crime among the residents of Davidson County. Based on these findings, a plan was devised to promote awareness and application.

THE PLAN

Clearly defined terms, policy, and objectives, which were viewed as proactive methods of policing, were constructed for the Metropolitan-Nashville Police Department in order to accomplish the goals of crime control. In addition to those strategies, community partnerships were implemented. For instance:

- The Crime Prevention Division of the police department developed a notice to citizens residing in the targeted areas explaining the reason for the increased police presence, and requesting their assistance in the crime fighting effort. The notice was distributed in both English and Spanish.
- Intelligence meetings were held at which nearly all police department components and outside agencies were represented. These meetings oc-

---

[3]Mitchell was charged with alerting staff of the establishment to the presence of an undercover officer, with violating department rules forbidding immoral conduct and the patronizing of undesirable establishments, with failing to report the activities inside the club to his superiors, and with being untruthful when interviewed by Assistant Chief Charles Smith regarding the goings-on inside the business. An undercover officer who investigated the club reported that he witnessed consensual sex, but did not see prostitution or drug use. (*Source:* METRO web site, http://www.nashville.net/~melissaj/vcr/2000/january/01102000.htm.)

cur twice a month. In addition to sharing information about ongoing investigations, computer-generated maps were used to monitor crime trends throughout the county so that the appropriate law enforcement resources could be directed to hot spots.

"While I strongly believe these initiatives will be effective, they are by no means all that we will be doing," Chief Turner stated. The chief also directed the units from several other marked police department components, including Traffic, Identification, and K-9, to make their presence known in the targeted hot spots when they are not otherwise responding to calls for service.

The plan included a written philosophy statement, procedures for implementing the various components of community oriented policing, and a lesson plan for training officers and supervisors. Written guidelines for establishing community ties and working relationships with community groups, merchant associations, and neighborhood watch groups were produced. The rationale was that officers require written guidelines to help them better understand community policing and to help their supervisors and management support teams aid their efforts to properly implement community-oriented policing. It was realized that written guidelines had to be put into action and, therefore, a definition of terms had to be created and a guide had to be developed to disseminate relevant information. As a result, it was hoped that community members of Davidson County would experience more law enforcement cooperation and an earnest effort by the members of METRO to help solve problems in their neighborhoods.

DEFINITION OF TERMS

METRO defined community-oriented policing as a proactive, problem-solving style of law enforcement achieved through personal interaction with citizens and by responding to their needs as defined by them. The mission statement of the department now reads:

To provide community based police services through crime prevention strategies and partnerships, to ensure a safe and peaceful Nashville.

Values
In carrying out our mission, members of the department will continue to value:

* organizational excellence and professionalism
* the impartial enforcement of the law
* the people we serve and each other
* problem-solving partnerships
* open communication
* ethics and integrity

COMMUNITY POLICING GUIDE

The following information was offered as a guide for **METRO** personnel to successfully aid in the development and maintenance of its community policing initiatives.

Objectives

Metropolitan-Nashville Police Department formally adopted the philosophy of community-oriented policing (COP) as its preferred method of providing law enforcement services to the citizens of Nashville-Davidson County, Tennessee. This philosophy was in direct opposition to the traditional "response-oriented" method of law enforcement that had been practiced for more than 50 years. This is the primary written instrument of **METRO**'s guidebook that will eventually be distributed to all **METRO** personnel.

Definition

The department's official definition of community-oriented policing is:

a proactive, problem-solving approach to law enforcement intended to reduce crime and increase the quality of life for the citizens of the community.

Rationale

COP is accomplished by providing community-based law enforcement services through application of proactive preventive and enforcement strategies derived from partnerships within the community. The official rational behind COP states:

Metropolitan-Nashville Police Department will strive to provide the best community-based law enforcement service possible. The members of the department will work diligently to address and resolve, as much as possible, the problems defined by the citizens of Nashville.

PHILOSOPHY

COP is a way of doing business—a different way of providing police service. It is not a program nor does it consist of a specialized unit responsible for a specific mission. However, COP must be supported and conducted by every member of the department regardless of rank or grade. Community-oriented policing is a return to the "beat cop" style of policing. COP is dependent on officers who communicate the mission to community members for the purpose of building relationships. Officers, supervisors, and managers are tasked with the responsibility of building relationships with other agencies, organizations, businesses, and the citizens of the community, too. These relationships place the burden of solving neighborhood problems equally among all parties involved.

The police department and its officers are the most visible form of government. Because of this, the line officer bears the burden of initiating the contact with the public and is responsible for reaching out to build positive relationships. Officers face the dilemma that many government employees rarely face—street contact with the public. While most people are eager and willing to work with the street officer, some community members easily remember past problems and broken promises from previous "traditional" police managers. Time and commitment are the only things that will change the thinking of skeptics.

"Who Are You Going to Call?"

Although the primary goals of COP are law enforcement and public order, some of the most important issues expressed by community members do not relate to either goal. Because COP officers frequently have face-to-face contact with residents, they are often called on to solve problems such as potholes, downed wires, and everything that might impact the lives of community members. Officers must build a repertoire of resources and connections among municipal and state agencies that can aid a vast array of resident problems. Often, just knowing which governmental agency can solve a problem will help eliminate the problem. For instance, a dispute among neighbors over property lines can be resolved by contacting either Codes or the Tax Assessor's office. An officer can obtain a copy of the plat map and help determine the actual property line. Thus, knowing who to call for community concerns might make a difference to the well-being of community members.

Furthermore, COP officers make decisions that require latitude and upper management confidence in order for COP officers to implement new and innovative ideas when responding to the needs of the citizens.

Community Support

Law enforcement is the business of providing a police service to the community. Community policing is a "total quality service" approach designed to reduce crime and the fear of crime among community members through a partnership. The effectiveness of this partnership rests on the credibility of the police department and the officers implementing the community policing initiatives, especially at community meetings. Although some residents might demonstrate inappropriate behavior at those meetings, many are there to interact with officers who take a genuine interest in their concerns. An effective tool in gaining community support, therefore, is to provide convenience and enthusiastic concern.

When community meeting members raise questions about prior police integrity, COP officers should acknowledge those past inadequacies of the department but firmly outline future community policing objectives. Officers should clarify that there was no one to blame; no reference should be made to a specific individual or group of individuals for those inadequacies. Officers should suggest that it might be best to move on to the present agenda. Officers could remind community members that past situations cannot be changed, yet a partnership can be used to help shape future actions and behaviors. One purpose of conceding to those past weaknesses of the department is to prevent those atypical events from occurring again and to enhance the credibility of the officer, which ultimately affects the credibility of the department. If community members trust the officers, the mission of COP is closer at hand.

COMMUNITY MEETINGS

Many people have never had the opportunity to express their approval or disapproval with the police directly, so this often occurs at community meetings. It is best to clarify that the police were not always wrong in specific incidents anymore than it means that the police were always right. Officers should not take community member comments personally nor should they be defensive.

To effectively diffuse situations when community members attempt to turn a meeting into a police bashing melee, officers must acknowledge the police imperfections of the past (see Community Support section). An officer can state that he or she was not present and could not address the complaint with a great deal of confidence, or try this: "One of the reasons we are here is to try to avoid those situations and improve communications." Professionally diffusing antagonistic persons will add a great deal of credibility to a police officers reputation. If an officer can remain calm when dealing with an antagonistic community member, another result might be to gain new friends.

Community members must sense that their involvement is essential to community policing efforts if any long-term relationship is to be accomplished. Methods of gaining their trust include protecting their interests—all of their interests, including those situations that do not include law enforcement prerogatives. When citizens accept the idea that their input can have a real effect in their neighborhood, community policing can succeed.

Officers should solicit and accept input from community members. They should allow community members time to define their problems. What police officers see as problems in the neighborhood may or may not be what the community members who live there sees as a problem. To be successful, law enforcement agencies must be prepared to respond to the needs of the community without compromising the law.

COMMUNICATION

Communication is vital to the success of a community policing strategy. Communication entails the sharing of information within the police department as well as an ongoing exchange of information with members of the community. Several things are required to begin the information sharing process:

1. **Accessibility:** Officers must be accessible to the members of the community. This requires officers to be available to the community through a more immediate point of contact than a radio call routed through a dispatcher. The use of substations, enterprise offices, cell phones, pagers, voice mail, and e-mail are all examples of increasing an officer's accessibility.

2. **Willingness to communicate:** Officers must be willing to take time to talk with people. This includes informal one-on-one conversations, formal talks to community groups, and talking with children at school, on the playground, or in the neighborhood. Meeting with business owners at their establishments or attending business association meetings is also vital.

3. **Reporting of actions:** Officers should not be hesitant to explain police actions when circumstances allow. Operating under the secrecy of police "professional autonomy" leads to mistrust and wariness. Explaining the reasons why certain actions were taken in a given situation can enhance citizen understanding and can increase trust and support of the project. Officers should find ways to relay information to community members when the information is something that may be of concern to the neighborhood.

4. **Feedback:** Officers should solicit feedback from the citizens in the community. This will allow officers the opportunity to evaluate how the citizens feel about the police department. This does not mean that everyone will be happy. This also does not mean that officers will have to change the way they have handled situations, but it will provide the officer an opportunity to clarify why certain things were done and this will improve understanding as outlined earlier.

5. **Citizen input:** Soliciting input from the community is extremely important to the problem-solving process. It is incumbent on the citizenry to become involved and to define the problems and concerns. The problems identified by the police department may not be as important as the problems identified by the citizens. Many times the problems will overlap, but often there will be some variance. The perception of safety is just as important as the actual crime rate. If citizens do not feel safe, they are not safe.

STREET OFFICERS IMPLEMENTING COMMUNITY POLICING INITIATIVES

Any officer can perform the functions necessary to successfully implement community-oriented policing if he or she possesses two personal traits: knowledge and desire. Knowledge is supplied through guidelines, but desire is something that she or he must obtain in other ways. A list follows of characteristics that might be used as a predictor of a successful community policing specialist:

- Compassionate and caring attitude;
- Understanding of people in general;
- Problem solver;
- Professional "take charge" attitude;
- Ability to make sound and rational decisions;
- Ability to read people, discern between the average citizen and the criminal, and act accordingly;
- Honest, straightforward, and trustworthy;
- Impartial and fair;
- High level of self-discipline;
- Committed to mission of the department and are entrusted with the task of performing their duties since they work unsupervised;
- Willing to flex their shifts to meet the "clocks" of the community; and
- Ability to recognize changes in crime patterns.

However, supervisors should remember that the more empowered an officer, the more likely he or she is able to take a leadership role in solving the problems of the community. Therefore, the above characteristics should aid a supervisor in recommending those officers who are more likely to succeed at COP than those who are not.

SIMPLE STEPS FOR BUILDING RELATIONSHIPS

The word *relationship* is one of those words that seems "warm and fuzzy" to most officers. The fact is, human beings are social creatures. Most human beings rarely go through a day without engaging in some level of social interaction. Building a relationship does not mean that an officer puts aside his or her duties. Relationships are the focal point of human interaction. Officers should encourage interaction within the community. Building relationships is the centerpiece for building trust and mutual respect. Officers who take time to build relationships with community members are more likely to receive their support and assistance when needed. Officers should begin establishing relationships before they need support and assistance. Below are some simple steps for building and maintaining relationships with community members:

1. **Build relationships one at a time:** There are no shortcuts. Relationships are built through personal interaction, one person at a time.

2. **Be friendly and approachable:** Officers who are open and seem approachable will begin making friends quickly. No one wants to be around a grouch, so maintain approachability and people will be more receptive to you.

3. **Ask question:** People usually like to talk about themselves and express opinions. Officers who take the time to listen attentively will quickly gain an ally and friend.

4. **Tell people about yourself:** The more people get to know you, the more likely they are to trust you. This does not mean that an officer needs to reveal details about his or her life, but the more human you appear, the more approachable you are.

5. **Go places:** Officers cannot sit in the office or the patrol car and expect to meet and interact with people. Go to the community meetings, block parties, schools, community center, ball games, and wherever else the people are.

6. **Assume other people want to form relationships:** People are social creatures who require human interaction. People usually have a curiosity about police officers. Most people have limited knowledge about police officers and law enforcement. Many only know what they see on television. While there may be some mistrust, many people would like to get to know an officer and gain some understanding about law enforcement.

7. **Do not fear rejection:** While officers will encounter some people who do not want to talk or be involved with the police, officers should not take it personally. Most people who shy away from the police are doing so either from mistrust or because of possible criminal involvement.

8. **Be persistent:** It takes time to establish rapport and build trust. Determine if a person is reluctant because of mistrust or because they are attempting to hide a criminal act. Then act accordingly. Situations involving mistrust can be changed if you are persistent, open, and honest.

9. **Learn about the neighborhood:** Every neighborhood has its history and its culture. The more an officer knows about the neighborhood, the more likely she or he is to establish rapport with residents.

10. **Maintain contact:** Relationships cannot be built on one meeting. Stay in contact with as many people as possible. The more interaction, the stronger the relationship.

11. **Communicate openly:** Most problems in relationships stem from poor or no communication. Talk to people and let them know what is going on and what the police are doing in their neighborhood.

12. **Understand different views:** Everyone sees things differently. Part of that difference is due to cultural diversity, and officers need to understand that each of us possesses a different perspective. A lack of understanding that differences exist can lead to a miscommunication between an officer and a community member. Also, an officer does not have to agree with an opposing viewpoint nor does an officer need to sacrifice his or her own principles. Understanding that different points

of view are an American perspective that made this country strong in the first place is a great starting point.

13. **Maintain respect and professionalism:** Officers represent themselves and the department. Officers should maintain a level of professional respect toward everyone and, in return, most individuals will treat the officer with respect.

14. **Enjoy yourself:** Knowing the people in the neighborhood, forming relationships, and helping solve problems can be rewarding and provide enhanced job satisfaction.

COMMUNITY MEMBER OFFICER EXPECTATIONS

To understand what residents expected from METRO officers, surveys were conducted throughout Davidson County. The respondents rank-ordered the following expectations. Results showed that the participants expected police officers to do the following:

- Take time to listen and to show true concern for their situations.
- Share information with neighbors about crime activity.
- Provide a rapid response to calls for assistance.
- Reach out to the community.
- Work to defuse potentially violent situations.
- Problem solve with members of the community.
- Be equal partners with the community.
- Become stable members of the neighborhood.
- Be committed to the idea of "community policing."
- Be viewed as "real" people.

Surveys in Davidson County also provided information about what community members did not expect from METRO officers. Participants did not want to experience the following items:

- "Us versus Them" mentality,
- Verbal abuse or demeaning of community residents,
- Untimely feedback about incidents in the neighborhood,
- No sense of ownership of the neighborhood,
- Instability in the neighborhood (police are frequently moved from one neighborhood to another),
- Poor communication channel with community residents,
- Officers who do not know people who live and work in the community,
- Rude dispatchers,
- Defensive explanations, and
- Keeping anonymous information anonymous.

In summary, trust, stability, commitment, and good communications can be a solid foundation of community policing initiatives. While some resident problems seem invalid from a police perspective, they are nonetheless monumental to the person(s) having the problem. Officers who take time to talk with the residents will be respected and liked if they respect the people they interact with and like the assignment. Officers leave a lasting impression on community members, and how an officer conducts him or herself reflects on the every member of the department.

IDENTIFYING AND UTILIZING RESOURCES

One of the most effective tools in an officer's "tool kit" is his or her knowledge of community resources that are available to aid community members in solving some of their concerns. That is, some community concerns are not necessarily police-related issues. The more resources at the disposal of an officer, the more likely the officer can help community members solve their problems. Results can be as encouraging as the assistance provided by community members that led to the arrest of a man who abducted and raped an 11-year-old girl in a vacant apartment as she walked to school through Cheatham Place Homes. Youth Services detectives responded and, after relating the description of the suspect given by the victim to citizens, were given the name of a suspect. The suspect, Shawn Oceole Johnson, 18, could not be located, but citizens notified officers late in the evening that he had returned to the area. He was charged with three counts of child rape, criminal impersonation, possession of drug paraphernalia, criminal trespassing, resisting a police stop, and violation of the terms of a previously imposed community corrections sentence.

Police Resources

Many officers do not know or understand all of the functions of the different sections within the police department itself. Officers should take time to learn about DARE, Crime Prevention, Police Athletic League, Chaplain's Office, Victim Intervention, Combat Auto Theft, and Join Hands with the Badge. Knowing the functions, capabilities, and limitations of these programs may provide an avenue of solutions not previously considered.

Resources from Outside Agencies

Learning about the different programs offered by the various federal and state governmental agencies can also be advantageous. Most agencies have brochures and flyers that describe their different functions. Many of the agencies can be accessed online. Officers can contact any agency and request information. Officers may contact the police department supply office or Metro Government's Central Printing and request a METRO telephone directory. This will save the officer valuable time when researching telephone numbers or contact persons.

Community Resources

Virtually dozens of private agencies and organizations provide a wide range of services within Davidson County. The Council of Community Services has compiled a directory that lists these various programs and services. Each Patrol Detail and the four Enterprise Zone supervisors have been issued a copy of this directory. Individuals who wish to purchase a copy of this directory may do so by contacting the Council of Community Services.

MANAGING ENVIRONMENTAL ISSUES

One of the most common problems officers face is the use of abandoned and dilapidated structures as "crack houses" and places for prostitutes to conduct business. Drug dealers, addicts, and hookers seek refuge in places where they feel safe. Because officers cannot see into structures from the street, and because of stringent constitutional laws regarding houses and searches of homes, this problem is common in every community. It is more pronounced in inner city neighborhoods because the attendant socioeconomic conditions can result in unattended "absent owner" rental or abandoned properties. An officer can take several actions to reduce or eliminate this problem. Locate and contact the property owner. Inform him or her of the problem and offer several possible solutions. These include, but are not limited to the following:

- Provide a "trespassing waiver." This will allow officers to prosecute violators on behalf of the property owner. The owner should also be encouraged to post No Trespassing signs on the property.
- Request the owner to secure the property by boarding up the windows and doors with plywood. Whenever a property owner is unwilling to do this, the officer should seek assistance from the Department of Codes. This action is necessary to prevent drug dealers and addicts from using the property, and to protect the neighborhood children from venturing into these structures and possibly injuring themselves.
- Assist the owner in contacting the appropriate division of the Metropolitan Development and Housing Authority (MDHA) to research the availability of rehabilitation grants. This may provide the owner with the necessary funding to repair the property and rent it to qualified tenants.
- In those instances where the owner does not qualify or rehabilitation grants/loans are not available, the owner may be willing to release the property to MDHA. This process, if available, will allow MDHA to acquire the property and repair it with their own funding sources or transfer the property to another person who will be willing to repair the property.
- In instances where businesses continually tolerate or further crime on the premises they can be declared a public nuisance and closed.

One example occurred on May 1, 1998, when METRO and the district attorney general took action to shut down and padlock a Dickerson Road motel that was a refuge for prostitutes and drug dealers. The Esquire Motel, 2706 Dickerson Road, had been declared a public nuisance in a temporary injunction and padlocking order signed by Criminal Court Judge Cheryl Blackburn. Judge Blackburn's order provided that the motel's nearly 30 rooms and office were to be padlocked, and prohibited the owners and operators of the motel, Kiran J. Patel, Parbhubhai N. Patel, and James C. Patterson, from entering onto the property until a hearing was held. The temporary injunction directed police officers to remove all "guests" from the motel, and provided that the district attorney's office could use its funds (to be recovered later during court proceedings) to refund the registration fees of duly registered and bona fide guests. The temporary injunction also directed officers to search the premises, including each room, for evidence of criminal activity related to promoting prostitution and the possession of controlled substances.

Abandoned and Junk Cars

Abandoned vehicles cause problems similar to those of abandoned houses. Drug dealers use these vehicles for hiding drugs. They also offer some protection from view of the police. In addition, children have a tendency to find new and exciting ways to alleviate boredom. Abandoned vehicles offer them another "toy" with which to play. This can be dangerous for the children. While Codes is the agency that is primarily responsible for identifying and removing abandoned vehicles, there are some things that officers can do to assist with this problem:

- Document the location and description of all abandoned vehicles in the neighborhood and provide this information to the codes inspector that is assigned to their area. This will be invaluable to the codes inspector. This can be done with a Safety Hazard Notification form or by compiling a list.
- Whenever possible, locate the owner of the vehicle and request it be removed.
- Often the owner cannot be located or neglects to remove the vehicle, but at times the owner will comply with a request from an officer. Some of these vehicles will be in violation of traffic and parking laws. In these instances, the officer can write a parking ticket and have the vehicle towed. The officer should have the vehicle towed to the lot of the wrecker providing the wrecker service and not to the tow-in lot. Whenever possible, provide the towing company with the owner information.
- In some instances the owner of the vehicle does not know what to do with the junk car. In these instances, officers can assist the owner in contacting a local recycling center that may purchase and remove the vehicle. The officer may also suggest to the owner that he or she may contact the local Kidney Foundation. They will arrange to pick up the vehicle and the owner may be eligible for a tax deduction.

Trash, Debris, and Community Cleanups

Community cleanups provide an excellent tool for helping the officer achieve two major goals within a community. First, it brings the residents together with a common purpose. Regardless of specific goals of the different community groups and organizations, almost all will agree that the condition of the neighborhood is a common concern. This may provide the avenue needed to begin networking and creating the partnerships necessary for residents to make positive changes in their neighborhood. Second, community cleanups provide the residents with a sense of pride in their neighborhood.

While many residents may be hesitant to become directly involved in other areas of neighborhood improvement (i.e., crime issues), most do not feel threatened when participating in community cleanups. As with any endeavor, there are problems with organizing community cleanups. The apathy that is prevalent among most people is a difficult obstacle to overcome. Officers must be careful not to be caught in the trap of doing the cleanup work for the residents. The main objective is to get the residents working together to improve their neighborhood.

There are several things the officers can do to overcome apathy and boost citizen participation. Below are some suggestions:

- Ensure that the various community leaders are committed to the project and are willing to actively solicit participation. They should be tasked with the responsibility of bringing participants to the cleanup. One way to improve participation is to find a local businessperson who might wish to donate a prize to the organization that brings the most people to help.
- Get the word out. Advertising is very important. Organizing a community cleanup is a lot like advertising a grand opening for a business. The more people who know about it, the more likely there will be active participation. Metro Beautification, a division of Parks and Recreation, will provide flyers, gloves, hats, and garbage bags free of charge. Begin the planning and organizing at least four weeks in advance. A reminder notice should be distributed at least one week prior to cleanup day.
- Secure the vehicles, tools, and extra personnel needed to conduct a successful cleanup. Coordinate with Davidson County Sheriff's Office, (DCSO). They will provide trash and dump trucks for hauling the trash and debris. The trucks will be staffed with inmates who can be utilized for removing bulk items, such as water heaters, old appliances, and old furniture. Contact Public Works and request they provide a truck for removing hazardous material, such as tires, paint cans, and old car batteries. These items cannot be taken with the other items. DCSO will also supply rakes and shovels. Additional prisoners for general cleanup can also be requested from the Sheriff's Department or from Juvenile Court. Neither government employees nor prisoners can perform cleanup work on private property. Because guards will be difficult to obtain without causing disruption to DCSO staffing, police personnel will have to as-

sume responsibility for supervising inmate activity. While these are low-risk inmates (DUI, child support, etc.) inmates should not be left unattended, nor put under the supervision of a resident or other participant. There should never be more than 10 prisoners assigned to one officer. Whenever prisoner transport becomes a problem, Metropolitan Transit Authority (MTA) is usually a reliable source for vans or buses.

- Time limits and specific areas are needed to conduct a successful cleanup. Three to four hours should be the maximum time limit for performing a community cleanup. While this may seem like a short time, much can be accomplished in this time frame. Most people are not able to donate an entire day or weekend. Keeping the time shorter will help boost participation. Scheduling multiple cleanups with shorter times is much better than having fewer cleanups that take longer.

- Schedule a social event after the cleanup. Contact local churches, businesses, and organizations for assistance in providing food and drinks for the participants. These can be given out as a reward to participants and to boost their sense of belonging. This is also the time when any awards can be distributed. This will help boost participation for the next scheduled cleanup as the event begins to become a social event and not just hard work.

The Neighborhood Notifier

METRO's newest community policing tool is the Notifier. It is a computer system that can deliver a recorded telephone message to hundreds of people in a specified geographic area in just a few minutes. It can be used for emergency evacuations, searches for missing children, and dozens of other purposes. Here's what Assistant Chief Charles V. Smith said about it: "No doubt the Neighborhood Notifier is the most far-reaching and positive step taken by METRO Police Department in its efforts to communicate with the Nashville community. Everyone but criminals benefit when citizens and police can communicate."

The Neighborhood Notifier uses the One Touch Mapping® system developed by Dialogic Communications Corporation of Franklin, Tennessee. It was purchased with a community policing grant. The system resides in a server located at the communications center. It is networked over the department's local area network (LAN) to six client workstations. They are located at all sector stations and at Crime Prevention and Youth Services. In addition, supervisors at the communications center have access to the system. A trained user at each location can call up a map on the computer screen, define a notification area, and record a message through the PC's sound card.

The Neighborhood Notifier is connected to 18 telephone lines, and can call a thousand telephone customers in 30 minutes. It uses a map overlay generated by the computer-aided dispatch (CAD) system, so it contains all valid Metro addresses and street number ranges. The telephone customer database is from a commercial source and is updated every quarter.

The Neighborhood Notifier system was actually installed in 1998, but there were delays in implementation due to the nature of the department's network. The police department's LAN was larger than any other Dialogic customers to date. The system is now operational, and had been used three times as this chapter was developed.

Community policing through a partnership with its clients is working in Davidson County to reduce crime and to create a safe environment.

Bike Patrols

Bike patrol started in the Enterprise Zone, which began operation in 1995 and is contained within the larger Enterprise Community consisting of the Edgehill, Vine Hill, and J. C. Napier/Tony Sudekum neighborhoods of David County. These areas are patrolled by bike officers who are daily practitioners of community policing. Bike patrol officers work in pairs with one patrol car assigned to each pair. The officers ride their bikes and work together to determine who will transport prisoners; at times an officer may have to return to the office to obtain a car for prisoner transport. Supervisors maintain the office for the most part, and we try to have our people in the field where they can be most effective. Officers work flex shifts to address problems. The benefits from bicycle patrols are as follows:

- Officers are out of cars and accessible to the public.
- Subjects cannot generally outrun officers on bicycles.
- Officers can approach silently on the specially designed bicycles, which makes them excellent for drug "sting" takedowns (stealth).
- Much more ground can be covered on a bicycle patrol than on foot.
- Bicycles can go where cars are unable to go.
- Costs are lower for bicycles than cars.

PROACTIVE STRATEGIES WITH JUVENILES

"The best defense is a good offense" is especially true with regard to community policing initiatives. To solve problems, a proactive approach is best. Relying on the traditional "response-oriented" method of law enforcement will only act as a basis for maintaining the status quo. Because positive long-term changes in the quality of life are a predominant goal in COP, working with children and helping shape their perspective is a fundamental part of the job. COP is not a cure-all for the social ills of our society. Officers are tasked with doing their part, but they cannot replace family structure and the responsibility that is incumbent on parents to provide moral and parental guidance for their children. The objective for the officer is to show that there is more to an officer than the person who makes an arrest.

Numerous avenues can be tried with juveniles to promote a long-term change. For instance, "adopt a child," especially those between 6 and 12 years of age. Help him or her with schoolwork, visit the child at school, help the child get into sports programs or organized youth clubs. Officers can coordinate their efforts with local universities and colleges by soliciting for volunteers from the student body to help with these activities. Institutions of higher learning are great resources for volunteers who can provide homework assistance and other types of help.

Another thing an officer can do is to become familiar with Don't Follow Me or some other similar organization. Don't Follow Me is a group of ex-cons who tell their story in an effort to dissuade children from becoming involved in crime. They can be called on to speak at public functions such as block parties, school groups, neighborhood meetings, and summer camps. These individuals are passionate about their efforts and appear to be very dedicated to their cause. Don't Follow Me has an office on Jefferson Street near the Neighborhood Justice Center.

Other programs include the one that involved 2,500 middle school students in the Metropolitan Police Department's Gang Resistance Education and Training (GREAT) program in November 1999. The students assembled at the Municipal Auditorium for the Musical Ride of the Royal Canadian Mounted Police. Students were admitted free to the performance with the donation of one canned good, which benefited Second Harvest Food Bank. The Musical Ride is a troop of 32 mounties on horseback who perform precision riding maneuvers and traditional cavalry drills to up-beat western, jazz, and contemporary music. The event was sponsored by the police department's School Services Division.

Additionally, the Boy Scouts and Girl Scouts of America offer excellent programs that teach skills, morals, and values. Their programs are age specific and they have programs for children as young as 6, and the Explorer program (specific job-related programs) for teenagers. Officers might consider running a scout troop themselves or may solicit troop leaders from the adults in the community. These troop leaders may be volunteers from community groups, churches, or businesses or students from local universities as outlined earlier. Officers can provide role models for children that may very well help children make the right choices about their lives.

Neighborhood Meeting Challenges and Young Adults

While officers usually have regular meetings with neighborhood groups, there is one segment of the population that is often excluded. Young adults, ages 13 to 17, receive almost no interaction except through enforcement activities. These young adults have mostly negative perceptions of the police and often believe that no one understands or cares about their problems or concerns. Meeting with these young adults will also bring a realization that is shocking to most officers. There are numerous "good" kids in the community. Officers usually have very little interaction with this group of young adults, because much of their time is spent dealing with those who are committing crimes.

When attempting to hold community meetings with young adults, officers must be extremely careful about how the meeting is conducted. First and foremost, officers must never promise anything that cannot be delivered. One broken promise and an officer's credibility is overturned. Therefore, preplanning is vital. Officers should coordinate with community groups, churches, businesses, and other government agencies prior to organizing and conducting a meeting with these young adults (the same holds true for adults too). Representatives from each organization or entity should be present. Officers would be prudent to secure the assistance of an experienced facilitator. The tone of the meeting must be set immediately. The participants should be advised of the agenda and the rules of the meeting.

The emphasis of the meeting should be to identify the problems faced by the young adults and any possible solutions. The focus with this age group should be the same as with adults: active participation in solving the problems. The facilitator must ensure that the meeting does not become a gripe session or a forum for complaining about past deeds or acts of the police or any other agency or entity. When conducted properly, these forums can provide the officers with an avenue of communication to this segment of the population that is normally very resistant to any interaction with police officers.

Truancy/Curfew Reduction

Officers are to cite juveniles who are on the streets during school hours and hours prohibited by curfew ordinances. Once a juvenile has been cited, the juvenile should be taken home and parents notified of the juvenile's truancy and/or curfew violation. In those instances when the juvenile violator is uncooperative or combative, the officer should conduct an arrest. When parents are uncooperative, it may be appropriate to complete an incident report and forward the case to Youth Services.

One method that helps with truancy/curfew enforcement is to do an occasional truancy sweep. A recent sweep resulted in the arrests of 29 juveniles. The sweep was coordinated by the Metropolitan-Nashville Police Department, Davidson County Juvenile Court, and Metropolitan Public Schools. Ten adults were also arrested during the operation on a variety of offenses not related to school attendance. Officers concentrated on East Nashville, looking for school-aged children who were out and about during school hours. The sweep targeted the "Stratford cluster," made up of Stratford High, East Middle, Lockeland Middle, and Litton Middle schools. Several of the students arrested had checked in to Stratford High, but then left the campus without permission. The sweep was designed to send a message to students and parents alike that school attendance is important and the compulsory attendance law will be enforced. Similar sweeps will be held throughout the school year.

This type of program conveys a message to both the student and the parent/guardian that truancy will not be condoned. This type of action may help reduce the number of incidents of crime committed by juveniles during school hours.

Child Development Community Policing Program

Community policing initiatives have also impacted Child Development Community Policing. One program that is innovative in Davidson County was designed to intervene in the lives of children and families traumatized by family and community violence. METRO is one of four law enforcement agencies chosen by Yale University to replicate the highly successful Child Development Community Policing Program (CDCPP) begun by Yale and the New Haven Connecticut Police Department.

METRO teamed up with clinical social workers at Family & Children's Service, a not-for-profit family counseling agency, to provide trauma debriefing, follow-up counseling, and support groups for children who have been victims of or witnesses to community violence. Moreover the clinicians provide 24-hour consultation to the police officers responding to violent scenes where children are present.

Why is a partnership so critical? First and foremost, the consequences to children of chronic exposure to violence are tragic and devastating. Those experiences can produce depression, anxiety, stress, and anger. Alcohol abuse, academic failure, and the increased likelihood of acting out in an aggressive manner are examples of how the cycle of violence seems to hopelessly trap children. Police officers are all too familiar with this cycle of violence and how some families perpetuate it from one generation to the next. As first responders to scenes of violence and tragedy, police officers have frequent contact with the children and families most at risk. However, officers usually do not have training, practical support, or time to deal with the psychological aftermath of a child's exposure to violence. Mental health professionals, on the other hand, are trained to intervene so that the burden of trauma is significantly lessened. Unfortunately clinicians often do not have access to these children and therefore critical time is lost after a violent event. Forging a partnership between the two professions provides an opportunity to develop new collaborative approaches to problems that are beyond the reach of either profession when working in isolation.

Dr. Steven Marans at the Yale Child Study Center explains additional benefits when police, mental health workers, and neighborhood residents partner together on behalf of their communities. "At best, police can provide children and families with a sense of security and safety through rapid, authoritative, and effective responses at times of danger." The experience children have generally had with police officers prior to CDCPP aroused negative feelings. For example, the arrival of officers after a violent event can reinforce their uncertainty and helplessness. Through CDCPP they learn a new perspective about police officers.

Nashville's program began in the Enterprise Community (Napier/Tony Sudekum, Vine Hill and Edgehill neighborhoods) during the fall of 1996. During 1999, the program expanded to the Briley Parkway loop and eventually all of Davidson County. Currently, clinicians respond to cases out-of-zone whenever a child is a victim of or witness to violence and an officer believes METRO's presence is needed.

The most critical components of this program include the following:

- 24-hour consultation service staffed by clinicians responding to police;
- Officers' need for guidance in crisis interventions;
- Crisis response by clinicians for children experiencing or witnessing violent events;
- Trauma debriefing for children and families experiencing violent events;
- Ongoing groups for children/families on the impact of violence in their lives;
- Ongoing training seminars for police officers on childhood development, psychological and family response to trauma, indicators of child abuse, cultural competence, and other topics;
- Follow-up family/individual counseling by this staff or through referral; and
- Weekly consultation team meetings with police officers and clinicians to discuss referrals and strategies for more complex cases.

METRO's collaborative effort is also greatly enhanced by the participation of the clinicians from the Victim Intervention Program and the Domestic Violence Unit. These clinicians attend weekly meetings, provide training for the officers, and share invaluable insights with the Family & Children's Service clinicians involved in this program.

Overall, CDCPP provides opportunities for officers to minimize the negative experiences of victimized children and become their potential heroes. As CDCPP places officers on long-term assignments in specific neighborhoods, they are encouraged to work with community residents to analyze and solve problems. Those strategies allow officers to develop relationships and assume roles in the lives of children that would not necessarily be possible in a more impersonal, incident-driven policing delivery system.

Similarly, regular, nonconfrontational contact with a neighborhood officer may help some previously adjudicated juveniles to abide by court-imposed restrictions. Perhaps Chief Emmett Turner best summarized the importance of the CDCPP in Davidson County when he stated, "This program will allow us to better meet the needs of children exposed to violence for it is the goal of this program to intervene with youngsters quickly so that the violence they have witnessed whether it be in the home or on the street will not haunt them for the rest of their lives."

PROACTIVE ENFORCEMENT STRATEGIES

Largely, community policing initiatives must be linked with proactive enforcement strategies if METRO is to come closer to its mission of providing community-based police services to ensure a safe and peaceful Nashville. Therefore, in addition to random patrols and enforcement actions arising from incident-driven events, Chief Turner announced that METRO would embark on a sweeping, comprehensive plan to attack violent crime throughout Davidson County. The plan enlisted the assistance and support of all police department personnel and resources, as well as a host of other law enforcement agencies, including the Tennessee Highway Patrol, Bureau of Alcohol, Tobacco and Firearms, Federal Bureau of Investigation, Drug Enforcement Administration, Immigration and Naturalization Service, and Secret Service. The chief said, "I am very serious about ridding our neighborhoods of the gun-toting drug dealers, thieves, and other criminals who are terrorizing innocent citizens. The plan I am announcing today sends a clear message to law breakers that the war is on, and we intend to win." METRO's violent crime strategy consists of several elements, including these:

- High-crime hot spots and trouble areas have been identified in each of the four sectors by the respective commanders in each sector.
- The 40-officer Flex Unit has been divided into four smaller Flex Units, with each of the four sectors now having a unit to target identified hot spots.
- Drug Activity Response Team (DART) units have been established at each sector and are targeting drug houses and drug dealers. The DART units are made up of off-duty officers who are being paid overtime through a federal grant.
- The FBI Violent Crimes Task Force, which consists of officers and agents of METRO, the FBI, U.S. Marshal's Service, and Tennessee Highway Patrol, are utilized to assist METRO detectives in serving violent felony warrants, especially homicide warrants, on suspects on the run attempting to avoid capture.
- The Homicide and Murder Squad components of the police department established a policy aimed at the prevention of retaliation in homicide and aggravated assault cases. The policy makes the protection of witnesses against retaliatory acts a priority, and calls for assistance to witnesses in making emergency arrangements to help alleviate the threat of danger. The policy also calls for the involvement of the police department's Intelligence Division in helping prevent retaliation in any gang-related shooting incidents.

Other elements of Metro's violent crime strategy are discussed in the following subsections.

Undercover Buy/Bust Operations: Buy/busts are designed to target the street-level drug dealer. Undercover officers will purchase drugs from a dealer, then take-down officers will move in and make the apprehension. These operations are inherently dangerous due to the high number of drug dealers who carry weapons and/or make a practice of robbing drug buyers. Officers should never attempt to conduct this type of operation without the assistance and guidance of supervisors and officers. To ensure officer safety, this type of operation must never be conducted without adequate staffing. Unit supervisors will determine the number of personnel needed. This determination will be based on the circumstances such as location, number of suspects, number of available vehicles, available equipment, time of day, and weather.

Reverse Drug Stings: Reverse drug stings are designed to target the buyers who purchase their drugs from street dealers. The objective is to reduce the demand in hopes it reduces the supply. Reduce the number of buyers that frequent a particular drug area and the number of dealers will be reduced.

This type of operation is also very manpower intensive and the same guidelines listed above will be utilized by CSU supervisors to determine the number of personnel needed to safely conduct this operation. For instance, the police department's street drug enforcement efforts moved beyond the inner city in August 1998 as officers contacted a suspected drug dealer through his pager and arranged for the delivery of crack cocaine at a South Nashville motel. The sale was made to an undercover officer, and the dealer was arrested.

Immediately following the arrest, the cellular telephone of the dealer was called repeatedly by prospective crack buyers. Undercover officers answered the phone and wound up meeting a total of six prospective buyers at various locations in the city. The six were charged with soliciting the sale of a controlled substance after requesting varying amounts of crack cocaine from an undercover officer. In addition to the seven arrests made in this case, four vehicles were seized.

Undercover Prostitution Operations: Certain areas of Nashville have many prostitutes. Because prostitution is a misdemeanor, lengthy jail sentences are rare at best. Successful reduction or elimination of this problem requires constant pressure and a "no-tolerance" position. Constant stops, warnings, and field interviews by uniformed officers help drive prostitutes from a location. In addition, regular undercover operations in which officers are solicited by prostitutes and then make an arrest are also needed.

Citizen involvement is a necessity. When prostitutes know that the neighbors are reporting their activities and are assisting the police in prosecution, prostitutes are more likely to stop frequenting the area. When conducting the undercover operation, field supervisors and officers should seek the assistance of CSU personnel until they have gained enough experience to conduct these operations on their own. Officers should never conduct an undercover operation without an electronic monitoring device.

Reverse Prostitution Stings: This operation targets the individuals who frequent prostitutes or "Johns" and is intended to produce the same results as a reverse drug sting. By increasing the fear of discovery and arrest, suspects are deterred from patronizing a particular area of the community. Although this endeavor has a lower risk factor than drug operations, officers must not become complacent and must always ensure the safety of all officers involved, especially the undercover female decoys. These operations should always be video and audio taped. This operation must never be conducted without experienced officers. Decoy officers who have never performed this function should always be paired with an officer who has undercover experience and be afforded the opportunity to learn prior to operating in an undercover operation. Because rape and assaults of prostitutes are a frequent occurrence, cover officers must remain alert and prepared to protect the decoy. Supervisors should request assistance from CSU and/or Vice supervisors and officers when planning, organizing, and conducting a reverse sting operation.

Enforcement Roadblocks: Enforcement roadblocks are an effective way to conduct a high-visibility enforcement effort. Many criminals do not maintain a valid driver's license. This operation provides officers of the Tennessee Highway Patrol and METRO officers a tool for detecting and arresting large numbers of persons who are operating a vehicle without a license and usually without insurance. The purposes of those roadblocks are twofold: first, to arrest violators who are driving illegally and, second, to arrest violators who are guilty of other more serious offenses such as drug, weapon, and warrant violations.

Enforcement roadblocks are a joint operation with the Highway Patrol largely because neither department has enough officers to staff multiple roadblocks alone. Officers who wish to conduct this type of operation should coordinate with a supervisor from the Traffic Division to assist with scheduling. Representatives from the police department's Criminal Intelligence and Criminal Investigations Divisions, and other law enforcement agencies, including ATF, FBI, DEA, INS, and Secret Service will observe the roadblocks and will be prepared to interview and/or debrief felony suspects identified as a result of the license checks.

Let's look at some of the typical results from roadblocks. On August 20, 1998, four driver's license roadblocks were conducted in the Central and East sectors of the county. The officers checked approximately 945 vehicles, issued 256 citations, and made 20 arrests on charges including drug and weapon possession, DUI, outstanding warrants, and no driver's license. Contraband seized that Wednesday night included 3.5 grams of crack cocaine, 38 grams of cocaine, 3 grams of marijuana, and 1 semiautomatic pistol. The following night, two driver's license roadblocks were conducted in the West sector and resulted in the checking of 430 vehicles. Troopers and officers issued a total of 168 citations and made a total of 12 arrests. One stolen car was recovered.

Saturation Patrols: An effective tool for providing a high-visibility enforcement effort is a saturation patrol. A saturation patrol brings a large number of officers into a specific area to reduce street crime. This often requires coordination between sectors to bring sufficient resources. The best method for saturation is to utilize undercover officers to make buys from street dealers, then follow it with saturation by uniformed patrol and/or bicycle officers. The uniformed officers can make the arrest and identify other individuals who are associating with the dealers. This approach is recommended so officers are not targeting all individuals in a given neighborhood, just because they live there. Officers should be specific in their objective and target those who are engaging in illegal or suspicious activity.

Enforcement of "Quality of Life" Laws: While many officers feel that they are too busy or some laws are too trivial to deal with, these are the things that can make or break a neighborhood. Community policing is not soft on crime, rather it requires a zero tolerance with even the most minor of infractions. Officers must address all violations of the law. They should be willing to prevent and enforce such issues as prostitution, littering, open container, loud music, rock throwing, panhandling, and so on. While these may seem trivial, they have a direct effect on a neighborhood and affect the quality of life in a neighborhood. Not every instance will require an arrest, but the officer must take some type of action. The officer may elect to make a person pick up some trash that was discarded, demand that a person with an open container go inside their residence to drink, take a juvenile home who is throwing rocks, and so on.

Allowing minor infractions to go unchecked paves the way for more serious violations to occur. In those neighborhoods where panhandling and prostitution are a problem, the officer can enforce other laws on violators when they are unable to catch them actively engaged in the primary crime. Citing for trespassing, soliciting a ride, walking on the wrong side of the street, and so on are all valid citations that may cause the violator to cease their activities or at least move them elsewhere.

While elimination of a problem is the desired outcome, sometimes displacement is the only viable solution. Citizen involvement is important for success in these endeavors. Crime will flourish in neighborhoods where it is tolerated. Because police resources are limited, citizens must become actively involved in addressing the crime problems. This will add eyes and ears to the department. Citizens who are willing to actively address the problems in the neighborhood and who assist officers with prosecution will see a greater improvement than when the police are attempting to handle everything themselves.

When violators know that citizens are reporting them, they are more likely to seek neighborhoods where they can operate with less assertive enforcement actions taken against them. The more active the citizens, the greater the success of the police department. A few ways in which community members can directly assist METRO police are discussed next.

Parole Hearing Objection Committee: The majority of crimes that are committed in communities are committed by a small portion of individuals. Those criminals are usually not confined to prison for the duration of their original sentence. Most are released on their first parole hearing. This is because in most parole hearings, the only people present are the criminal and the Parole Board. Officers should establish a "committee" within the neighborhood in which they work. This committee should include some of the community leaders who are active in the neighborhood. The officer and this committee should build a rapport with the Department of Parole and request that they be notified whenever an inmate is to have a parole hearing and may be released into their neighborhood. The committee should then coordinate with the victim and/or victim's family to appear at the parole hearing and object to the release of the prisoner. This action will usually result in a denial of parole, at least on the first hearing, and will help keep an offender in prison a little longer.

Burglary Follow-Up: This action is conducted by patrol officers as well as officers assigned to a community policing unit. The purpose of this operation is to provide additional assistance to burglary detectives as well as providing a point of contact with the citizens. Officers return to the scene of a burglary one to two days after the burglary. The officer canvasses the neighborhood in an attempt to locate any witnesses who may have been present during the time of the burglary, but who may have been gone when the officer arrived to make the report. The officer documents the information on a supplement report and returns the report to the Burglary Section.

This endeavor has had some success in assisting detectives with solving crimes. It also gives reassurance to the victim that the police are doing everything possible to solve the crime and recover their property. While this will not solve all burglaries, it is far better than increasing a detective's already heavy caseload or doing nothing and giving a victim the impression that the police department does not care about them or their property.

Because every neighborhood is different, not all of the above proactive strategies can apply to each neighborhood. Officers can assess the situation in their respective neighborhood and determine which, if any of the above, may prove to be successful. If a program is not in operation in a particular neighborhood, notify your superior with your observations and suggestions on which programs might work.

SUCCESS STORIES

Success stories about community policing at Metro PD are centered on descriptions of arrests made by the department in league with the community. For instance, concerned citizens and quick action by Central sector patrol officers led to the shut down of a crack cocaine operation on South 7th Street in February, 2000. The police department was alerted by concerned citizens that cocaine was being cooked into crack at 617-A South 7th. Officers went to the apartment, knocked on the door, and were greeted by a man with a semiautomatic pistol. Officers quickly subdued the man and the five other persons in the apartment, and as they were doing so, noticed cocaine and related materials in plain sight in the kitchen area.

"I am thankful for the increasing number of citizens who are working with their police department to rid neighborhoods of criminal activity," Chief Emmett Turner said. "[This] is just the latest example of what can happen when citizens take the time to let us know illegal activity is taking place." The Metropolitan Development and Housing Authority is being notified of arrests being made in housing it owns so that it can take appropriate action regarding the residents.

Another example comes from community complaints about drug dealing in the West sector. As a result of the complaints, patrol officers seized one pound of marijuana in a rental unit. The marijuana was hidden inside the springs of a living room sofa and it was sniffed out by Barney, the police dog. In addition to the marijuana, officers also seized a .25 semiautomatic pistol, a .22 sawed off semiautomatic rifle with a pistol grip, a set of scales, a military-type flak vest (body armor), and a scanner programmed to pick up police channels. The landlord of the property has begun eviction proceedings. "I remind citizens to let us know of neighborhood drug problems," Chief Emmett Turner said.

Also, acting on community complaints regarding suspected drug activity, West sector patrol officers arrested a cocaine dealer and seized 88 grams of cocaine, $2,377 cash, scales, two loaded semiautomatic pistols, two loaded revolvers, and a 1988 Cadillac. Another case initiated by community participation put a cocaine dealer out of business and led to the seizure of three assault rifles and one pistol.

As a result of television coverage of the robbery of a local store, the Bordeaux Market, detectives received information from the community that led to the arrest of one of the suspects, Scott Newsome. Newsome was featured on the store's video surveillance system. The airing of the videotape prompted telephone calls to police identifying Newsome.

The police in partnership with the community can curb crime and in the process, can bring about a quality of life that minimizes crime and enhances public safety. Although these examples are not necessarily significant to outsiders, they might not have been possible in past decades due to a lack of trust in the police. Hopefully, many of those old memories of the police have been altered thanks in part to community policing initiatives.

SUMMARY

The METRO-Nashville Police Department evaluates their progress through arrest rates, zero-tolerance policy impact, and a mix of proactive environmental strategies and proactive enforcement initiatives towards juveniles and adults. It often appears as if those proactive strategies and initiatives are limited to a specific population and a specific geographical area within the county. For instance, 29 juveniles were arrested as part of a truancy sweep in East Nashville and most of those students attended Stratford High School. One major hurdle the department is trying to overcome is a lack of trust by both community members and police personnel. This chapter, in part, contains METRO's plan to help move them from a traditional incident-driven police agency to a proactive partnership with the community.

CONCLUSION

To combat a lack of police trust and to enhance police integrity, METRO initiated policies in specific geographical areas, targeted at a specific population. These policies might give rise to suspect police agendas by both the residents targeted and the officers who enforce those mandates. Although community policing is different in different departments due to a variety of reasons, there are distinctive commonalties found in most initiatives. That is, at the core of community policing is a department-wide philosophy equally effecting residents city-wide. Largely, the primary objective of community policing is prevention and proactive strategies which aid community members through an empowered partnership. The role of police is that of a facilitator as opposed to enforcer. In examining the pages of community policing prerogatives in Davidson County (assuming the validity of the information provided), it seems that police response is centered on a traditional incident-driven directive and that those mandates lack community member decision-making input. That is, METRO Nashville PD's policy seems to be, victim first—police response second. For instance, METRO's "proactive strategy" of Child Development in partnership with Yale University shows that a child must be a victim prior to police or clinical intervention. Also, deployment and zero tolerance responses appear to be purely police command decisions (supported by city council). These indicators suggest the department is more traditional or reactive in its orientation as opposed to modern and proactive in its approach to delivering police service. Trying to enhance trust and integrity, which are admirable objectives might be more transitory than anticipated in a department providing traditional police service. But, it should be recognized that ignoring day-to-day criminal activities and redirecting police resources will give rise to criminal frequency and crime intensity. Therefore, each police department has the enormous task of balancing reactive issues and proactive concerns with generally limited budgets and little genuine community support.

Do You Know?

1. What assumptions were made by **METRO** about police automobiles and their impact on police service and community outcomes? How accurate might those assumptions relate to police service and community outcomes? What about police vehicles and the relationship between officers and supervisors?
2. Identify the root causes for the lack of community trust that **METRO** attempts to resolve through community policing. In what way might you see those root causes effecting community life styles?
3. Describe some of the proactive environmental strategies other than community policing employed by **METRO** to reduce crime and the fear of crime.
4. Describe the most important aspects of community policing for a **METRO** community officer. In what ways do you agree or disagree with these aspects?
5. **METRO's** Guidebook tells officers that at community meetings police bashing is a normal experience. What recommendations are made to deal with this experience? In what ways do you agree or disagree with those recommendations?

6. Describe several communication components that are required to begin and to maintain the informational sharing process between community officers and community members. Which components might play the most important role within the communication process and why?

7. Describe several communication components that lend themselves well to the building of productive relationships between officers and members. In what ways do you agree or disagree with those recommendations?

8. Look over the results of the survey that provides information about what community members do not want from community officers. Which set of results might most hinder valuable police partnerships with the community? Why? What recommendations could you make that would help correct the results produced by that survey?

9. Describe some of the proactive enforcement strategies other than community policing employed by METRO to reduce crime and the fear of crime.

CHAPTER FOUR

COLUMBUS DIVISION OF POLICE

Columbus, Ohio

INTRODUCTION

The Columbus Division of Police in Columbus, Ohio,[1] services almost 700,000 individuals living in 212 square miles. Approximately 1,800 sworn officers are employed by the division, which is equivalent to 2.6 sworn officers per each 1,000 residents. Columbus is one of the fastest growing cities in the Midwest, and its downtown is evidence of its energy and distinguished character. New home buyers are glad to find that Columbus's livability is matched by its affordability and cost of living, with home prices averaging below national figures. It is the home of Ohio State University and the capital of Ohio.

The Columbus Division of Police (CDP; see Appendix 1 for the CDP organizational chart) under the command of Chief James G. Jackson views preventive policing such as community-oriented policing (COP) and problem-oriented policing (POP) as popular concepts among law enforcement agencies and researchers.[2] "Community policing and problem-oriented policing are concepts," Chief Jackson believes, "often described

---

[1]The Columbus Division of Police can be found on the web at http://www.police.ci. columbus.oh.us/

[2]Without the contributions of Commander Kent Shafer, Strategic Response Bureau, CDP, none of this chapter would have been possible. The commander can be reached via e-mail at kshafer@police.cmhmetro.net

as solutions to traditional policing strategies, and have become buzzwords and/or icons in many police and academic circles. The ideals of policing in collaboration with the community and policing to solve problems are sound principles that can hold promise for increasing the effectiveness of police agencies like the CDP" (see Appendix 2 for program highlights of other strategies). Yet, the CDP learned of the difficulty involved with actually realizing the goals of those concepts because they experienced the reactive–proactive transitional process. Although, the CDP is presently on a successful course, they did have to overcome obstacles.

CHAPTER OUTLINE

This chapter, therefore, is a description of the obstacles encountered by the Columbus Division of Police in their efforts to alter their method of police service from reactive to proactive initiatives. A precise description of the Mission Aligned Policing Philosophy and five assumptions that laid the ground work for community policing initiatives in Columbus are revealed. An outline of the obstacles encountered by the department is offered followed by a brief history of the transformational attempts of the CDP, leading to the division's establishment of both a new philosophy and a new bureau, the Strategic Response Bureau (SRB).

The SRB is highlighted to acquaint readers with the nuances of this unit and its components, which perform different tasks in relationship to community policing initiatives. The accomplishments of the SRB are offered as evidence of the bureau's efforts followed by the problem-solving and resistance to change experiences that led to evaluation and community meeting outcomes.

Questions are answered about community policing strategies to help better explain the department's partnership relationship with the community. In the last part of the chapter, training courses are described, and results are discussed from a study conducted by Commander Kent Shafer to measure the success of CDP's COP/POP initiative among patrol officers, community members, and other police agencies. Chief James G. Jackson offers his personal perspective about community policing in Columbus, Ohio.

OBSTACLES ENCOUNTERED BY THE CDP

During the transitional period, four primary issues arose. First, since there were as many definitions of community-oriented policing as there were agencies claiming to be "doing it," the CDP had to develop an appropriate definition of this concept and communicate it to personnel, officials, and community members alike.

Second, there existed neither a precise plan for implementation of the concept or a distinct tool to measure effective implementation and operational success. Therefore, the CDP had to create one that best fit the department's mission and the community's demographics. Results were often disappointing, since organizational attempts to implement community-oriented policing initiatives were frequently characterized by unclear objectives and lack of a shared vision, the CDP discovered.

Third, the often quoted dogma that "Community policing is a philosophy not a program" is not borne out in practice, the CDP learned. Therefore, most efforts at becoming more "community oriented" are, in fact, programs (walking patrols, bicycle patrols, door-to-door surveys) intended to improve relations between citizens and police. While those practices are helpful, they don't necessarily result in a long-term philosophical change in the way a police organization conducts business, the CDP now understands.

Finally, there is a desire on the part of many police agencies to "practice" an idealized policing strategy such as community policing, but that desire was stronger than understanding what the concept of community policing actually meant for the agency. The fact is that many attempts at community-oriented policing suffer from significant internal resistance, the CDP learned. As a result, those strategies can be short lived. Now, the CDP reports that a precise definition, plan of implementation, and a profile of benefits should be both in place *and* articulated to personnel, community members, and business and social managers prior to police agency transition. Putting together a piecemeal community policing program is not an efficient or effective method of transition.

One of the goals of the CDP in implementing a modern-day police strategy such as community policing or problem-oriented partnerships was to become a more effective organization and to enhance the quality of life standards for community members in its jurisdiction. The basic idea of policing in the community is not new. Sir Robert Peel (the "father" of Euro-American policing) suggested in 1829 in *Principles of Law Enforcement* that "The police at all times should maintain a relationship with the public that gives reality to the historic tradition that the police are the public and that the public are the police; the police are the only members of the public who are paid to give full-time attention to the duties that are incumbent on every citizen in the interest of community welfare."

Historically, the police have always policed the community—in the community. In recent times, some could argue, police agencies lost touch with the citizens they serve, operating independently of community needs and concerns because they are primarily incident-driven organizations. That is, some agencies have lost their vision of problem solving and react as crime fighters. It is the purpose of the Columbus Division of Police to move from an incident-driven, reactive crime fighter agency to a proactive community problem-solving agency without compromising public safety. Evidently, CDP's initiative to meet the needs of the community through problem-solving partnerships has served the community well as evidenced by community member surveys and a reduction in the overall crime rates (see Appendix 3). However, recent crime trends suggest that murder, robbery, and aggravated assault among other crimes of violence are rising (see Appendix 4). And, although the transformation is still in process, the change has not been without fault. What follows is a narrative about CDP's transformation—its success and its failures are reported to provide guidelines for other agencies should they wish to compare experiences.

OVERVIEW OF CHANGE
A Brief History of Transformation Within the Columbus Division of Police

In late 1994, the Columbus Division of Police applied for a COPS Ahead Grant to fund police officers for implementing community-oriented policing in Columbus. In early 1995, Columbus Police Chief James G. Jackson asked his staff to prepare and present various plans for best implementing COP. Several plans were submitted for evaluation.

In April and May 1995, community forums were held in various parts of Columbus, asking citizens to answer the following question: "If you had an unlimited budget to implement community policing efforts in your community, how would you spend the money?" While each community had concerns specific to their particular needs, there were considerable similarities in the overall desires of the citizens. In general, citizens wanted police services tailored to the individual needs of each community, better resolution of crime and safety problems, more police presence, greater input to and communication with the police department, increased enforcement of quality of life violations, and closer relationships with the officers working in the neighborhoods.

Among the proposals submitted for implementing COP in Columbus was a plan entitled Mission Aligned Policing Philosophy (MAPP). The plan was developed by Commander Kent H. Shafer and Lieutenant Fred C. Bowditch. The plan had also been reviewed and critiqued by former U.S. Attorney for the Southern District of Ohio and current Federal Judge Edmund Sargus, the Director of the Ohio State University School of Public Policy and Management C. Ronald Huff,[3] and Georgia State University professor and COP expert Robert R. Friedman. The MAPP concept is described in detail in a publication from the Columbus Division of Police titled "Mission Aligned Policing Philosophy, A Principle Centered Approach to Policing, Combining Traditional Policing Activities with Community Collaboration and Problem Solving." A general overview of the concept follows.

Mission Aligned Policing Philosophy (MAPP)

MAPP is based on the premise that the mission statement of the Columbus Division of Police already encompasses the elements of COP and the basic desires

---

[3]President of the American Society of Criminology, 2000–2001.

expressed by the citizens of Columbus in the 1995 community forums. The goal of the MAPP plan was to create a method of utilizing the talents and the resources of the division to better accomplish the organization's mission. The plan outlined these objectives for the organization's mission:

1. Working with citizens to deal with their problems,
2. Reduction of fear of crime,
3. An ongoing commitment to traditional law enforcement responsibilities,
4. Emphasizing a results-oriented and satisfying work ethic, and
5. Adherence to the high values of the agency.

The proposal also listed five basic assumptions that laid the groundwork for changes proposed in the plan, as discussed next.

Assumption 1: Traditional policing activities and community policing objectives are not mutually exclusive. Law enforcement agencies must simultaneously deal with the concepts of public safety and public perceptions. Public safety involves the traditional concepts of protecting life and property, preventing crime, apprehending criminals, regulating traffic and maintaining order. Public perceptions relate to the citizens' concerns regarding quality of life, fear of crime, and their opinion of the agency.

Assumption 2: Just as reliance solely on traditional enforcement responses to crime is insufficient and ineffective, it is equally unrealistic for the police to attempt to solve all of society's problems. Police agencies must focus their efforts on the tasks for which they are best equipped. Generally, investigation, enforcement, and crime prevention are the functions used by law enforcement to deal with public safety. These efforts, however, must reflect the concerns and needs of the citizens that the agency is designed to serve and protect.

The broad law enforcement mission involves three distinct categories of activities:

1. Conventional law enforcement duties and responsibilities,
2. Police responses specific to community problems and needs, and
3. Police input and support for community-based programs to address needs.

Assumption 3: Traditionally, law enforcement has maintained an independent relationship with the citizens. The police generally decide which crime problems are important and what to do about them. Some views of community policing would have police involved in a dependent relationship with the public where the police agency would be seen as responsible for "solving" almost every problem. The ideal is for the police and the public to be interdependent where each understands the other's needs and concerns; where the police listen to and respond to the concerns of the citizens consistent with their mission; and where the community understands what the police mission is as well as the constraints under which the police operate. This type of relationship between officers and citizens is built through an ongoing process of changing attitudes and developing skills, especially within the police agency.

Assumption 4: The CDP has created various special operations such as SCAT, ACE, and others with the specific duties of combating street-level drug and crime problems. As problems change and new concerns emerge, the division needs the flexibility to adapt its tactics. By encouraging and increasing input from the community into the planning of strategic operations, our public safety goals will be better realized and the public's perception regarding our response to their needs will be enhanced. In short, these operations can be improved by broadening their focus and increasing their responsiveness to the specific concerns of the public. This can best be accomplished by centralizing control of street-level enforcement, with a problem-oriented approach to these problems.

Assumption 5: The public and the media regularly raise their concerns regarding gangs, juvenile criminals, and violent crime. The same persons who belong to gangs and commit violent street crimes also create fear and concern in communities. Police response to community concerns and its response to street-level criminal activity are interrelated. The most effective approach to these problems will be a broad-based effort, capable of focusing on all aspects of the street crime problem rather than a number of specialized programs, each independently focused and operated.

A critical part of responding to street-level crime and community safety is focusing on gangs and related youth violence problems. Suppression alone will not adequately address the complex problems of juvenile crime and gangs. The police must work cooperatively with the entire community to provide the components of prevention, intervention, and suppression to respond to youth at risk and those involved in criminal activity and gangs.

Based on these assumptions and the objectives of the organizational mission statement, six goals were established for MAPP:

1. Establish and maintain partnerships with community leaders and groups.
2. Reduce crime through intelligence-based, directed tactics.
3. Investigate, through the use of zone assigned investigators, neighborhood-specific crime (misdemeanors) and solve these crimes through victim follow-up, witness contact, analysis, and forensics.
4. Target, apprehend, and prosecute career criminals who live a life of crime within the community.
5. Gather, analyze, and disseminate information and crime trends about groups that are affecting the safety and quality of life in Columbus neighborhoods.
6. Coordinate efforts within the CDP and with other government agencies to adequately respond to crime, safety, and quality of life issues.

In reality, the MAPP plan was more comprehensive than simply implementing a form of community policing. It proposed significant, long-term organizational change, aimed at improving community collaboration, emphasizing problem solving (problem-oriented policing), developing the information systems necessary to provide data for strategic use of agency resources to deal with crime and safety issues, and assessment and evaluation of the department's effectiveness in accomplishing its mission. MAPP included the concepts of community-oriented policing, problem solving, strategic (data-driven) policing, and evaluation of results.

The plan proposed three components of change for the division. First was a redistricting of the Patrol Subdivision with consideration to traditional neighborhoods and organized community groups. The intent of the redistricting was to create geographically oriented police services, based on established community boundaries, and to deliver services based on the needs of each neighborhood. Next, the plan called for the education and development of all patrol personnel to instill the Mission Aligned Policing Philosophy and cause officers and supervisors to acquire attitudes and skills that permit the philosophy to be implemented and fulfilled. The third component, and the foundation of the plan, was the development of the Strategic Response Bureau (SRB) to carry out the MAPP goal of providing police responses specific to community needs and concerns. SRB was designed to be a "boundary spanning unit," to begin the process of making the practices of MAPP the standard throughout the organization. In theory, SRB would be an organizational component intended to eliminate itself when its task of establishing MAPP organization-wide was accomplished. SRB consisted of a Community Liaison Section to foster communication with the community, and Investigative and Enforcement Sections designed to develop responses to identified community concerns.

STRATEGIC RESPONSE BUREAU

The Strategic Response Bureau (SRB), with a staff of nearly 100 officers and supervisors, was created to better identify problems related to the police mission and develop creative solutions to impact them. The difficulty came in getting officers to break the mold of "one size fits all" policing and learn to solve the problems that they faced creatively and collaboratively.

Commander Kent H. Shafer,
Strategic Response Bureau

The SRB has six primary functions:

1. Community liaison,
2. Enforcement,
3. Investigative,
4. Information,
5. Crime analysis (crime trends), and
6. Administrative (clerical support).

The Community Liaison, Enforcement, and Investigative Sections are each responsible for one component of MAPP, as discussed next.

Community Liaison Section

This section is staffed by one lieutenant, two sergeants, and 19 officers. Each sergeant supervises a unit consisting of 9 officers (one for each precinct on their zones) and is responsible for two zones. Each officer conducts community-oriented activities for their assigned precinct. Tasks include liaison with the community and the CDP, making contacts with area businesses and residents, attending community meetings and block watches, and identifying concerns and problems.

The secondary function is the education of the public and divisional personnel. Citizen concerns and problems can be referred by these officers to other units within CDP and other governmental agencies, boards, and groups for resolution. Community liaison officers also monitor the progress on these actions.

The goals of this section are as follows:

- Liaison with community groups and individuals regarding criminal activities and prevention and quality of life issues, and facilitate problem solving and follow-up.
- Develop MAPP within the Patrol Subdivision via education and development activities.
- Liaison with district officers and precinct sergeants to bring about responses to crime problems and quality of life issues.
- Liaison with other units within the SRB.
- Facilitate referrals about non-law-enforcement concerns.

Enforcement Section

The goals of the enforcement section are as follows:

- Address neighborhood crime problems with different, innovative, effective responses. Coordinate activities with precinct Sergeants and other units within the Patrol Subdivision and division-wide to address criminal activity.
- Formulate enforcement responses based on identified crime patterns and specific problems.
- Assess effectiveness of responses.

Investigative Section

Some of the goals of the investigative section are as follows:

- *Zone Investigator Unit.* Investigate neighborhood-related crimes (graffiti, vandalism, thefts, etc.) and solve them through witness contacts, analyses, and forensics.
- *Career Criminal/Liaison Unit.* Target and apprehend career criminals and coordinate investigations with the prosecutor's office, federal agencies,

and other units within the investigative subdivision.
- *Criminal Information Unit.* Collect, analyze, and distribute information to the Enforcement and Investigative Sections, divisional units, and community groups. Coordinate intelligence from the patrol zone intelligence coordinators, and maintain a computerized file of the criminal information. This unit gives special emphasis to the gang and monitors group activity and information.

Accomplishments

Here are some of the accomplishments of the SRB:

- Created resource manuals for the department.
- Provided community police relation training for neighborhoods.
- Provided problem-solving training.
- Provided recruit training.
- Built community partnerships, through events in the community such as the anti-burglary program at Ohio State University, the safe partying "walk-around" conducted by Campus Partners, and a Rape Awareness five-mile walk.
- Developed and implemented a criteria rating scale/criminal point analysis designed to identify violent career offenders. Designed a temporary database that included the names of 2,710 felons, 272 of which have reached career criminal status.
- One hundred eighty-eight cases were forwarded for review by the career criminal prosecutor as of September 1998. Of these, 28 were selected for vertical prosecution, 60 were rejected as F-5 drug cases, 45 cases were rejected for lack of merit, 30 are still under review, and 12 were foreign jurisdiction cases. Nine defendants of the 28 defendants selected for vertical prosecution have pled guilty to the indictment while 4 other defendants await sentencing.
- Led major investigations. For instance, the SRB assisted the Criminal Information Unit and Detective Bureau in the first state racketeering (RICO) investigation on a criminal street gang in Central Ohio, the Linden Avenue Crips. This investigation resulted in the indictment of 12 individuals on a total of 74 counts to include RICO, aggravated murder, manslaughter, and aggravated robbery. Eleven members of this gang have already been convicted or pled guilty to 30 counts and were sentenced to an average of 18.5 years in prison. The reputed leader of this group, Norm Jones, is presently in custody and awaiting trial.

A long-term investigation of the Latin Kings was spurred by a drive-by shooting at the 8/15 substation. CIU developed the intelligence information and conducted surveillance, which led to the arrest of Osvaldo Aponte, a fugitive from justice, who had been convicted of this shooting and was attempting to flee to Puerto Rico.

The unit also participated in major investigations of the Insane Viet Boys (IVB), a Sacramento, California, based Vietnamese gang that infiltrated the Columbus area and began committing burglaries and extortion. Officer Wildman coordinated efforts with the Sacramento PD in his investigation of this gang. This resulted in the execution of one search warrant, recovery of stolen property, and three arrests.

- Managed narcotics cases. Officer Sandford assembled a large intelligence package regarding a criminal drug gang operating in Zone I, which led to the opening of this case management. This long-term project will be worked in conjunction with Narcotics, Patrol, SRB Enforcement, and coordinated by the Franklin County Prosecutor's Office.
- Conducted state racketeering (RICO) investigation with assistance from the Detective Bureau into a Central Ohio burglary/safe cracking ring operating in Ohio, Pennsylvania, Kentucky, and West Virginia. This resulted with the indictment of four individuals on a total of 36 counts to include RICO, burglary, theft, and receiving stolen property. The four individuals arrested still face 54 criminal counts in the state of Pennsylvania. Five search warrants were executed during the course of this investigation.
- Conducted state racketeering (RICO) investigation with assistance from the Detective Bureau and the FBI into a stolen auto/motorcycle, burglary, chop shop, theft ring operating in Central Ohio, Dayton, and the state of Kentucky. This resulted in the indictment of nine individuals on a total of 185 counts to include RICO, burglary, theft, and receiving stolen property. Twenty-five search warrants were executed during the course of this investigation.

SRB officially began operation in June 1996. Prior to the actual start-up of the bureau, information sessions were held for personnel inside the CDP and for citizen groups. Support for the new operation was high within the community, but mixed within the division. After the new bureau began operations, citizen support continued to increase. This was due, in large part, to the increased access to the police and the results of many successful problem-solving efforts. Division personnel responded more slowly to the new concept. In 1998, both citizens and CDP officers were surveyed. Officers indicated a 65 percent approval rating of the community liaison component of SRB, while citizens reported approval ratings as high as 97 percent with regard to some aspects of the new program.

Two critical issues needed to be addressed before the new concept could officially be declared effective. First was the difficult transition from reactive, statistics-driven policing to proactive problem solving. Beyond that challenge came the larger issue of overcoming resistance to substantial organizational change.

Implementing Problem Solving

To accomplish this transition from crime fighting to problem solving, SRB management engaged in three major activities. First, it was necessary to introduce the concepts, and teach the requisite skills of problem-solving. Problem-solving models were discussed and applied. Crime data and other information were collected, analyzed, and disseminated to officers, along with instructions on how to utilize this information in the problem-solving process. Second, officers were given the opportunity to work collectively to discuss problems, propose alternative solutions, and collaboratively select and implement what appeared to be the best solution. Citizens were often included in these problem-solving discussions. Third, the officer's activities and results of their actions were monitored and evaluated to determine the effectiveness of the solutions implemented, as well as to observe the problem-solving process itself. Through the repeating cycle of skill development, application, and feedback, participants gradually started to develop the ability and desire to become good problem solvers.

Police literature is replete with claims that police agencies fail to measure what is truly indicative of successful performance. Fyfe 1988 argues that the quantitative measurements tracked by the police do not reflect the quality or effectiveness of police services. Alpert and Moore (1997) discuss the traditional police performance measurements of arrests, reported crimes, and response times. These numbers, while easy to track, are not characteristic of police effectiveness. Alpert and Moore suggest that measurements of how much the police agency is oriented to the community and how well they problem solve are much more important in determining the extent to which the agency is effectively accomplishing its mission.

To measure the effectiveness of new problem-solving efforts, reliable monitoring systems had to be developed. Forms and routine paperwork were changed to accommodate tracking of problem solving. And, finally, a citizen survey was implemented to gauge the extent to which these problem-solving efforts impacted the community. While many CDP officials and officers preferred to focus on the traditional measures of arrests and calls for service, new information began to emerge that shed light on the strengths and weaknesses of the problem-solving efforts. During the change process, the value of problem-solving techniques became apparent to more and more officers and staff. Thinking in terms of analyzing and addressing problems, rather than simply responding to calls, became more of the norm. Ultimately, how well crime and safety problems are addressed, and the satisfaction of the community with police services, will be the most important indicators of quality police service. Yet, this process encountered its obstacles.

Resistance to Change

The concept behind the SRB was well grounded in the literature and highly supported by the public. The program was highly publicized and poised to be an immediate success story. In reality, the first two years that followed the glamorous introduction of the program were rife with struggles, frustrations, and unexpected circumstances. During these two years, excitement and enthusiasm were present in the beginning, yet they gave way to disappointment, anger, and uncertainty, as everyone involved struggled to see their vision unfold.

Bridges (1991) describes what he calls the "neutral zone" a very difficult time where the boss is getting impatient and asking "How long is it going to take you to implement those changes?" In retrospect, the neutral zone seemed to be one of the experiences of men and women of the CDP, too. Top brass wanted to see quantifiable results and increasingly put pressure on the new bureau to demonstrate success. Meanwhile, members of the new operation felt the pressure to produce, yet they found themselves unable to follow their own plans of operation. Even the principal planners seemed unable to successfully implement what they had designed. Many began to question the virtue of the plan itself and the ability of those involved to carry it out. Little did they realize that what they were experiencing was a normal part of a process of change, the neutral zone.

Bridges (1991) lists six steps to survive the neutral zone:

1. Protect people from further changes.
2. Review policies and procedures.
3. Examine reporting relationships and organizational structure.
4. Set short-range goals.
5. Do not promise overly high levels of performance.
6. Help supervisors and managers learn what they need to function successfully.

The time in the neutral zone can actually be a creative period if proper actions are taken to make it so. Without the benefit of Bridge's advice, members of SRB eventually discovered these steps for themselves and acted to turn things around. Decisions were made to minimize further changes within the bureau and concentrate on making the current plan work. Policies and procedures were examined and rewritten with the input of workers and supervisors. These new procedures took advantage of lessons learned to streamline operations and avoid problems experienced previously. Unproductive reporting relationships were changed and the organizational structure modified to make communications easier and maximize the ability of the various components to accomplish their tasks and collaborate with other units. Each unit was asked to develop short-term goals and focus on accomplishing those goals. Efforts were made to establish more reasonable expectations as to what the new bureau could deliver and communicate these new, less ambitious promises to stakeholders. Finally, opportunities for skill development were provided for officers and supervisors, equipping them to perform well in their assignments. Nonetheless, it was a very difficult time for the CDP and everyone involved with its new direction.

Had the members of the Strategic Response Bureau initially been exposed to Bridges' work (1991) on transitions, perhaps the department could have emerged from the neutral zone sooner and experienced fewer setbacks. Yet, it is a hard call since the change itself was department-wide including changes in the very backbone of policing principles of the CDP. Now, members of SRB have succeeded and are witnessing positive changes toward proactive policing throughout the Columbus Department of Police and in the communities serviced by the CDP.

Evaluation

From the beginning of the new program, outside, independent evaluation was conducted by the Ohio State University Criminal Justice Research Center, under the direction of C. Ronald Huff. Professor Huff provided ongoing input into the operation, to SRB personnel, to the division's top-level managers, and to government officials. This evaluative effort not only provided an analysis of the program's success in accomplishing its goals, but also timely information that permitted rapid response to problems along the way.

Moving to the Next Level: Organizational Transformation

In 1997, representatives of the division examined the New York City Police Department's COMPSTAT program, designed to use computer-generated crime data to drive strategic application of the agencies' vast resources to reduce crime. The concept had resulted in a dramatic reduction in crime in New York City since its inception in 1994. After reporting to Chief James G. Jackson and the division's executive staff, the personnel were instructed to form a steering committee charged with linking the division's information system with the MAPP concept to improve the department's ability to strategically respond to crime and community problems. The committee was also given broad authority to identify goals, strategies, and methods required to transform the agency into a highly effective police organization within the philosophy of mission aligned policing. The new initiative was dubbed MAPPSTAT.

The MAPPSTAT Steering Committee identified the primary objectives of the initiative, and then worked to gain support within the division, the city administration, and the community. A plan was then developed to create a road map for change within the division.

MAPPSTAT CRIME STRATEGY MEETINGS

In late 1997, the division began to hold MAPPSTAT Crime Strategy Meetings, examining crime in each of the four patrol zones. All bureaus of the division are required to attend the meetings and to provide needed assistance, information, and guidance to assist the patrol commanders in addressing the problems in their zones. The division's Crime Analysis Unit, housed in the Strategic Response Bureau, provides the needed crime data and related information that drive the crime strategy process. The division's ability to solve crime problems, as well as its capacity to work collaboratively, has been significantly improved by the meetings.

Information Program

The first formal step taken by the steering committee was to provide information regarding the concept to the rank and file of the division. A videotape presentation was created and distributed to all personnel, along with literature providing additional information on this concept. Information sessions were also held for division supervisors and citizen groups.

Focus Groups

After information on the MAPPSTAT concept and the division's plans had been distributed, the steering committee held focus groups, designed to solicit input from within the organization. Ten focus groups were held, each with 25 employees, sworn and nonsworn, from all ranks and assignments. Questions were structured to gain insight into current problems, suggestions for organizational improvement, and other concerns of the personnel involved.

At each focus group, a high-ranking person from the steering committee provided an overview of the goals and ideas of MAPPSTAT, and this person then became a "listener" as they recorded the input of the focus group members while a facilitator guided the group. At each focus group session, individuals from management and labor jointly participated in leading the group. This alliance is significant and important to the overall success of this endeavor. Involved personnel began the meeting reluctantly and with some uncertainty, but by the end of the four-hour session, most present had contributed to the process and a great deal of valuable input was obtained.

Reengineering Teams

The results of the focus groups were compiled into a lengthy report, containing literally hundreds of concerns and suggestions. From that report, the committee identified 46 core issues, and divided them into nine categories. For each category, a reengineering team was formed. Each team was led by a member of the steering committee, but was made up of various personnel, representing all ranks and subdivisions of the agency. Each team was charged with researching the issues assigned, and preparing a report outlining their findings and making and justifying recommendations for changes to address the issues. Each team was scheduled to present their report to executive staff in the fall of 1999.

Reengineering Report

A comprehensive report, literally an action plan for change, will be compiled from all of the recommendations made by the reengineering teams. After the recommendations have been approved by executive staff, an implementation matrix will be developed, detailing the timetable and priorities for the changes, those responsible for developing and implementing the changes, and a reporting system to keep executive staff and others within the division informed as to progress being made.

Crime Report

In reviewing a nine-year crime report (see Appendix 3), there appears to be no marked improvement in the reported crime levels in Columbus, Ohio. That is, despite minor changes in the population base, the crime rate per 1,000 population has been consistently around 90 for the past four years and at 88 for the two proceeding years. Therefore, it could be argued that the crime rate has not necessarily reflected a significant change from 1990–1998. More crime has been reported in 1999 and greater crime is expected in 2000 (see Appendix 4).

NINE HARD QUESTIONS ABOUT COMMUNITY POLICING INITIATIVES

Question 1: What methods were employed to ensure that typical members of the community are represented in the community policing process?
Initially, community forums were held, including every established neighborhood, soliciting input into what type of police services and police department were desired. After the program concept had been developed, information sessions were held on each zone for input from citizens. Since the program has become operational, interaction is continuous at community meetings and through other forums. Surveys are also used regularly to gather input and citizen perceptions.

Question 2: In what way are community residents included in the decision-making processes associated with community policing? Explain the feedback and/or the decision levels of community members in the following areas:

- Deployment strategies relevant to activities such as foot patrols, mini stations, bike patrols;
- Crime-targeted strategies, activities such as neighborhood crime watches, owner notification, criminal trespass; and
- Collaborative strategies such as advisory councils, crime prevention councils, police disciplinary committees.

Input from citizen groups and individual citizens is a primary factor in deployment of nonemergency resources and in deciding what types of crimes and problems are addressed. The community liaison officers are the primary link between the citizens and the Division of Police. The division's mission statement identifies citizen concerns and fear of crime as the first two major objectives of the division, therefore, citizen input and concerns greatly influence operational decisions. A Community Advisory Board meets bimonthly; representatives from major neighbor groups, police management, city administration, schools, business, faith community, and so on meet to discuss problems and concerns and decide on potential responses.

Question 3: What are the elements and/or conditions that will sustain the active involvement of residents in community.

This is an ongoing challenge. In Columbus, as in many other cities, citizens stay involved as long as they feel they are threatened and need the police to solve a particular problem. Absent immediate crime or safety concerns, citizen participation dwindles. Through the Community Advisory Board and the use of special events (National Night Out, community cleanups, etc.), the division works to maintain citizen interaction and involvement with the police.

Question 4: How will your organization pick up the slack from federal money when it runs out, assuming some part of your community policing program is being funded or subsidized?

Funds have been allocated in the annual budget to continue *all* operations that were originally funded with federal grant monies. Our grants agenda is not driven solely by what federal funding is available, but by the needs and goals of the division. We see federal COP grants as assisting us in our goals of practicing COP/POP, not as the impetus for such actions.

Question 5: What were the historical events that influenced organizational decisions to establish a community policing agenda at your agency?

No major community crises precipitated the movement to COP. If any one factor can be identified, it was the initiative of several City Council members who felt citizens were not being fully served (or heard) by the division and that the police needed to be more aware of and responsive to citizen concerns. These councilpersons established the community forums that provided information regarding what types of police services (and police department) citizens desired. The other factor was growing recognition within the division (especially at middle management levels) that reform was needed. The reform-minded managers utilized the report from the community forums to develop the current Mission Aligned Policing Philosophy. The COPS Ahead Grant from the 1994 Crime Bill caused the transformation to occur more quickly than would normally be possible because it provided funding needed for manpower, which served as a major incentive to division leaders and city administration to move ahead with the changes.

Question 6: What methods are used to assess and/or evaluate the progress of the community policing effort?

Surveys were utilized, inside the division and with the public, to assess the impact of COP. Additionally, research was conducted between September 1998 and August 1999 to evaluate COP both within CPD and across 45 larger police agencies in Ohio and nationwide. This report (*Evaluating the Impact of Community Ori-*

ented Policing in Larger Departments by Kent H. Shafer) is available through CPD. The Ohio State University Criminal Justice Research Center also conducted a process evaluation of the program during its first two years of operation. Ongoing feedback and a final report were made available to CPD personnel.

Question 7: How does your agency determine the success or failure of your community policing effort?
Success was measured primarily by two factors. First was citizen perception of the quality of police services as they relate to addressing their crime and safety concerns. Next was the extent to which officers within the division embrace and practice the tenets of COP/POP. Additional background on this evaluative approach is available in the above-mentioned paper by Shafer.

Question 8: In what way have any community policing programs been changed or altered as a result of community policing assessments?
The CPD sees community policing as part of an ongoing philosophy that includes responsiveness to citizen concerns and perceptions. As a result, we regularly adjust our operational strategies and tactics based on citizen input. It would be difficult to give examples of which specific programs were altered because we view programs (strategies) as being fluid and flexible, being modified as needs and input dictates.

An example would be use of walking and bicycle officers. Where the officers are assigned and what type of activities they conduct vary regularly based on the needs and concerns of the area, including citizen concerns.

Question 9: In what way has decentralization been accomplished in keeping with community policing efforts?
The agency is just beginning to tackle the issue of decentralization. For the past two years, CPD was involved in a major reengineering effort, involving personnel from all levels of the organization. Decentralization, geographic operational focus, and increased emphasis on patrol operations are the major objectives of this effort. A new organizational structure and staffing proposal is under consideration by the division's executive staff that would result in a radical redesign of the agency that would decentralize operational resources and strategic decision making to the geographic patrol areas.

TRAINING ISSUES FOR COMMUNITY-ORIENTED POLICING/PROBLEM-ORIENTED POLICING

Implementing COP or POP within a police organization requires changes in the fundamental practices of the organization. Among these changes were the methods and focus of training personnel.

Training all personnel, whether civilian staff or sworn officers, regarding the changes in the police department's thrust in providing service to the community is essential. Just as developing partnerships within the community is important, the development of operational partnerships within the organization is critical to the successful implementation of COP/POP.

In the Columbus Division of Police, every sworn officer received an overview of the implementation of the division's community policing effort. Additionally, each patrol officer received eight hours of training in the SARA problem-solving method while all nonpatrol officers were provided a four-hour block of the same training. This was accomplished with the assistance of the Tri-State Regional Policing Institute in Cincinnati, Ohio.

Commander Larry M. Rod, Training Bureau

Every member of the civilian staff received similar training to imbue them with the knowledge of what changes were taking place and how those changes were going to affect them.

Of particular concern is the necessary change in training for new officers while they are in the training academy.

First, there must be a movement away from a stress-type academy where new officers post for senior officers, expected to do only what is instructed. Individuality and free thinking must be appreciated and fostered. Without this change, it is unreasonable to expect our officers to be able to creatively problem solve for the community they serve. Certainly it is important that officers respond appropriately during emergency situations, and any organization must be confident that its officers will operate within the parameters of accountability established by the organization. Modifications in training programs are able to develop the traits desired in officers who will now be providing increased focus on customer service and will be initiating partnerships within the community.

Second, the curriculum of the training program needs to be reviewed by the training staff to ensure the material presented contains a relational basis to the COP/POP goals of the department. Otherwise the courses will not reinforce the department's commitment to COP/POP and the effort to plant the seeds of change will bear no fruit.

Within the Columbus Division of Police there has been a change in the training program to foster community policing training.

Each recruit class is now instructed for 12 hours of community policing training. The course allows for a four-hour block that covers the introduction to community policing. Included in this part of the program are the philosophy of community policing and the evolution of that philosophy within the Division of Police. An important part of this class is an explanation of how the officer will benefit in the application of community policing. This assists with the development of community ownership by the officer.

The first part of the community policing training takes place near the beginning of the particular recruit class program. Near the end of the training program, just prior to graduation, the recruits are provided an eight-hour class on the SARA problem-solving model. This reinforces those concepts presented as the recruit began the police career and helps prepare the recruit to engage in problem solving on the community level.

In any police agency, the implementation of COP/POP is a process that may take several years to accomplish. While changes in the management structure of a police department implementing the community policing philosophy are an absolute, such changes without a corresponding alteration in the way new officers are trained will be insufficient and doom the long-term goals of the change.

Chief James G. Jackson Talks About Community Policing December 6, 1999

James G. Jackson, Chief of Police

It is my pleasure to share with you some of the benefits I believe the Columbus (Ohio) Division of Police has enjoyed regarding our commitment to community policing. The process for developing the division's commitment to the COP philosophy, and the corresponding process for implementing the mechanics, is time consuming and often problematic. Changing attitudes and responses in the policing business requires patience and persistence. However, it seems this is the direction we in law enforcement should be going and, more importantly, it appears this approach will prove to be (long-term) effective and efficient.

Community policing with the Columbus Division of Police probably began, as it did with most agencies, with our old Crime Prevention Unit. While very popular with the community groups it trained and interacted with, and effective as far as it could be within its limited scope and range, most community members were not dramatically impacted by its efforts.

Our fairly recent commitment to the COP process via the creation of the Strategic Response Bureau has provided our division and the community with a fresh approach to addressing community problems and concerns. With the inclusion of a number of service units under one umbrella bureau, our goal is to permit a comprehensive approach to dealing with often endemic and long-standing challenges. Additionally, other division resources including traditional patrol officers, community resource officers, bike patrol officers, and walking officers supported by other division and outside re-sources all help to round out our ability to assist our community members.

Not surprisingly, in-house responses to nontraditional, proactive and problem-solving oriented strategies have been mixed, however, it is my be-lief that with both officers and community members alike seeing improv-ing results from community responsive policing, there will ultimately be greater general support for our efforts. In conclusion, there is little question that COP is the philosophy for law enforcement agencies of the future. The challenges are many and sometimes difficult to overcome, however, with persistence and commitment, the challenges facing COP will prove to be the stepping stones to success.

AN EVALUATION OF CDP's COP/POP EFFORTS

Commander Kent Shafer conducted an extensive exploratory study about COP/POP initiatives within the Columbus Division of Police. The commander wanted to measure the COP/POP attitudes of three groups of individuals: 40 CDP uniformed patrol officers who had little direct contact with COP/POP ini-tiatives, 70 community members in Columbus who had direct contact's with those initiatives, and 36 commanders and related personnel in major police departments in Ohio and similar departments across the United States. A sep-arate format was used in a questionnaire designed for the groups through trial and error. It contained a number of open-ended and closed questions. Ques-tionnaires were distributed and collected through the principal researcher's of-fice via both U.S. mail and CDP services. This test was conducted two years af-ter CDP established its COP/POP initiatives in Columbus, Ohio. The data, once collected, were placed in computer grinds to determine if any distinctive pat-terns arose among the participants.

Results

Survey 1: CDP Patrol Officers   When the data of the patrol officers were polled, distinctive patterns arose. For example, the following typical response from a patrol officer typified the reports of a majority of the patrol officers con-cerning the community liaison officers (CLO). They "have the hardest job be-cause they deal with the public and the police." "Liaison officers were accessi-ble to to people and (patrol) officers to answers questions." Liaison officers "help explain what patrol is really all about."

Accordingly, the statistical evidence supported these comments in that more than one-half of the patrol officers reported that they felt confident about the Strategic Response Bureau and the bureau's liaison officers specifically as-signed to interact with community members, community organizations, and CDP personnel such as the patrol officers themselves. The respondents wrote additional comments that seemed to suggest that the CLOs were able to identify with community problems and that, therefore, the community liaison officers had become "a positive force" for police community relations.

Evidently, patrol officers see the SRB and CLOs as assets to both the community and the department. Negative responses from the patrol respondents were typified by the one respondent, who stated that there's "a lot of turnover in the unit." Apparently, patrol officers don't appreciate liaison officers being rotated out of a specific area. Perhaps these officers see the advantage in assigning liaison officers on a permanent basis in certain communities. This finding is linked to a similar finding among community member respondents and is discussed below.

The data further suggested that the liaison officers provided assistance to patrol officers on all shifts. Negative comments generally reflected concern over a lack of communication and follow-up between patrol and liaison officers, a lack of sufficient contact by liaison officers, and a lack of accessibility of the patrol officers with liaison officers.

Survey 2: Community Members   Specifically, several remarks seemed to typify the primary issues addressed by the community member respondents. For example, the efforts of the community policing liaison officers were typified in one respondent's statement that "The liaison officer in our community has been very effective and supportive of our concerns." Another respondent added, "He comes to all meetings and is well respected for his response to our needs." Another made the CLO's efforts clear: "There was an incident with a rental property across the street operating a grass company business and the officer took care of it as it was against code. He called me and let me know. It provides a better sense of security knowing we have these individuals and also seeing the patrol car."

Accordingly, the statistical results were no surprise when 95 percent (67) of the respondents reported that COP was a change for the better for Columbus, yet only 48 percent (34) felt that CDP was doing all it should be regarding COP. Seventy-two percent (50) of the community members polled reported the CDP was effective in solving crime in their neighborhood and 76 percent (53) felt that police effectiveness had improved since the inception of COP. When asked specifically about the SRB and the COP Program, most of the respondents were aware of the program and 87 percent (61) felt the program improved police service. Regarding the CLOs, almost all of the participants reported that liaison officers provided assistance in problem solving, that better information was available due to those officers, and 91 percent (64) felt that the officers were an improvement in providing police services. Most community member participants thought that the COP should be expanded.

The following three remarks typify the many issues some of the respondents offered that might be a challenge to community meetings in general: "I attended the community police relations sessions and it was a big step in getting to know police problems better." "We need a stable CLO—we have gone through three in the past couple of years." And, "It is unfortunate that there is not more support for community policing from the top-top (the chief)." One way to interpret these three comments is that while community policing meetings are productive for residents, there are discussions about police matters that may or may not lend themselves to the mission of community policing.

Community members felt comfortable and that might mean they feel safer when they have a stable CLO in the area. Yet, appropriate recruitment and professional training of CLOs might be one method of solving instability as well as the issues raised by Respondent Number 58: "Need officers committed with good attitude like Officer Beard. Former liaison officers projected a negative attitude and pessimistic outlook to solutions for residents." Clearly, the best community plans can go haywire if the CLOs don't follow through in an appropriate manner.

And last, somehow community members felt that top management should be involved with the grassroots efforts of community policing which in large cities like Columbus might be geographically difficult. Yet, this is an issue top management might want to review.

Survey 3: Other Police Agencies   Of 36 similar sized police agencies, 88 percent (32) of their commanders endorsed COP and most reported experiences similar to those of CDP. Of those agencies, 28 of them had a department definition consistent with community policing objectives, and they had modified their training programs to facilitate COP expectations. Also, most of those agencies included problem solving as part of their community policing objectives, and strategic response initiatives, but fewer had a method of evaluation instituted to help guide the decision-making process. Additionally, agency commanders generally supported COP; midlevel managers and patrol officers were less likely to support COP initiatives. Least supportive were line supervisors, detectives, and special unit officers. Overall, problem-solving skills were the most valued concepts of COP initiatives reported by all of the agency respondents.

Discussion

The data reveal meaningful information about the effectiveness of COP as gauged by the attitudes of typical patrol officers and community members in Columbus, Ohio, and commanders and middle managers from other departments across the United States.

Concerning the major focus of that study, community members supported CDP's COP initiatives. Community members reported that the department was effective in solving neighborhood crime, and that COP was more effective than traditional police practices prior to COP initiatives in Columbus, Ohio. Quantitative data, along with a qualitative perspective provided by residents indicate that citizen perceptions of the Columbus police, their satisfaction with police services, and their relations with COP officers are all highly positive. One implication from these findings is that community members feel safer in their neighborhoods since COP was instituted.

There is clearly a need for more extensive research to provide conclusive findings on community perspectives on COP initiatives. Preliminary findings from this study, argues Commander Shafer, suggest the following recommendations.

1. Agencies should prepare for the neutral zone experiences through planning and via communications to all individuals—community members, police officers, and civic leaders.

2. Departments should prioritize training that leads to better understanding of the concepts and benefits of COP, and provide opportunities for officers, especially patrol officers, to be involved with citizens in solving problems. For agencies with designated COP officers, policy should encourage other officers to accompany the COP officers and become engaged in COP activities.

3. Involvement in COP-related activity serves two distinct purposes. First, it allows officers to experience firsthand the satisfaction of having an impact on some of the crime and safety problems that concern residents and to put into practice the concepts and strategies learned in training. Second, the interaction with citizens helps officers learn the value of developing relationships and working collaboratively with the citizens they serve.

4. Citizen comments and responses indicate that the more involved the police agency is in COP, the more positively citizens view the agency. Often, however, citizens lack awareness of improvements within their local department unless they have had an occasion to be involved with officers engaged in problem solving or other COP activities. Officers who have the opportunity to observe firsthand the benefits of COP indicate an enhanced sense of safety and high levels of satisfaction with police services. Police agencies need to aggressively market their COP efforts, communicating through all appropriate medium their philosophies, activities, successes, and so on. Follow-up with citizens regarding actions taken in response to concerns and problems also enhances citizen awareness of agency effectiveness.

5. Officer and first-line supervisor attitudes toward and support for COP are clearly linked to their perception of the extent agency executives support and are genuinely committed to the concept. Chiefs and upper-level mangers need to express and demonstrate clear support for COP at all levels within their organizations. Their support needs to be genuine, public, and consistent. Survey results indicate that where support for COP is high at top management levels, officers and supervisors are likely to be highly supportive as well.

6. Chiefs need to quickly get middle managers involved in implementing COP reform. Middle mangers generally recognize the value of COP and can be important change agents within the department. Middle managers can communicate the chief's support for COP to lower organizational levels, serve as coaches and mentors to teach new methods of dealing with problems, and foster attitudinal and behavioral changes at operations levels.

7. COP needs to be an organizational norm, rather than an another program created within the department. Police agencies with organization-wide communication and involvement in COP experience much higher levels of officer support. In larger agencies, it may be appropriate to begin such an effort with a boundary-spanning unit intended to begin a localized effort and expand it throughout the department. It should be clear from the beginning, however, that the intent is for eventual organization-wide change.

8. Police departments committed to COP must develop performance measurement systems that track the important dimensions of COP and then use the resulting data to evaluate program and agency effectiveness. Evaluation can include both the processes used to accomplish operational objectives and the outcomes of those efforts. In addition to quantitative data, attitudes and perceptions of citizens and officers can be useful in the evaluative process. Many police agencies are currently expanding their use of information technology. Often the new technology is simply used, however, to automate the same types of information that have been tracked and recorded in other ways for many years. Agency heads need to establish performance objectives and then determine what information is necessary to evaluate the accomplishment of those objectives. This often means finding ways to quantify, measure, and record new and different types of information. New technology can then be helpful in evaluating operational effectiveness if it is used to record the proper types of information and make that information available in useful forms.

SURVEY CONCLUSION

As a result of implementing the Mission Aligned Policing Philosophy the Columbus Division of Police has strengthened its relationship with the community, involved citizens in efforts to address crime and safety problems, and enhanced its ability to effectively police the City of Columbus. The division has become a high-performance police organization, focused on not only increasing effectiveness in dealing with crime and safety problems, but also on fostering ongoing learning, encouraging innovation, and maximizing the use of information technology to improve law enforcement.

The reengineering undertaking is among the most comprehensive change initiative ever attempted by an American law enforcement agency. It promises significant, long-lasting, "bottom-up" change that will continue to increase the productivity of the Columbus police, expand police interaction with the community, and make the job of a Columbus police officer a truly rewarding and challenging one.

SUMMARY

During their transitional period, five issues arose: (1) There were many definitions of community policing. (2) There existed neither a precise plan for implementation of the concept or a distinct tool to measure effective implementation and operational success. (3) The often quoted dogma that "Community policing is a philosophy not a program" is not borne out in practice. (4) There is a desire on the part of many police agencies to "practice" an idealized policing strategy. (5) Individuals involved with community policing implementation go through a "neutral zone" where little gets accomplished, ultimately producing frustration and anger.

Most attempts at community-oriented policing suffer from significant internal resistance of all types. How did the Columbus PD solve their problems? They developed a precise definition, plan of implementation, and a profile of benefits and articulated them to personnel, community members, and business and social managers prior to their second attempt at a transition. They learned that putting together a piecemeal community policing program is not an efficient or effective method of transition. The CDP went back to the planning stages many times. Despite their successes with community policing, management may eventually experience difficulty in explaining why crime levels have not been significantly changed over a nine-year period.

CONCLUSION

With the resources of the Columbus Division of Police and Ohio Sate University, an initial community policing plan still met with misfortune because management was unaware of a natural, but expected condition referred to as the "neutral zone." Link that finding with an unaffected nine-year crime rate, and there may be some cause for concern. However, CDP management has received high marks from patrol officers, community members, and other justice agency personnel through what appears to be a professionally engaged survey.

DO YOU KNOW?

1. Community forums were held in various parts of Columbus asking citizens "If you had an unlimited budget to implement community policing efforts in your community, how would you spend the money?" The results showed considerable similarities in the overall desires of the citizens. Describe those similarities and make an attempt at explaining why those similarities exist. If a similar questionnaire were distributed in another city of similar size such as Nashville or Boston, how similar might the results be? Why?

2. The Mission Aligned Policing Philosophy (MAPP) addressed five assumptions that laid the groundwork prior to establishing community policing strategies in Columbus, Ohio. Describe those five assumptions and explain how each of them affected community policing initiatives.

3. The first two years of the community policing initiatives in Columbus were described as a period of excitement and enthusiasm that turned to disappointment, anger, and uncertainty, as everyone involved struggled to see their vision unfold. What was this period called and what might

have been different if the department had planned for this period?

4. In what way were community residents included in the decision-making processes associated with community policing in Columbus? Explain the feedback and/or the decision levels of community members in police deployment strategies, crime-targeted strategies, and collaborative strategies such as advisory councils, crime prevention councils, and police disciplinary committees.

5. Describe the methods used to assess and/or evaluate the progress of the community policing effort in Columbus, Ohio.

6. Commander Kent Shafer conducted an extensive exploratory study about COP/POP initiatives within the Columbus Division of Police. The commander wanted to measure the COP/POP attitudes of 40 CDP uniformed patrol officers. Describe the findings of the patrol officers and explain the impact the attitudes of the officers had on community policing initiatives.

7. In what way was decentralization accomplished in keeping with community policing efforts in Columbus, Ohio?

REFERENCES

Alpert, G., & Moore, M. (1997). *Critical issues in policing*. Prospect Heights, IL: Waveland Press.

Bridges, W. (1991). *Managing transitions: Making the most of changes*. Reading, MA: Addison-Wesley Publishing Company.

Fyfe, J. (1988). Police use of deadly force: Research and reform. *Justice Quarterly*, 5, 166–205.

APPENDIX 1   Organizational Structure

The Columbia Division of Police is made up of several sections:

- Administration
  - Personnel
  - Standards
  - Internal Affairs
  - Training
- Investigation
  - Detectives
  - Juvenile
  - Intelligence
  - Narcotics
- Patrol East
  - Zone One
  - Zone Two
- Patrol West
  - Zone Three
  - Zone Four
  - Traffic

- Support Services
  - Communications
  - Strategic Response Bureau
  - Special Services
  - Technical Services

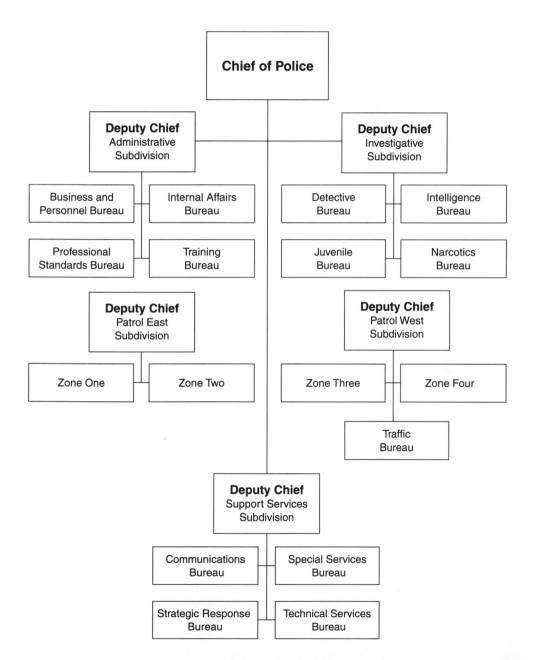

APPENDIX 2   Program Highlights of the CDP

The Citizen Police Academy graduated 64 Columbus citizens in 1998 who now have a better understanding of the Division of Police and its many activities and responsibilities.

The DARE Unit celebrated 10 years of providing Drug Abuse Resistance Education lessons to Columbus public and area Catholic schools in 1998. The DARE Unit also continued to provide this service to six City of Worthington elementary schools. Project Shield, the program designed by Columbus officers for the middle schools, was implemented in all Columbus public and area Catholic middle schools as well as one Worthington middle school. These two programs impacted more than 10,000 schoolchildren with more than 5,800 graduating from DARE and more than 3,000 completing Project Shield. During the past 10 years, the Columbus DARE program has graduated more than 56,000 fifth-grade students.

The DARE Unit hosted three roller skating events with United Skates of America, two DARE concerts, and appeared at more than 40 community functions, such as church-sponsored drug prevention seminars for youth, summer day camp programs, and neighborhood awareness programs. Another program, Project Kidtown, a safety program for young children, was developed and presented four times by DARE and Hot Pursuit over the summer.

In one year, the Hot Pursuit Band presented the Safety City Program in 93 area elementary schools, performed at two middle school concerts, five DARE concerts, Red White and Boom, Secret Santa, a summer program for the mentally retarded, the Hilliard Police Department, the Kids Expo, and the Midwest Hostage Negotiators' Conference.

The Police Athletic League (PAL) is designed to foster interaction between police officers and children ages 7 to 17, and to reduce juvenile crime throughout the community. PAL sponsors a variety of sports and educational programs. PAL's showcase activities for 1998 were two six-week tutorials for the Ninth Grade Proficiency Test, and a first place for the 12-year-old boys' basketball team from Columbus PAL at the state PAL Basketball Tournament.

The Columbus Police Reserve is an all-volunteer organization whose mission is to aid and augment the Division of Police by providing an additional source of law enforcement officers. Seventy-five officers donated nearly 20,000 hours of police service to the citizens of Columbus in 1998.

APPENDIX 3   Uniform Crime Index Offenses, Nine-Year Comparison

CRIME	1990	1991	1992	1993	1994	1995	1996	1997	1998
Murder	92	139	113	105	100	78	90	83	79
Rape	647	651	685	658	679	636	571	696	668
Robbery	3,541	3,747	3,595	3,887	3,599	3,330	3,318	3,104	2,615
Aggravated assault	2,735	2,686	2,859	2,496	2,383	2,582	2,238	2,103	2,040
Burglary	14,982	16,398	15,064	13,055	13,088	13,146	13,013	13,453	13,526
Theft/larceny	32,387	32,989	31,051	29,051	29,776	31,905	34,244	35,882	36,338
Vehicle theft	8,466	8,874	7,136	7,070	6,720	7,038	7,610	7,118	7,343
Arson	926	875	995	1,029	1,035	915	808	778	813
Total	63,622	66,359	60,503	57,351	57,378	59,630	61,892	63,217	63,422
Population	632,910	638,533	643,028	646,933	647,860	657,487	657,045	696,849	696,849
Rate per 1,000 population	100.7	103.9	94.1	88.7	88.6	90.7	91.7	90.7	91.0

Source: The Columbus Division of Police.

Appendix 4   Crime Reports 1999–2000

Offense	March 2000 Totals	Year 2000 Totals	Year 1999 Totals
Murder/Manslaughter	16	29	113
Rape	44	151	650
Robbery	232	726	3,026
Aggravated Assault	164	479	2,046
Burglary	1,007	3,041	14,070
Larceny over $500.00	740	2,133	8,919
Larceny under $500.00	2,223	5,992	25,740
Vehicle Theft	520	1,648	7,277
Other Assaults	1,875	4,561	19,306
Forgery	254	707	2,268
Fraud/Embezzlement	227	599	1,906
Indecent Exposure	11	19	150
Molestations	30	58	249
Other Sex Crimes	20	38	193
All Other	1,791	4,365	19,585

Source: The Columbus Division of Police.

CHAPTER FIVE

LANSING POLICE DEPARTMENT

Lansing, Michigan

INTRODUCTION

Lansing is the capital of Michigan and home to Oldsmobile, Lansing Community College, and the Lansing Lugnuts Class A Baseball; Michigan State University is its next door neighbor in East Lansing. The Lansing Police Department (LPD.www.lansingpolice.com) employs 268 sworn officers (and 101 civilians) who serve a population of approximately 127,000 individuals (or approximately 2 officers per 1,000 residents) living in 33 square miles. The official mission of the LPD is to suppress crime, apprehend criminals, maintain order, and safeguard public peace and tranquility. The department divided the city into two precincts each with its own command staff and objectives: the North Precinct consisting of 115 sworn personnel servicing approximately 48,000 residents, and the South Precinct consisting of 116 sworn personnel servicing approximately 80,000 residents. In late 1998, each precinct was geographically changed to allow the department to be more responsive to the needs of the citizens of Lansing. An interstate highway separates the precincts, each of which is divided into nine team areas. Each has its own commander. Patrol lieutenants administer shift assignments and oversee a sector for problem solving. Individual patrol sergeants are each assigned a team area with several officers. Overall, the LPD claims that it is dedicated to community policing and problem solving. They continually strive, their website reports (http://www.lansingpolice.com), to work closely with Lansing's communities and neighborhoods through ongoing problem-solving initiatives.

CHAPTER OUTLINE

This chapter is an introduction to the Lansing Police Department's evolutionary process of instituting community policing and problem-solving initiatives.

Observations and influences that impacted community policing initiatives are revealed and include massive top management retirements, decentralization issues, and active civilian interaction. In part, the transformation process was directed by middle managers who were guided by academic advisers from a nearby distinguished university. One result is that crime rates are down in Lansing and community members are somewhat satisfied with the quality of police service they receive. The philosophy and mission of policing initiatives are discussed from the perspective of the current chief of police who also offers his vision of police service.

Community services are briefly reviewed from a LPD viewpoint and are followed by discussions about each of the two precincts, which operate independently in Lansing but follow similar guidelines. That discussion includes identifying the respective neighborhood organizations that participate in Lansing's partnerships with the police. Questions are answered about LPD's community policing agenda. An overview of a typical community officer's annual activities and information about community policing training programs are shared. The chapter ends with a closer look at LPD's truancy monitored program, a community assessment of Neighborhood Watch, and a comprehensive explanation of the Mentor Program. A community president addresses community policing and a new program that involves collaborating with parole officers. Finally, a citizen survey measuring community satisfaction levels with police services is reviewed.

COMMUNITY POLICING OBSERVATIONS AND DEPARTMENTAL INFLUENCES

Chief Mark Alley. Photo courtesy of Officer Lori Baukus. Lansing Police Department.

The LPD believes, according to their new chief, (2000) Captain Mark Alley[1] that their community policing efforts have reduced crime and spurred neighborhood and business cooperation. In a review of Lansing's five-year arrest records, that appears to be a reality (see Appendix 1). More important, as the LPD moves from a specialized programmatic approach of police service to an operational philosophy, and more aspects of their internal decision-making process are enhanced in the neighborhoods, community levels of satisfaction as determined through surveys also improved.

The LPD continues to look for new and innovative ways to deliver police services and increase their accessibility to neighborhoods and businesses. Their purpose is to reduce crime and calls for service, while increasing their overall citizen satisfaction levels. Former Chief Robert L. Johnson says that it was his pleasure to present the community

---

[1]In 2000, Captain Mark Alley became the Chief of Police of the Lansing PD. In 1999, when this researcher started collecting data for this chapter he *was* the commander of the South Precinct.

policing perspective of Lansing Police Department. However, he wishes to point out that 1998 was a year of tremendous changes, challenges, and opportunities for the department, including his appointment as police chief in March 1998.

The retirement of many senior, experienced police officers of all ranks and classifications left the department with nearly half of the sworn staff having five or fewer years of experience; 75 percent of the senior command staff were new to their positions in 1998.

Chief Johnson's challenge was to manage this relative young and inexperienced department in such a way as to maintain the quality of services that the city of Lansing had come to expect from its police department. "But," the chief comments, "the opportunity to effect change and move the department to an opera-

Former Chief of Police Robert L. Johnson, Lansing Police Department

tional philosophy of 'community policing' was greater than ever before." In that regard, a lot of time and effort have been expended during the past years in "reorganization." Patrol forces were increased almost 20 percent through the reassignment of nearly 30 personnel from non-patrol duties. Average patrol staffing levels were increased as much as 30 percent. Technology advancements, including crime mapping, and equipment acquisitions have helped the LPD work smarter and more proactively. Among the results of these changes have been noticeable decreases in crime, increased visibility of neighborhood patrols, and stronger, more cooperative partnerships with Lansing neighborhoods.

Vacancies brought on by retirements have also given the department an opportunity to broaden the racial, gender, and cultural diversity of the department's entire workforce. The "face" of the LPD has come to truly represent the fullness of the city's diverse population.

"You will see and read about many of the department's accomplishments of the past years from personnel issues," the Chief continues, "that have impacted community policing and problem-solving partnerships. But much more remains to be done if LPD is to attain the vision of Lansing as a 'world class' city. I have no doubt the men and the women of LPD are truly committed to that ideal," the Chief states.

When Robert L. Johnson succeeded Chief Police Jerome G. Boles II, he offered a clear direction for the Lansing Police Department to reduce crime, reduce calls for service, and increase community satisfaction. Chief Johnson implemented three strategies to accomplish his goals. First, he reorganized the department. Police resources were returned to the neighborhoods and the business areas from inside desk jobs. Second, he instituted GIS (crime mapping) to identify hot spots. Third, patrol command staff became responsible for the reduction of crime and calls for service and for the increase of citizen satisfaction in their areas.

Chief Johnson planned on utilizing new crime fighting technology to its fullest. Increased police presence in hot-spot crime areas and attention to quality of life issues reduced crime, he argued. Deterring potential perpetrators by removing them from circulation would also affect crime. Chief Johnson reasons that the public in the United States has enjoyed a steady decline in violent crime since 1994 and police policies are a major component impacting those downward trends.[2] It appears that LPD's primary community policing initiatives are through community policing-type programs.

For example, during the spring of 1997, officers at the Lansing Police Department heard repeated complaints from Lansing residents about school-aged juveniles skipping school and roaming through their neighborhoods and businesses. Further analysis of that problem showed that on average, 10 percent of the 18,500 Lansing School District students were absent every school day. Some of these absent students were involved in criminal activities, such as stealing vehicles, breaking into homes, or stealing from businesses. Others were absent for a variety of personal reasons such as peer pressure, learning disabilities, and family problems. It became clear the community-wide problem of truancy would take a multidimensional community-wide approach to solve. The program created to serve this purpose is presented in detail later in this chapter.

COMMUNITY SERVICES

The Community Services Unit provides support and resources to residents of Lansing. This includes teaching DARE (Drug Abuse Resistance Education) to grade-school children, CUTT (Citizens United to Track Truants) monitoring student truancy, Neighborhood Watch groups providing senior citizens with safety tips, running the Citizen Police Academy, offering crime prevention seminars to businesses and residents, monitoring false alarms, conducting home security surveys, and using McGruff the Crime Dog to spread the crime prevention message. Each year the Community Services Unit sponsors several events to encourage neighborhood participation and to raise awareness about crime prevention. The Community Services Unit helps develop partnerships between city residents and the police department, a key component of LPD's community policing initiative. The LPD works to start community organizations. LPD community officers attend meetings and encourage participation by citizens. Largely, the LPD relies on community leaders in the various areas to pass out flyers, make phone calls, etc., to keep participation up. The Community Services Units operate independently in the two precincts.

Both precincts accept the mission to expand and enhance the concept of targeted enforcement to identify and address specific problems and criminal activity. Yet, the precincts add that the identification and apprehension of criminals and the solving of crimes depends heavily on the follow-up investigations

---

[2]Lowering crime and lower calls for service are the by-products of problem solving for the LPD. These two scales are looked at as concrete measurements by the department. Using surveys, the LPD can see how satisfied people are with the performance of the officers and how they view their neighborhoods.

Head Start teacher Melanie Glasscowe and her students. Photo courtesy of Officer Lori Baukus. Lansing Police Department.

conducted by skilled, trained investigators.[3] Captain Alley comments that the "North and South Precincts operate independently, but under the same general guidelines of the organization. They are not mirrors of each other, but organized basically the same. The officers think they are different, but an outsider would find them more alike than different. We both operate under the same mission and vision statement."

North Precinct

The North Precinct's concept of community policing is specifically directed toward increased interaction with the community and neighborhoods so that they can partner with residents to solve problems and arrive at solutions. More than 1,000 hours of work time was spent attending meetings, working with established neighborhood organizations, and listening to citizens. Community policing officers gather information about community problems at those meetings and, by working with community members, prioritize solutions to those problems. When in doubt, the team sergeant gives input and ultimately has to answer for problems not being worked on. Problems and solutions are offered to the North Precinct Advisory Board, which meets on the third Thursday of

---

[3]For instance, in 1998, North Precinct investigators averaged a case intake rate of approximately 450 to 500 cases a month. Of that number, anywhere between 200 and 300 cases per month were assigned to the 13 detectives and two sergeants in the North Precinct Investigations Unit. Investigators were able to close approximately 100 cases per month while obtaining an average of 65 to 80 arrest warrants per month.

every month. However, the major function of the board is to assist the precinct captain in prioritizing major problems/projects that affect the entire precinct.

Neighborhood Organizations

The North Precinct's neighborhood organizations which participate in community policing initiatives include:

Association for the Bingham Community
Capital Hill
Cherry Hill Neighborhood Association
Downtown Neighborhood Association
Eastfield Neighborhood Association
Eastside Neighborhood Association
Edmore Park Area
Fairview Areas Interested Residents
Genesee Neighborhood Association
Green Oaks
Hosmer Street Neighbors
Hunter Park West
Mount Vernon Resident's Council
North Lansing Community Association
Northtown
Northwest Neighborhood Alliance
Oak Park Neighborhood Association
Old Forest Neighborhood Association
Old Oakland Neighborhood Association
River Forest Neighborhood Association
Shepard Street United Neighbors
Sparrow Estates
Walnut Neighborhood

The North Precinct's Special Events/Traffic Enforcement Unit, in a partnering effort with the community, coordinated a variety of special events in Lansing. For example:

47 Parade permits
51 Street closing permits
77 baseball games requiring police presence
155 Traffic citations
35 Verbal warnings

Michigan Parades Into the 21st Century

Lansing Lugnuts games

Riverfeast

North Lansing Octoberfeast

Holiday parades

Melling labor strike

Heritage Festival

Fourth of July activities

Fest Eve

Jazz Feast

Halloween Fright Nites

Lights for Life

North Precinct's Neighborhood Youth Activity

The Neighborhood Youth Activity (NYA) coordinator spent 1998 & 1999 working within nine targeted neighborhoods and with the community policing officers within the targeted areas.

SOUTH PRECINCT

One of the primary goals of the South Precinct is to increase citizen satisfaction. The precinct established the following guidelines to accomplish this mission:

- Officers will continue to act professionally during all contacts with citizens and each other.
- Personnel will continue to network with other city services to provide the best possible service to the citizens.
- Procedures will be updated to be user friendly for the officers and citizens.
- The Mentor Program (details later) will continue to expand to meet the needs of all new employees. The changes to the FTO Program, and the department-wide emphasis on training, will continue to increase proficiency.
- Officers will continue to attend neighborhood and team meetings to share information and work out solutions to problems with the affected citizens.
- The South Precinct Network Center will continue to provide valuable social programs to residents as well as make the gymnasium available for citizen use.
- Team assignments will remain consistent with as few changes among team members as practicable. This will increase our officers' knowledge base of their assigned areas, and will minimize confusion among citizens about whom to contact regarding neighborhood issues.

Neighborhood Organizations

During 1999, four new neighborhood organizations were formed in the South Precinct, and four nonactive neighborhood groups were dissolved by the Lansing Neighborhood Council. Each of the four new organizations has active Neighborhood Watches associated with them. Some of the organizations are:

- Churchill Downs Community Association
- Colonial Village Neighborhood Association
- Fabulous Acres
- Forest View Citizens Association
- Lansing-Eaton Neighborhood Organization
- Maplehill Neighborhood Association
- Moores Park Neighborhood Organization
- Neighbors United in Action
- Potter/Walsh Neighborhood Organization
- Riverpoint Organization
- Sagamore Hills Neighborhood Organization
- Wexford Heights Neighborhood Association

Neighborhood Watch Groups

Twelve new watches were formed, and 14 inactive watches were deleted, bringing the total number of watch areas in the South Precinct to 92. Community policing officers gather information about community problems at meetings and, working with community members, prioritize solutions to those problems. When in doubt, the team sergeant provides input and ultimately has to answer for problems that are not being worked on.

Problems and solutions are offered to the South Precinct Advisory Board, which meets on the fourth Tuesday of every month. The major function of the board is to assist the precinct captain in prioritizing major problems/projects that affect the entire precinct. The advisory board has been active in providing insight on what they expect of the police and policing priorities for South Lansing, including Neighborhood Network Centers, public health issues, and ways to reduce the number of domestic calls that occur in South Lansing.

South Precinct Programs

In 1997 the Citizens United to Track Truants (CUTT) program was started as a means to solve the truancy problem in Lansing. As of February 1999, there were 45 CUTT volunteers. Captain Mark Alley, Lieutenant Julie Williams, and Officer Elizabeth Bonello assist in the administration of the program, along with John Grant from the Public Safety Department of the Lansing School District. Lieutenant Julie Williams provides an in-depth discussion about CUTT later in this chapter.

Capital Area Response Effort (CARE) is a volunteer-based program that operates out of the South Precinct Network Center to assist victims of domestic violence. The mission of CARE is to reduce family violence in the city of Lansing and Ingham County.

The South Precinct Network Center is a shared facility occupied by both neighborhood and agency representatives. Its purpose is to help neighborhood residents reclaim and improve their physical and social environment, and to increase access to health and human services by placing various "resource coordinators" who can develop personal relationships with the people in the neighborhood. Building on those relationships, resource coordinators subsequently identify and broker services for neighborhood residents as needed, and ensure the inclusion of the neighborhood perspective in service delivery.

Neighborhood Youth and Parent Prevention Partnership (NYPPP) continues to serve as facility coordinator for the South Network Center in the South Precinct. Other functions maintained by the NYPPP include establishing a system for use of various portions of the facility, assisting in the development and facilitation of neighborhood groups that may use the center, and regularly interacting with other personnel who use it. Additional functions include facilitating discussion of miscommunication or conflicts between various entities, reporting any problems regarding custodial maintenance, utilities, etc., to the facility owner, and meeting occasionally with the facility coordinators of the other network centers for mutual support and strategy development regarding the goal of making each network center a hub for neighborhood-based, community-involved, collaborative service delivery.

The South Neighborhood Advisory Board was formed in 1998. Members developed their mission and vision statements, goals, and by-laws in preparation for a south side Neighborhood Summit. This group meets the third Wednesday of the month at the Ingham Regional Medical Center. One of their functions is to set priorities for police duties.

EIGHT HARD QUESTIONS ANSWERED ABOUT COMMUNITY POLICING INITIATIVES

Question 1: What methods are employed to ensure that typical members of the community are represented in the community policing process?

We have worked diligently to make sure that members of the community have been and are involved in policing issues that affect their neighborhood. Each precinct has an advisory board that meets on a monthly basis with the precinct captain to discuss community policing issues. We have two officers who coordinate the Neighborhood Watches, one for each precinct. Each policing team has a set schedule for team meetings (usually every other month) that the public is invited to attend. During these team meetings neighborhood problems are discussed with an understanding of what will be done to fix the problem. Team officers attend neighborhood meetings to identify and respond to neighborhood concerns.

We have conducted citizen surveys to better ascertain how we as a police agency have done. We operate under the philosophy that every contact with a citizen (call for service, traffic stop, investigation, etc.) is an opportunity to initiate community policing and solve problems. Lansing has many community groups including more than 100 Neighborhood Watches. Each community group has elected leadership (president, vice president, secretary, treasurer). The members contact people in the community for representation to the meetings and functions.

Question 2: In what way are community residents included in the decision-making processes associated with community policing?
In addition to the information listed above we rely on the citizens to assist us in policing their neighborhoods and businesses. We have had an evolution in the department where citizens have been representatives on various decision-making boards. A neighborhood citizen sits on our cadet advisory board. This board makes decisions on where police cadets are assigned in the organization and they review the cadet's performance. The Board of Police Commissioners is a civilian oversight group that reviews all of our new policies and procedures, reviews Internal Affairs investigations, reviews the budget, and is represented in promotional processes.

Question 3: What are the elements and/or conditions that will sustain the active involvement of residents in the community?
We have been fortunate that when one leader of a community group steps down a new leader is willing to step forward and take an active role in that neighborhood. Citizens need to believe that they have valuable input in the policing process. As long as that occurs we will have citizens willing to volunteer their time to make their neighborhood city a better place to live and work.

Question 4: How will your organization pick up the slack from federal funding money when it runs out, assuming some part of your community policing program is being funded or subsidized?
We have decided that it is time for us to take the next step in community policing: moving from a "program" to an organizational philosophy. As an organization we need to maximize all of our resources and the only way to do that is to make every officer a community policing officer. As money runs out to sponsor CPOS we have not replaced those positions with general fund dollars. Rather, we have put the responsibility on the team officers and command officers to make sure that community policing in those neighborhoods continues.

Question 5: What were the historical events that influenced organizational decisions to establish a community policing agenda at your agency?
We were fortunate to have the founder of community policing, Dr. Robert Trojanowicz, five miles away at Michigan State University. Dr. Trojanowicz educated many of the organizations' command staffs from the 1970s through the 1990s. This influence was critical for our move to community policing.

Question 6: What methods are used to assess and/or evaluate the progress of the community policing effort?

We have three overlapping goals at the department: (1) Reduce crime, (2) reduce calls for service, and (3) increase citizen satisfaction. The first two goals are judged using crime statistics. The third goal is measured by citizen surveys and the overall comments we get from citizens when we have contact with them.

Question 7: In what way have any community policing programs been changed or altered as a result of community policing assessments?

This chapter highlights several programs that have been adopted as a direct result of citizen input and the need to have a positive effect on our three main goals. (See sections on the CUTT program on truancy, parolee program, and mentor program.)

Question 8: In what way has decentralization been accomplished in keeping with community policing efforts?

We have decentralized the field operations in the community by creating two police precincts. Both precincts have a gym and meeting rooms for citizens to use free of charge. In addition to this, we have network centers and community offices throughout the city.

A Community Officer's Activities

Officer Paul Arnold reported to Captain Mark Alley that in terms of community-related functions, in 1999 he accomplished the following activities in addition to many other policing functions:

- 4 Central Michigan crime prevention meetings
- 6 Ingham County Triad meetings (senior citizen, law enforcement meetings)
- 7 Neighborhood Watch Advisory Board meetings
- 4 Financial institution meetings
- 3 Gang Task Force meetings
- 23 Crime prevention presentations
- 11 Neighborhood Watch-related functions, meetings, parades, etc.
- 8 Security-related inspections
- 4 Crime prevention audio-visual presentations for TV stations
- 4 Team typing for audio-visual presentations for community education on TV
- 3 meetings with military installations regarding security and alarm testing on arms and munitions vault
- 4 Crossing guard training sessions

Lansing Police Officer Mobley and neighborhood children. Photo courtesy of Officer Lori Baukus, Lansing Police Department.

COMMUNITY POLICING TRAINING

Table 1 provides a sample of the type of training LPD officers received to prepare them for community policing activities. The number of officers attending is shown as well as the length of time each of these four programs generally takes. Although there are about 10 different courses, the ones shown in the table are the most in depth.

COMMUNITY POLICING STRATEGIES

Citizens United to Track Truants Program

Citizens United to Track Truants (CUTT) was implemented in October 1997 as a result of a community-wide approach to solve the problem of the high truancy rate in Lansing. Specifically CUTT is a partnership between the Lansing School District, Lansing Police Department, and Retired Senior Volunteer Program (RSVP). The CUTT volunteers, all senior citizens, work out of an office located in the Lansing Police Department, South Precinct Network Center. Volunteers staff a telephone hotline, 272-CUTT, where they take calls from residents and businesses reporting suspected truants. The CUTT program focuses on middle-school-aged students. Volunteers get an absence report every school day from all Lansing School District middle schools. The volunteers then make follow-up telephone calls to the parents of these students to see if they are aware that their child is not in school. The volunteers keep detailed records of the absences so the Lansing School District Department of Public Safety (LSDDPS) and the LPD can make home visits to the chronic truants and their parents.

Other CUTT volunteers are paired in donated vehicles patrolling Lansing neighborhoods and businesses looking for truants. Volunteers are equipped with a LSDDPS radio and cellular telephones to call in suspected truants. For safety reasons, the volunteers do not approach the suspected truants, but keep

Table 1   Community Policing Training

Program	Date	Number Attending/ Hours	Course Description
Community policing series	Spring 97/98/99	15/80	A five-part, weekly series focusing on the development, implementation, and administration of community policing areas. Participants also receive a three-day segment on planning, developing, and presenting a presentation.
Team building	Spring 99	28/16	A two part in-house training program designed for supervisors to review the department's focus on team policing and how it incorporates the fundamental philosophy of community policing.
Skills training/design	Spring 98	256/8	An ongoing training series conducted on a quarterly basis designed to address current organizational, administrative, legal, or operational changes that have occurred. The training is designed to follow adult learning methods with strong emphasis on solid content and quick moving material. Referral information and community policing/team policing components are always incorporated into each session.
Dialogue circles	1996/97	399/10	Two-hour sessions are held once a week for five weeks. Employees follow a program that encourages communication, self-expression, and active listening.

them in sight until an officer from LSDDPS or LPD can arrive to check the person. All volunteers complete a 16-hour training program covering truancy law, safety, use of equipment, and expectations.

CUTT volunteers developed a brochure that details the truancy problem, who is and is not a truant, and how the CUTT program works. The volunteers also developed a flyer which showed the CUTT logo and told how to report a suspected truant. Volunteers distributed this literature as they made their daily contacts with businesses. This literature was also distributed to parents through the schools and to Neighborhood Watch groups.

The program currently has 46 active senior citizen volunteers who are outfitted with a CUTT uniform including pants and the CUTT uniform patches on a shirt, baseball cap, and coat. The volunteers were also given a Lansing School District picture identification card, which they are required to wear while on duty. All of the money and equipment to operate the CUTT program was donated by 16 Lansing businesses. Getting donations for the program was surprisingly easy. The sponsors have been extremely generous in their support of the program and are recognized in the CUTT brochure.

Truancy Sweeps: This community-wide effort to attack the truancy problem in Lansing has increased the cooperation between the Lansing School District (LSD) and the Lansing Police Department. This new cooperation has led to bimonthly truancy sweeps. Twice a month the LSD and the LPD schedule six to eight officers to work in a joint effort to locate truants. An officer from each organization is paired in a vehicle and given a section of the city in which to look for truants. Each team is also given addresses to check for chronic truants.

When located, the truants are brought to a central location on school district property. The student's parents are located and summoned to that location. Upon the parent's arrival, a screening is done to determine why the student was not in school. If intervention is appropriate, referrals are made. The student and parent then meet with an assistant prosecuting attorney who explains the law to both parties and reinforces the seriousness of the offense. If this is a first-time offense, the student is issued a ticket for truancy. If it is a second time or greater offense the student is issued a ticket for truancy and the parent is issued a ticket for Failure of Parental Responsibility. In either case, the student is then released to the parent to be taken back to school. The CUTT volunteers do follow-up and track the attendance of students picked up during the sweeps. On average, 30 to 50 students are picked up on sweep days.

Strategy Conclusion: During the first year of these truancy initiatives (September 1, 1997, through February 28, 1998), Lansing experienced an 11 percent reduction in the number of juveniles accused of crimes Monday through Friday from 7:00 A.M. to 5:00 P.M. as compared to the same time frame for 1996–1997. During the second year (September 1, 1998, through February 28, 1999), Lansing decreased the number of juveniles accused of crimes committed Monday through Friday, 7:00 A.M. to 5:00 P.M., by 27 percent as compared to the same time frame for 1997–1998.

Over the course of two years, juveniles accused of crimes committed during school hours has been reduced by 35 percent. Complaints from citizens of school-aged truants walking their neighborhoods have greatly diminished. The Lansing School District has also seen a marked increase in school attendance. During the second semester of the 1996–1997 school year, 34 percent of students missed more than 10 days of school, but by the second semester of the 1997–1998 school year, only 23 percent of the students missed more than 10 days of school.

Wesley G. Skogan defined community policing in terms of problem solving and community engagement. Lansing has used these two basic principles to combat the long-standing problem of truancy. We are optimistic that this community-wide effort will reap future dividends in that a better educated workforce will result.

Recently a CUTT volunteer was interviewed by a local television station. He was asked by the reporter how many truants he needed to find to make it a good day. The volunteer responded, "When we don't find any, it's a good day." The LPD encourages other communities to emulate what they have done to combat truancy, which in turn impacts crime and criminal activity.

Neighborhood Watch

In 1978, Landing community members, in conjunction with the LPD, launched a city-wide Neighborhood Watch program. Fifteen years later, 151 watches had been organized and were serving more than 11,500 households. Two officers are responsible for establishing new groups, facilitating existing ones, and disseminating information to all. The officers carry the responsibility for updating and taping the Lansing Police Department's Neighborhood Watch Information line four times a week to keep citizens informed of crimes reported the preceding day.

In March 1995, Lansing Police Chief Jerome G. Boles reorganized the department to make officers more accessible to the citizens they serve, and enhance communication and problem-solving potential. Boles divided the department into north and south precincts. Because the citizens in the North Precinct were organized and had numerous active neighborhood organizations in place, his staff concentrated on those groups in the south that needed strengthening. They established 12 problem-solving teams in the South Precinct and encouraged citizen participation.

Each of the 12 teams was represented by a sergeant and many officers from each shift. The sergeants explained the department's reorganization to the watch coordinators and introduced each team's officers. Before long, the coordinators were openly sharing their operational concerns about the watch program. Many felt the information line was insufficient and not specific enough to be useful. In addition to asking for suggestions on how to improve the watch information line, the officers used this interaction to get feedback on how the coordinators perceived the department's reorganization.

The teams formulated a questionnaire to gather information. The anonymous survey used a combination of Lickert scales, dichotomous fill-in values, and open-ended questions. In early August 1998 the department mailed surveys to all 91 South Precinct watch coordinators. The surveys were accompanied by a cover letter explaining the survey's purpose and a self-addressed stamped envelope for returning it once completed. Fifty-seven of the 91 questionnaires were returned—a response of 63 percent. After the data had been analyzed, a committee of Neighborhood Watch coordinators and a police sergeant met to make recommendations for improving the program. This step ensured that citizens shared in every aspect of the program.

Survey Findings: One of the most interesting findings was that nearly one-half (48 percent) of the respondents rated the performance of their team as "unknown." Also, results showed that a strong correlation existed between a coordinator having contact with a team and the coordinator's positive feelings toward a team approach to problem solving. Conversely, a lack of communication between the police organization and the citizen was shown to be a primary reason for a lack of support by watch coordinators.

Policy Solutions: The committee who reviewed the results of the survey developed some recommendations for improving the Neighborhood Watch program. They stressed that better communication between the team officers and the coordinators was essential. They proposed that the Neighborhood Watch teams have a separate voice mailbox at the police department to provide specific crime information about each team area. The committee further suggested that coordinators attend the officers' monthly team meetings, which would enable them to discuss neighborhood problems with team members and improve communication with the officers. The group also encouraged coordinators to "ride along" with their team officers to get a better idea of what the officers do in the field. Finally, the committee asked that the department start a mentor program to assist in the development of new watch groups.

Policy Solution Conclusion: The Lansing Police Department works with its citizens to provide the best service possible. The LPD involves coordinators in the decision-making process as it continues forward with improvements and reorganization. Line officers and citizens are still working on breaking down the communication barriers and will continue to do so until both sides are comfortable communicating with each other. Lansing Mayor David Hollister recently acknowledged this need while addressing a community group. He reinforced this message in his statement that "decentralization of the police department is not being done as an end in itself; it is being done to help foster open and honest communication between the police officers and the citizens they serve. This open communication leads to the identification and solving of problems, which in turn makes Lansing a better place to live and work." As part of those recommendations, the LPD Mentor program was established.

Lansing Police Department Mentor Program[4]

In spring of 1996, the Lansing Police Department was in the second year of a department-wide reorganization. Not only was the organization flattening out, it was literally spreading out—to separate precincts for the first time in its 103-year history. A philosophical emphasis and transition to community- and team-based policing was in high gear. Tremendous change was occurring all at once.

---

[4]This section was written by Captain Julie Williams of the LPD.

The organization was being rocked by an average retirement rate of 5 percent. The sworn personnel departure rate of nonprobationary personnel from 1992 to 1996 was 30 percent. A wealth of experience and technical knowledge was walking out the door at a crippling pace. New hires were arriving at an average rate of 8.5 percent per year and throughout the department 67 percent of sworn personnel had been hired between 1992 and 1998. All indications were that this trend would continue for years to come.

The organization was at a critical juncture in its history and its survival. A structured method was needed to increase the retention of new hires and facilitate the transmission of critical knowledge and experience from senior sworn personnel to police cadets, recruits, and sworn new hires.

The perfect remedy appeared to be a mentor program, given that research projects over the years had documented the capability of a formal mentor program to transmit organizational knowledge, experience, and values from person to person. It was recognized that the design and implementation of a successful mentor program at the Lansing Police Department would require the input of a diverse group of individuals from varied backgrounds, assignments, experience levels, and ranks within the organization. What followed was a series of focused group meetings in the fall of 1996. Each meeting had an agenda and purpose. Input was gained on program design, goals, mentor criteria, mentor–protege pairings, meeting and feedback parameters, program evaluation criteria, training and compensation for mentors, and departmental mentor program operational guidelines and policy. Most importantly, participants believed that the emphasis of the mentor program should be doing what can be done to uphold departmental standards and assist new hires in meeting those standards.

In December 1996, a survey was designed and distributed in an effort to obtain input on program design from all sworn personnel. The survey responses were anonymous. The wealth of information provided by the survey assisted in defining the scope and nature of the problem and gave valuable insight in what to aim for in program structure, goals, and implementation strategy. Since initial program implementation in April 1997, a number of additional surveys were designed and disseminated to obtain additional feedback on mentor training and various program components, as well as overall program progress. Feedback was constantly sought and encouraged in an effort to improve the program and maximize potential.

The first LPD mentor training session was attended by thirty mentors. Soon thereafter, others began to impatiently urge that another training session be conducted, resulting in a total of 49 mentors by the end of 1997. Due to an ever-increasing number of new hires, the mentor pool was increased to a total of 68 mentors with the completion of a third mentor training session in January 1999.

The LPD Mentor Program structure consists of a mentor coordinator, an advisory team, a pool of mentors, and proteges. Involvement in the program is voluntary and requires completion of a Mentor Program questionnaire if accepted. Involvement commences for the new hire upon hire with the organization and for the mentor upon receipt of formal training by the mentor coordinator. Mentor–protege pairing recommendations are made by the advisory team to the mentor coordinator and are based on compatible values, goals and needs, similar backgrounds and interests, race, and gender.

The mentor coordinator reviews the mentor–protege (M–P) pairing recommendation and confers with the proposed mentor prior to approving the M–P pairing. Upon approval of the M–P pairing, proper notifications are made to human resources, staff, mentors, the field training officer (FTO) coordinator(s), and the protege. Meetings are held as needed by the advisory team and mentor coordinator to address M–P pairings, critical developments in protege progress, timely response to protege needs, and program feedback and oversight. Semiannual meetings of the mentor coordinator, advisory team, and mentors are held. This is supplemented with one-on-one meetings between the mentor coordinator and mentors on an as-needed basis. The mentor coordinator meets one-on-one with each protege at the time of hire to review the program parameters and answer new hire questions about the program.

A mentor program newsletter is issued monthly to provide mentoring tips, program updates, reminders, and spotlights on particular mentors, proteges, or mentoring relationships. A highlight of each issue is a featured article submitted by either a mentor or protege sharing their insight, knowledge, experiences, thoughts, strategies, and general excitement about the program and their M–P relationship. Each article is packed with sincerity and sensitivity.

Program goals are broken down into three categories: organizational, protege, and mentor. Organizational goals are to increase employee retention, better assimilate new hires into the agency, increase job satisfaction and loyalty, develop a professional identity, provide a support system for employees, facilitate professional development of the protege, and teach the organizational culture, values, mission, and standards to proteges. Protege goals include successful completion of the probationary period, smooth transition into LPD, enhancement of current skills, the learning of new skills, identification of career goals, and career development. Mentor goals seek to recognize the critical service mentors provide to LPD in the attainment of program goals and the pivotal role mentors play in a protege's successful completion of the LPD probationary period. Additionally, mentor goals seek the professional development of junior employees, enhancement of mentor skills and knowledge, a reinvigoration of the mentor's career, and an installation of a sense of pride and accomplishment.

Mentor training consists of a one-day program that is mandatory for all mentors. The Mentor Program guidelines delineate the need for mentors to assist, guide, familiarize, prepare, facilitate, initiate, and communicate as they perform as a confidante and role model to a protege. They communicate that being a mentor should be viewed as an honor. The Mentor Program policy encourages program involvement of all new hires. It explains that the mentor coordinator and assigned mentor will determine the necessary time commitment of the mentor to the protege during the initial phase of the protege's development. The policy also facilitates commanders in scheduling on-duty time for mentors to assist the new hire during their first week of employment at LPD.

Program evaluation criteria include the resultant impact the program bears on retention rates for new hires, survey/questionnaire feedback, and an increase in the mentor pool. The meetings, newsletter, stated program goals, mentor training, program guidelines, and program policy are designed and intended to clearly communicate employee roles and responsibilities for program members and for those responsible for coordination of effort between divisions and program personnel. A mechanism is in place to properly deal with disciplinary matters that arise as a result of the mentoring relationship. This mechanism is designed to maintain program and departmental integrity while also respecting the nature of the mentor–protege relationship.

A Mentor Program video was made to introduce new hires to the program and encourage their involvement. It features several mentors and proteges providing their personal insights about the program. This video not only serves as a helpful guide for human resource personnel during the application process, but also captures and communicates the special nature of the mentor–protege relationship to new hire candidates.

The two primary goals of the Mentor Program are to capture some of the experience and knowledge being lost as a result of employee departures and the improvement of retention rates of new hires. Survey feedback from mentors, proteges, field training officers, and nonprogram personnel consistently indicate that solid inroads are being made in these areas. The long-term result is an employee who "fits" in the organization, is committed to it, and is retained by the organization as a valued, productive employee. Survey responses note that proteges feel "connected" to the organization. This is supportive evidence of the attainment of program goals of assimilation, job satisfaction and loyalty, professional development, as well as, the enhancement and learning of skills.

The unique value of the LPD Mentor Program lies in the fact that this program was intentionally and specifically designed with replication and easy adaptation in mind. The goal was to create a program that could and should be adapted for any workgroup, anywhere. Indeed, survey feedback repeatedly cites expansion of this program to other LPD workgroups as the sole item for program improvement. Logically, this has led to the expansion of the Mentor Program in March 1999 to the Communications Center at the LPD.

The willingness of the mentors to reach out to assist junior employees has been heartwarming. With each individual success comes the potential that today's protege will become tomorrow's mentor. Indeed, a number of Lansing Police Department personnel have brought the process full circle, evolving from protege to mentor. They are seeking to share with new hires what was generously provided to them by their mentors: support, understanding, advice, encouragement, humor, and the giving of oneself.

A COMMUNITY PRESIDENT ADDRESSES COMMUNITY POLICING

"At first it took a little getting used to," said Diane Pendell, "a police car parking in my driveway. The neighbors were a little leery of what was going on. But curiosity got the better of them and soon they began to venture over. By the time our Neighborhood Watch was activated, part of the Lansing-Eaton Neighborhood was already involved in community policing before it was officially introduced to Lansing. Neighbors talking to neighbors, working with the police to resolve and prevent future problems.

With the introduction of community policing to Lansing, just about every neighborhood organization had hoped to obtain an official community police officer (CPO). But with limited grant money there were just not enough officers for every neighborhood. When the Lansing-Eaton Neighborhood (LENO) did not get an official CPO, there was only one option left, to create our own, unofficial, CPO. Team officers were invited to neighborhood meetings and I volunteered to be the neighborhood police contact person.

Not wanting to be one of those dreaded "neighborhood people," I decided to do some homework. By attending the Lansing's Citizen's Police Academy I learned a lot about law enforcement from a policing perspective and about other city departments that could assist on nonpolice neighborhood issues. I was also granted ride-alongs with wonderfully patient officers, who answered endless questions, who taught me how to work with them, and let me observe how calls for police assistance were handled. This education was taken back to the LENO neighborhood. The better educated the community, the easier it has been to work not only with the police department, but also with code compliance and other City Hall departments. Very quickly the neighborhood became dependent on the dedication of the team officers to resolve and prevent problems. And within the team, there have always been officers willing to be our unofficial CPOs, giving more than just the call of duty to the neighborhood.

Has community policing worked in the Lansing-Eaton Neighborhood? The drug houses are gone, so are the problem houses, teenagers are not hanging out on street corners, crime is down. But most importantly, the fear is gone. There are joggers and dog walkers in the neighborhood from dawn to dusk. Families are out bike riding and in the parks children are enjoying the new playground equipment. Few houses go up for sale and those that do, do not stay on the market long because LENO is a "safe neighborhood." Community policing in LENO's neighborhood not only reduced crime and quality of life issues, but also created a more positive attitude toward and trust and faith in Lansing's Police Department. I could write a novel stating examples of good deeds by Team 16's officers, but my favorite stories involve the officers and neighborhood children.

After settling a neighbor dispute, police officers noticed a group of young children clustered together watching them leave. One of the officers went over to the small group of children and produced a handful of shiny junior police stick-on badges. With their badges adhered to their shirts, he swore them all in as junior officers and left them with a sense of pride in their new badges and a trust in the police.

Another officer was talking with a group of neighborhood boys, when he noticed a University of Michigan flag flying from one of the boy's house. The officer, a former MSU football player, mentioned the "offensive" flag of his former rival team. The owner of the flag was quick to point out that if the officer were truly an MSU fan, then why does the officer drive around in a car with U of M colors? (The police vehicles were painted in U of M colors) Touche! The officer laughed, admitting his defeat and the boy smiled knowing the man in the uniform is human, even if he is a MSU fan.

The officers of the South Precinct, from patrol to captain, through community policing, have helped to make the Lansing-Eaton Neighborhood a great place to call home. These officers and especially those who have and are serving as our unofficial CPOs, deserve our thanks. And maybe a chocolate chip cookie or two!

Diane Pendell, President Lansing-Eaton Neighborhood Organization. Photo courtesy of Officer Lori Baukus, Lansing Police Department.

COLLABORATION WITH LANSING PAROLE OFFICERS

On July 13, 1999, Captain Mark Alley distributed the following notice to all personnel of the South Precinct.

Beginning Cycle 8, 1999,[5] the South Precinct officers and Lansing parole officers will begin working together in Lansing Police cars. At this time there are eight parole officers who can participate in this program, because it is voluntary for them. We anticipate that each parole officer will work with us about once a month. They will have the opportunity to work any of our four shifts. I anticipate that only 1 parole officer will be working with us at a time. On these dates the shift lieutenant will put the parole officer with one of our officers and put the team on special assignment for the shift. The team will spend the shift checking on parolees in the city of Lansing. The parole officers will have their list of parolees assigned to them that they would like to check. Since the parolees can move, they are not assigned by geographic area. The parole officers are going to concentrate on parolees living in the South Precinct. You are allowed to check individuals living in the North Precinct.

---

[5]*Cycles* are what the LPD call scheduling months. Most cycles are 28 days and two are 42 days, thus they don't start and end at the beginning and ends of months. Cycle 8 is August.

The concept of parole officers and police officers working together on this type of initiative is not new. These types of programs have been very successful in the cities of Boston, Minneapolis, Phoenix, and Mobile just to name a few. We know that a small percentage of the population is responsible for the vast majority of crime. If these parolees are not involved in crimes themselves, chances are their associates are. That is why it is imperative that during these home visits we initiate a dialogue with the parolee about their knowledge of criminal activity. This interviewing tactic, referred to as "debriefing" in New York City, has produced outstanding information and results. If questioned, many of these parolees will divulge criminal information about their associates and acquaintances.

To assist in monitoring the effectiveness of this program and acquiring the debriefing information officers will be required to complete a Lansing Police & Parole Officer Contact Sheet for every home visit. The original forms will be left on the desk of our detective sergeants and a copy of the forms will be given to the shift lieutenant and precinct captain.

Captain Williams and I met with all of the parole officers on July 8, 1999, and reviewed the program with them. They all signed a ride-along waiver and watched the ride-along video: They understand that they are not police officers and do not have police powers. On the flip side, parole officers have powers of arrest and search that we do not have. For example, on a biweekly basis we are called to the parole office at 2101 W. Holmes to pick up parolees who has violated the terms of their parole and transport them to the Mall. The parole officer does not need a warrant to have the arrest made. During these home visits we expect that some of the parolees will be in violation of their parole and we will be transporting them to Detention.

I want to reiterate that this is not a ride-along/observer program for the parole officers. We will be accompanying them on their site visits and assisting them in making sure the parolees are not violating the terms of their parole. We also want to use this as an opportunity to gather information from the parolees on criminal activity that they are aware of. The parole officers will be carrying their normal equipment with them. For some of them this includes a handgun. They have procedures that they follow on use of force. If you are dispatched to a call for service or come across another incident while participating in this program the parole officer will not be considered a "back-up" police officer. In these circumstances officers should consider themselves as working alone and call for back-up as needed.

CITIZEN SURVEY

Other ways of measuring Lansing community response to community policing initiatives is through surveys. Surveys administered by the LPD measure community response to services provided by the LPD.

Lansing residents whose homes or businesses were broken into (breaking and entering/ B&E) over a nine-month period expressed a high degree of satisfaction with the service provided by the Lansing Police Department. This was one of the primary findings of the first Lansing Police "Citizen Satisfaction Survey," conducted in 1999 under the direction of Chief Robert L. Johnson by the department's Administrative Services Division and Dr. Michael Reisig, a criminal justice professor and survey research specialist at Michigan State University.

The survey involved 300 resident telephone contacts who filed home invasion or business break-in complaints between April and December 1998. A total of 715 citizens were telephoned during January 1999. Approximately 52 percent (300) of the sample population were willing to participate in the survey.

Respondents were asked a series of questions to measure their expectations as compared to actual police service received after reporting their victimization. The difference between what was expected and what actually took place offered a window, the researchers believed, to measure what the participants considered important and how satisfied they were with the service provided by the LPD. In addition, respondents were given the opportunity to rate their level of satisfaction with police services on a 1–4 scale (4 meant they were very satisfied, 3 represented a satisfied response, 2 a dissatisfied response, and 1 represented a very dissatisfied response).

The survey revealed that 81 percent (243) of the participants were satisfied or very satisfied (average score = 3.28) with the service they received from the LPD after they reported their B&E complaint. In response to the question "How satisfied are you in general with the LPD?," again, 81 percent (243) of the participants reported they were satisfied or very satisfied (average score = 3.25) with the general services of the department. Ninety-four percent (282) of respondents reported the officers to be courteous; 93 percent (279) reported that responding officers took time to listen to them; and 88 percent (264) of the respondents reported that responding officers took their situation seriously. Minority victims expressed a slightly higher rate of satisfaction than Caucasian victims with the LPD service relative to their B&E victimization (average score = 3.26 as compared to 3.24); and 90 percent (270) of those surveyed reported they were satisfied or very satisfied with the way the LPD Dispatch Center handled their 911 call for service (average score = 3.54).

Despite the strong satisfaction level reported by the respondents, the survey demonstrated that there was room for improvement in the way the LPD provided follow-up services to B&E victims. Only 57 percent (171) of those surveyed reported that they were called after their initial report was taken and informed of the status of their case; 36 percent (108) reported that they were called and told of the final status of their case. While almost 80 percent (240) of the respondents reported they were given advice on how to prevent future break-ins, only 70 percent (210) reported that LPD personnel provided information concerning available resources such as victim's services. In addition, female complainants were less satisfied than males with the way the LPD responded to their B&E calls (average score = 3.19 for females compared to 3.40 for males).

The LPD is currently analyzing and discussing the survey results throughout each of its divisions with the goal of improving services and increasing citizen satisfaction. An active plan to address the deficiencies discovered through the survey will be developed and implemented in the near future. A follow-up survey of B&E victims will take place in the near future to assess the progress the LPD has made.

SUMMARY

The intention of the LPD to move from an incident-driven programmatic approach of police service to an operational philosophy grounded in problem-solving strategies was documented. The department was challenged by many obstacles including top management turn over leaving less experienced officers to manage the department. The North Precinct and the South Precinct of the LPD were emphasized and their many neighborhood organizations and programs were outlined. A community officer's activities and training were detailed. Some of the LPD's community policing strategies such as Citizens United to Track Truants, Neighborhood Watch, and a mentoring program were detailed. Many letters of community policing support were presented from neighborhood organizational presidents, police, and correctional personnel. A survey of 300 residents was conducted providing data toward LPD's community policing initiatives. The results showed that a high percentile of the participants were satisfied with the services they received from the LPD.

CONCLUSION

Community policing strategists argue that it is an outreach by the police to the community through facilitative leadership to develop a partnership to enhance public safety, reduce the fear of crime, and to improve the quality of life. Priorities of community policing focus on a preventive response to public order through a level of delegation of authority as a response to future crime as opposed to a response after crimes have occurred. That is, police executives must demonstrate facilitative skills as opposed to enforcer skills should they wish to move their agency into a 21st century policing model. While there were indicators that the Lansing Police Department wanted to move from an incident-driven bureaucratic department to a proactive partnership, there was little evidence that it succeeded. Perhaps the major administrative changes in the organization which left the agency with few experienced managers had something to do with this thought. While the department utilizes community member surveys as one method of evaluating community policing initiatives, they seem compelled to use incident-driven measurements and icons such as arrest rates and response time to ascertain their progress towards a community policing philosophy. Maybe, younger commanders feel more confident with those assessment scales because they are easy to articulate to the public and the policymakers, and it may be exactly what those groups want to hear. Yet, if management continues to emphasize an inadequate method of measuring police performance, would they become, in a sense, another obstacle in instituting a community policing philosophy in Lansing? Winning public trust through short term methods might produce long lasting effects that could hamper quality of life issues and crime control concerns.

DO YOU KNOW?

1. Identify three of the LPD's major programs. Which one of them might be the most productive for the community? For the police?
2. In what way does the community benefit from some of the innovative programs the Lansing Police Department supports?
3. In what way might the community be disadvantaged by a program-driven police department?
4. Decentralization plays an important role in community policing, but, given the manner in which the LPD operates, what disadvantages might result from having two precincts? What advantages?
5. Empowerment of community members is vital to community policing strategies. Can you identify how the citizens in Lansing might be empowered concerning police deployment?
6. Many departments institute community policing by first establishing a department-wide community policing philosophy. But that was not the case with the LPD. What might have prevented the LPD from following traditional methods of instituting community policing policies? What advantages might be gained by developing programs first and philosophies second?
7. Can you identify the primary components that promote crime and crime control strategies in the LPD as compared to prevention strategies practiced by many other agencies?

APPENDIX 1   Lansing Five-Year Arrest Record

TYPE	1994	1995	1996	1997	1998
Murder/manslaughter	12	14	11	16	10
CSC/1&3	142	144	163	154	125
Robbery	349	344	343	265	280
Felonious Assault	1,163	1,200	1,210	1,086	885
Burglary	1,537	1,502	1,607	1,698	1,606
Larceny	6,120	5,938	5,953	5,858	4,982
UDAA	972	700	538	506	507
Arson	71	55	68	59	67
Total	10,366	9,897	9,893	9,642	8,462
Population	125,513	125,875	126,324	127,321	127,825
Arrest rate per 1,000	8.25	7.86	7.83	7.57	6.61

*Source: Lansing Police Department Web Site.

Note: Year ending 1999, Felony arrests 1,686; Misdemeanor 11,639; Total arrests 14,325; Lansing's jail lodged more than 16,500 subjects in 1999.

CHAPTER SIX

HARRIS COUNTY PRECINCT 4 CONSTABLE'S OFFICE

Harris County, Texas

The Harris County Precinct 4 Constable's Office is located at 6831 Cypresswood Drive Spring, Harris County, Texas 77379.[1] The chapter was prepared, in part, by Assistant Chief Ron Hickman.

CHAPTER OUTLINE

The first section of this chapter explains the function of the constable and describes Precinct 4's demographics, mission statement, events leading to community policing initiatives, and rationale and description of programs. Precinct 4's history about their hiring practices through their Contract Deputy Program is clarified. Profiles of the Texas Law Enforcement agencies and Precinct 4 are given. Precinct 4's response and reported crime statistics are highlighted, and a review of their police units and their organizational chart are illustrated. A constable's experience and his comments about community policing are offered followed by the deputy chief's (who is running for the constable's job) experiences, comments, and reports on training and assessment of programs are explained. Last, precinct trainers, officers, and community members share their perspectives.

FUNCTIONS OF A CONSTABLE

The office and responsibilities of the constable vary greatly from region to region, and each office can utilize its power of authority differently. Texas's constitution

---

[1]The Harris County Precinct 4 Constable's Office web site is
http://www.co.harris.tx.us/pct4.

provides constables with authority similar to that of a county sheriff, without the responsibility for managing a jail facility. In some areas, the constable has been identified as an elected official who is responsive and responsible to constituents, which can be a highly motivating component in quality law enforcement service. Constable Dick Moore is the elected official for Harris County Precinct 4, and the Texas Code of Criminal Procedure designates the constable and deputy constables as Texas peace officers. Deputy Chief Ron Hickman was the primary contributor to this chapter.

DEMOGRAPHICS OF PRECINCT 4

Harris County is the third largest county in the United States with a population of more than three million people consisting of 1,788 square miles in size including Houston, Texas. There are eight precincts within the county. The Precinct 4 Constable's Office is one of those eight precincts. It serves 16 justices of the peace in Harris County, Texas. Precinct 4 covers a geographic area of more than 540 square miles in northern Harris County and serves a population of approximately 750,000 residents. Its general boundaries are from the Houston city limits north to Montgomery County and from US 290 east to Liberty County. Precinct 4 has in excess of 232 full-time and 70 reserve sworn officers. There are also 144 contracted deputies (a distinction that is discussed later in the chapter). Thus, the department strength can be considered to be 376 full timers and 70 reserves.

Several other law enforcement agencies operate in overlapping, concurrent jurisdictions with Precinct 4. These include the Harris County Sheriff's Department; the city police departments of Houston, Tomball, Humble, and Jersey Village; the Metropolitan Transit Authority Police; school district police from the Spring and Klein Independent School Districts; and the Texas Department of Public Safety Highway Patrol. Precinct 4 has interagency agreements with all of these entities to promote efficient community service, and cooperation is the norm between these agencies. However, Precinct 4 is the dominant law enforcement agency within the jurisdiction through, in part, the Contract Deputy Program.

MISSION STATEMENT

The mission of the Harris County Precinct 4 Constable's Office is to provide consistent quality in the delivery of all services available to the community. To excel in the delivery of these services, the stated Departmental goals must be achieved:

- To act effectively as the service and enforcement arm of the judicial system.
- To protect all segments of the community from criminal activities through innovative crime prevention and suppression techniques.
- To provide for the safety and protection of the employees of the department by all reasonable means.

- To preserve the peace and dignity of the community.
- To provide traffic enforcement directed at safe movement of the public throughout the community.
- To exercise diligence in the recovery of loss.
- To provide community programs directed toward assisting the public with education and awareness.

In achieving these goals, progressive techniques and strategic planning are exercised to maintain a proactive posture. Utilizing professionalism and courtesy, integrated with compassion and ethical standards, Precinct 4's officers strive to understand and meet the needs of their community.

In the achievement of this mission, the Precinct 4 Constable's Office of Harris County provides a level of service that exceeds the expectations of the community. Through this mission, the department continues to be a leader in the professional delivery of these services.

EVENTS LEADING TO COMMUNITY POLICING

The department, by necessity, focused on policing at the community level since Constable Dick Moore took office in 1981. As a locally elected official, the need to relate to and meet the expectations of that constituent base has required the constable to work with and identify issues at the lowest geographic level, that of a community or the individual. By identifying the specific unique needs and issues that are the major concerns to these small geographic areas, the department ensures its continued success. Even before community policing was identified as an acronym or label for a specific style of meeting community needs, Constable Moore was already working in that mode of operation by establishing programs in the community that helped define community problems that impacted the quality life for those individuals, and then his officers found solutions to those quality of life issues. However, programs are but one of two techniques that Precinct 4 utilizes to further quality of life issues in Harris County. The second technique is as a "hired-out agency" to communities who desire quality police service and cannot get it from the jurisdictional authority due to a number of variables discussed in this chapter.

PROGRAM RATIONALE

The public's expectations of their public service agencies have continued to increase along with the educational and economic progress of their communities. A more educated populace is less tolerant of crime and more interested in direct involvement in the manner and in the style of policing in their communities. During the 1990s, across the county we have seen a change in the relationship between the police and the public. From an era when police rode in steel boxes on wheels and law enforcement was perceived as distant from the public it policed, we have arrived at a time where an attitude of "we're the cops and you're not" is out of place and inappropriate. More and more of the types of programs that are provided by law enforcement to communities are indicative of law enforcement's desire to create partnerships in policing. We provide educational and informative programs to better prepare and equip the citizenry to deal with crime and their reaction to it. We have also become more proactive in programs such as DARE and GREAT where we target "at-risk" preteens.

This approach to policing has become more social in nature and places the police squarely within the reach of the community as a positive resource. Precinct 4 looks more at programs that are "helpful" to the public it serves. Precinct 4's programs, such as the Domestic Violence and Victims Assistance Programs place them in direct contact with a previously ignored segment of the population. Before this time, victims were pretty much left to recover and survive on their own. Now, agencies such as Precinct 4 step in and assist victims to recover compensation or direct them to the legal or family counseling processes with the intent of returning them to a pre-incident level of functionality. Specifically, our Victims Assistance and Domestic Violence Programs personnel review all incident reports involving violent crimes daily. Precinct 4 makes personal contact with the victims to see what types of aid can be provided. In many cases the victim is unaware of potential help, so this proactive approach is a very effective community service tool.

In a competitive environment, budget dollars are scrutinized and programs weighed for their success and public acceptability. To continue a program, it has to be successful and provide a meaningful purpose to the community. Not all services in law enforcement enjoy the latitude of being a necessary evil and with the proliferation of policing agencies, success in police programs is very important.

The staff of the Precinct 4 Constable's Office ensures that Harris County residents receive the highest level of service available. They are dedicated to the concepts of community-oriented policing and community interaction through the use of their programs and Contract Deputy Programs.

PRECINCT 4 PROGRAMS

Precinct 4's community-oriented policing programs include the following:

> *Citizens Police Academy.* A 13-week overview of the responsibilities, authority, and procedures of the Precinct 4 Constable's Office. Constable Dick Moore created Precinct 4's Citizens Police Academy (CPA) to help educate the public about the roles, training, and duties of law enforcement professionals. CPA cadets undergo an encapsulated version of the standard peace officer academy, including firearms training, basic investigation, and even a field training session with an on-duty deputy. Over a 13-week period, they are introduced to all aspects of law enforcement by seasoned instructors. Classes are held one evening per week with firearms qualifications being held on one Saturday. After completing the CPA, graduates are issued certificates during a formal ceremony.

Rape Aggression Defense (RAD) programs. A defensive tactics course provided to prepare younger girls and women to handle an attack. Separate programs have been designed for each group.

Junior public safety program. A week-long summer program for "at-risk" teenaged kids that deals with the responsibilities of various public service and emergency response agencies.

Bicycle safety programs. Precinct 4's bike patrol and crime prevention personnel put on bike safety rodeos to teach general safety precautions for children. They also do bike engraving.

Crime prevention. Precinct 4's certified crime prevention officers do home and business inspections, give safety talks to homeowner and business groups, and assist in coordinating implementation of crime watch groups.

Vacation Watch Program. Precinct 4 receives notices from area residents who are going on vacation and patrol personnel make routine visits to their address to check the general welfare of the home.

Victims Assistance Program. Trained personnel review offense reports and handle referrals for victims of serious crime. These advocates assist the crime victim in the application process to receive compensation from the State Crime Victim Compensation fund. To date, almost $400,000 has been provided to victims as a result of this intervention.

Domestic Violence Program. Officers trained in dealing with domestic violence review offense reports and provide referral for victims to ease their movement through the legal process as well as help them in acquiring needed family and peer counseling.

DARE program. Drug abuse and resistance education is taught through area schools in one of our school districts through a cooperative agreement.

GREAT program. This program of gang education and resistance to violence is taught throughout nine different school districts in our precinct. The program, begun by the Alcohol, Tobacco, and Firearms Bureau, has been widely accepted as a medium with which we can reach at-risk kids.

HISTORY OF PRECINCT 4'S HIRING-OUT PRACTICES

Constable offices have been traditional agencies in Texas since the time of the Old West. In more recent times, at least in Texas, counties have begun utilizing them as a resource, due to their locally responsive position in communities, for other types of police activities. In Harris County, one of the largest and most densely populated Texas counties, the increase in patrol utilization for constables came about as a response from communities for a need to increase field personnel. This occurred at a time when county jail inmate populations continued to grow as a result of the state mandating that county offenders remain in county jails. Working under a Texas Supreme Court mandate limiting the number of state prison beds, many of the sheriff's county jails had to hold an increasing jail population, too. Working under a separate court ruling that mandates the jail guard-to-prisoner ratio, much of the existing resources went to guarding county jail inmates. This left fewer and fewer personnel to patrol the streets and respond to calls. An opportunity existed for aggressive law enforcement agencies that wanted to service a larger community.

CONTRACT DEPUTY PROGRAM

As the Sheriff's Department focused on staffing jails and the population in Harris County exploded, the quality of police service was at risk. Budget cuts reduced the possibilities of personnel increases to the sheriff's Patrol Division. Thus, the Sheriff's Department was unable to adequately perform some of the more basic proactive law enforcement functions, such as neighborhood patrol and traffic enforcement. The precinct was in a high growth state, with many people migrating from the city of Houston to more suburban settings. These people brought with them an expectation of police service based on their experiences living in a municipality. Unfortunately, they also brought a measure of their own problems in the form of a savvy criminal element. The lack of routine patrols was surely evident to this group, who quickly took advantage of an underprotected populace. When public outcry for increased neighborhood patrol and more deputies met with little or no results from the county, communities began looking for other solutions.

They turned to their Homeowners Associations and civic groups for answers. Because these representatives harbored the same concerns as their constituents, a solution was quickly found. They discovered a mechanism that allowed them to subsidize the cost of increased law enforcement by "contracting" with the Constable's Office to pay a percentage of a deputy's cost, with the county picking up the balance. The terms of the contract allowed for the subsidized deputy to be assigned to the contracting subdivision, performing a corresponding percentage of patrol and law enforcement duties within their boundaries, or on their behalf. The balance of the deputy's time was available for law enforcement activities in the county at large. This created a blanketing effect of the more populous areas with deputies who also responded to calls outside of their assigned area. The overall result was increased law enforcement visibility throughout Precinct 4 and faster response times. The contract methodology permitted rapid increases of personnel at a fraction of the cost of deploying them at full expense to the normal county budget, resulting in a win–win situation for the county and the community.

Hundreds of local communities have requested police service through the Contract Deputy Program. Precinct 4 has a strong reputation for being responsive to the community, and has acquired 68 such contracts, including one school district, with 144 contracted deputies (sworn officers) assigned to them.

Those personnel owe their assignments and geographic responsibilities to the contract areas, and due to the manner in which Precinct 4 has come to relate to them, this program has continued to increase in popularity and effectiveness. There are approximately 85 subdivisions in Precinct 4's jurisdiction and many of those subdivisions have jointly contracted to form a cooperative alliance. The population of the precinct is approximately 750,000 and these communities comprise about 55 percent of the area.

One example is Northampton subdivision. They have a Community-Based Constable Protection contract with Precinct 4. In the early 1970s, when Northampton subdivision consisted of some 400 homes, a decision was made to contract with the Harris County Precinct 4 Constable's Office for regular patrol within Northampton subdivision. By 1999, Northampton had grown to more than 1,400 homes with an estimated population of 4,000 residents. Precinct 4 continues to provide a safe and secure environment for the Northampton community.

Fred Parrow, president of the Northampton Maintenance Fund, is convinced that the high visibility of constable patrols within the subdivision sends a clear message to potential perpetrators of crimes that Northampton will not tolerate any type of criminal behavior. Additionally, the sense of security that residents have knowing that a Northampton-dedicated constable can respond within minutes to a security matter is most comforting.

Northampton has established a reputation for being a safe environment in which to live and raise a family, said Parrow. Unquestionably, there is a strong relationship between the low incidence of crime in Northampton and vigilant patrol by the constables assigned to Northampton. "We intend to keep our community-based security partnership with the Precinct 4 Constable's Department in place for as long as contracted security continues to represent our most effective deterrent against crime," Parrow said.

Another example is Bridgestone Homeowners Association. Its president hired Precinct 4, too, and their president, Jerry Thomas's, remarks follow:

I have been the president of the Bridgestone Homeowners Association for the past six years and prior to that I was the security director for four years. For the first three years that I was security director, Bridgestone relied on the county district units for police protection. During that time, we never saw a deputy in our subdivision unless they were on a call, serious crime was extremely high, crimes were virtually never solved, response time for the police was at least one hour if not longer, and the community had a lack of trust in the local police force. Since becoming involved in community-based policing we see a constable in our subdivision continually, serious crime has fallen to almost nothing, virtually all crime is solved, response time for police assistance has dropped to less than five minutes, and the community once again has trust and respect for the local police department.

Community-based policing makes the officer a part of our community, not just a nameless face. People within the community become friends with the officers. The people are more apt to speak freely with an officer they know rather than with a nameless face. The officers are able to learn what cars go with what houses, who leaves lights on when they're not home, who works late, and many other things about the community that an officer who never enters our community would know. All of this helps the officer know when something does not look right and should be investigated, which in turn either deters crime or solves it; either way, I'm happy.

I have spoken with numerous presidents of other homeowners associations and they all have the same opinion that I do: Community-based policing makes the local community a much safer place to live versus local district units.

Each subdivision and/or contracted area has representatives who provide input on their needs and general expectations. Their input is limited as to the scope of operational issues. Deployment is covered by contract details as to the general area of assignment. Operationally, Precinct 4 maintains a reasonable limit as to the distance they will take calls from their contracted assigned area.

More than 400 of Harris County's law enforcement personnel can now attribute their existence to this program and three-fourths of these are Constable's Office personnel. Precinct 4's specific approach to dealing with the services provided to the community has earned the Constable's Office a distinctive reputation in local law enforcement. Another result is that it has some of the best trained and specialized personnel in the business of law enforcement. The increased popularity of the Contract Deputy Program created a vacuum of qualified law enforcement professionals in the county. Precinct 4 continues to process employment applications at an unprecedented rate, in most cases selecting seasoned officers who applied from other agencies. Former troopers, retired municipal police officers, and federal agents all have found a home as officers in Precinct 4, and many of them hold advanced degrees in many fields.

Once this foothold in local patrol responsibilities was established, growth in this area followed the construction of new neighborhoods and population increases in our area. As Precinct 4 began to provide more and more service to the community, the need to diversify these services also became evident.

TEXAS LAW ENFORCEMENT

To better understand Texas law enforcement experiences, it should be acknowledged that peace officers in Texas face a high risk of assault and/or death, reports Sam Houston's Criminal Justice Center. For instance, in 1993 with a total full-time force of almost 42,000 sworn officers in the state from all jurisdictions, there were 5,191 assaults among those officers, a ratio of 1 out of 8.0. Furthermore, there were 1,952 assaults with injury, which represents a ratio of assaults with injury to number of officers as 1 out of 21. Approximately, 3,000 deputies are employed by constable departments throughout

Texas. Last, the amount of violent crime in Texas per 100,000 ranked it thirteenth compared to all the other states.

Profile of the Precinct

The Patrol Division, in addition to being the largest division within Precinct 4, is the most visible part of the Constable's Office. The duties of the Patrol Division include high-profile marked patrols, emergency and nonemergency response to calls for service, on-scene and follow-up investigations, crime prevention, and traffic enforcement.

There are 187 full-time uniformed deputies who patrol the 520 square miles of territory. Precinct 4's fleet has 146 patrol cars. In addition to the public roadways, our deputies are responsible for law enforcement in the county parks, the Hardy and Sam Houston toll roads and Cy-Fair ISD school facilities. Many subdivisions opt to participate in the Contract Deputy Program as a way to supplement existing law enforcement services, which accounts for the majority of our uniformed personnel—deputies who would otherwise not be on patrol.

The Patrol Division is supported by an Emergency Communications and Technical Services Division staffed by 19 employees. Precinct 4 is one of the most technically progressive departments in Texas, utilizing wireless data communications from laptop computers to permit field officers to access remote databases for offense reports and computerized dispatching. We have specialized groups such as Victims Assistance and Domestic Violence Units to provide direct assistance to victims of domestic violence and serious crimes to receive proper referrals or aid from the state's Crime Victim Compensation Fund. Our accident investigators and accident reconstructionists are some of the most highly trained and specialized in this area of Texas and have special equipment for plotting and drawing a computerized reconstruction of an accident scene. Precinct 4 has crime scene photographers and videographers, an honor guard with a bagpipe player, and drug and search canines. Our Citizens Police Academy routinely reaches many of the communities we represent, giving us a cross section of the population and a strong support group. These resources and many others assist us in reaching into the community as a participant, not apart from the people we serve.

Precinct 4's primary focus remains the local law enforcement officer working in neighborhoods through community policing techniques. This places the field officer in a strong position to acquire information on crimes that happen in his or her local community and helps to solve crimes.

Responses to Crime

Arrest and crime statistics are shown in Tables 1 and 2, but because of the dissimilarities in the modes of operations and priorities, any comparison with a similar jurisdiction would probably prove meaningless especially without a deep review of the socioeconomic differences in the areas. Furthermore, some agencies are better suited to report crime and other agencies may not make crime reporting a priority. Last, any in-depth review of jurisdictions is beyond the scope of this work.

Often, Harris County Precinct 4 officers receive the recognition they deserve. For instance, on February 27, 1999, while responding to a weapons disturbance on the west side of Precinct 4 deputies came across more than 3,000 pounds of high-grade marijuana with a street value of more than $1.5 million. Even though the suspects had tried to wrap the bricks of marijuana with oily residue, this did not keep the narcotics dogs from finding the contraband. This marijuana won't be in our schools this year or on your street corner.

PRECINCT UNITS
Mounted Patrol

Our Mounted Patrol Unit is staffed as a volunteer operation with both regular and reserve personnel. They have been trained specifically in search and rescue operations and working with and around crowds. Each member and his or her mount go through rigorous training in preparation for their activities. They are used in static displays and demonstration in addition to their regular duties.

TABLE 1   Precinct 4's Arrests, Calls, Stops

CATEGORY	ANNUAL 1998	MAY 1999 MONTHLY
Contract calls	47,470	7,051
District calls	50,219	7,753
Self-initiated/support calls	286,400	52,224
Total patrol responses	384,089	67,028
Reports	23,145	3,714
Felony arrests	699	64
Misdemeanor arrests	7,720	687
Citations	49,503	8,204
Warning citations	34,760	3,147
Recovered property	$3,165,456.00	$366,967.00
Miles driven	2,691,763	420,216
Traffic stops	39,100	19,152

TABLE 2   Precinct 4's Crime Statistics

CRIME CATEGORY	1998 ANNUAL	FIRST HALF 1999
Assault—simple	1,394	671
Assault—aggravated	66	68
Assault—sexual	91	51
Burglary—residence/business	1,346	614
Burglary—motor vehicle	1,477	766
Criminal mischief	2,198	1,017
Robbery	87	34
Missing persons	67	59
Runaway juvenile	851	421
Telephone harassment	590	284
DWI / DUID	99	74
Terroristic threat	597	321
Theft	3,944	1,709
Stolen vehicle	733	286
Recovered stolen vehicle	198	78

Canine Unit

Our canines are qualified for patrol and search operations and have been used successfully for locating lost and missing persons. The teams have been very helpful in tracking fleeing suspects and in building and residential searches. The narcotics dogs have been used widely by the department to locate and seize narcotics.

These teams, canines and their handlers, are recognized by local and federal agencies and are frequently used for searching suspect vehicles and buildings. Each K-9 lives and works with his or her handler and becomes a part of their family, working with the deputy like a partner. These units use volunteers who must pass a strenuous selection process and are responsible for regular patrol duties as well.

Domestic Violence Unit

The Domestic Violence Unit is a specialized division that falls under Victims Assistance and has similar duties. Whereas the Victims Assistance Unit deals with the victims of all crimes after the fact, the Domestic Violence Unit targets domestic violence incidents and will respond to those calls in progress. This allows them to conduct an on-the-scene evaluation of the situation and to assist the complainant in the filing of protective orders, charges, and compensation claims as needed. They also offer referral to resources within the community.

Bike Patrol

The deputies currently assigned to bike patrol responsibilities operate as highly visible and mobile units that can respond to special terrain or area problems that are inaccessible to standard patrol vehicles. These units are widely accepted and welcomed by area residents and frequent the jogging and bike trails that have been a haven for mischief and criminal activity in the past. The bikes are specially designed for patrol activities and personnel have been trained in the tactical use of the bikes for these types of specialized operations.

CONSTABLE DICK MOORE—"A LIFETIME IN PUBLIC SERVICE"

Constable Moore has dedicated over 42 years of his life to law enforcement. He holds a Master Peace Officers Certificate from the state of Texas and is a past president of the State Justice of the Peace and Constable's Association of Texas.

He began his career with the Texas Department of Public Safety in 1958 working the Harris County area as a public safety trooper. He resigned from that position to run for constable in a small county and was elected in 1965. He has since been elected to eight terms as a Harris County constable. He is currently responsible for the largest of the precincts covering unincorporated Harris County. When Constable Moore took over the reins at Precinct 4 in 1981, there

Constable Dick Moore

were 42 employees with limited responsibility and the community had a limited respect for the office of constable. This office now has more than 400 employees, enjoys an excellent reputation with the communities it serves, and prides itself on being the most advanced and progressive agency of its kind in the state of Texas.

The office is comprised of a full-fledged Emergency Communications Division, Warrant and Civil Divisions, Records Division, Patrol Division, Technical Services, and Training, as well as Victims Assistance, DARE, and GREAT Units. Constable Dick Moore has initiated bike patrols directly targeted at improving visibility within local communities, and is believed to have created the first Citizens Police Academy by a constable in Texas.

Constable Moore is recognized in both the law enforcement community and local community as a progressive and professional leader. Constable Moore's office was the first to become active in the Harris County Law Enforcement Computer System and was actually the first to go online with the Computer Aided Dispatching and Offense Reporting portions of the system. He was the first department in the county to field laptop computers in patrol vehicles and continues to top the list of technically advanced agencies in Texas.

Constable Dick Moore's strong leadership position has proved invaluable in directing the success of Precinct 4, the programs we support, and the communities we serve. His progressive attitude and leadership set a benchmark for others in law enforcement to follow and reflects his lifetime commitment of service to the citizens of this area.

Constable Dick Moore says:

Community Policing demands and methodology vary from agency to agency as the needs and expectations of communities vary from place to place. Establishing strong communication links with various members and groups within the communities we each represent is vital to being able to identify the expectations that they have for their public servants. As front-line representatives of local government, we are often called upon to answer questions and deal with situations that are not routinely police in nature. We must be attuned to dealing with problems down to the smallest level of the community.

Looking for long-term solutions to all types of problems requires a different manner of thinking and policing. Responding to situations where finding solutions in the best interests of the community, its members, and the legal system is often a complex and difficult task. Simply looking for the best "legal" answer is not always the only approach. In order for this philosophy to be widely accepted and appropriately applied, it must first be ingrained into both field personnel and supervisors through a training program designed to establish an understanding of the department's community-oriented philosophy. This training must be reinforced with administrative support for the decisions and activities required in the field. Part of that support involves programs that are of a direct benefit to the community. We must develop programs that seek to inform and educate them about public service activities, matters of public interest, and programs that serve to assert our position as more than just outsiders to the community are of paramount importance. Being a part of the activities and day-to-day involvement in the community are important in maintaining the working relationships that police form there and to build strong communication and understanding with community members.

We have learned to look for "hot button" issues for different areas. The issues are the ones that are most commonly the main concerns for residents in a specific community. These issues may vary greatly from place to place. One area may want increased focus on traffic in and around school zones, another is highly concerned about the welfare of a flood control levee that keeps water from damaging their homes. Issues of drug activity, late-night teenage parties, and abandoned or neglected property all serve to provide negative influences on property values and the standard of living for the community. These "hot button" issues can provide direction and focus for law enforcement activities that most effectively address the community's expectations.

Being involved in community policing means becoming a member of the community. It's like being in the picture, not just the picture frame or being a piece of the puzzle.

DEPUTY CHIEF RON HICKMAN

Working on the development team for the county's first attempt at a consolidated computer-aided dispatching system, Chief Hickman provided crucial input for building a computer system that supports a strong cooperative environment among all the county's law enforcement agencies. This consolidated system has been in place for a dozen years and houses the offense reporting, dispatching, alarm permits, and towed vehicle systems. Expanding on his knowledge of computerization, Chief Hickman set out to build a local-area network for the Precinct 4 Constable's Office. Extending the computer resource to the numerous remote offices was an important step in enhancing the administrative capabilities of the office.

The changes in technology soon permitted computerization to go mobile, and as laptop computers and communication systems became sufficiently advanced, Precinct 4 was at the forefront of progressive application of technology in patrol vehicles. Utilizing cellular digital packet data (CDPD) technology to communicate to remote computer mainframes from laptops in the cars has significantly extended research and information abilities to field personnel. "Sharing experiences and offering guidance to other agencies is important as a participant in the brotherhood of policing," says Hickman.

With a strong emphasis on community policing, Chief Hickman continues the practice of two-way communication with community leaders and members of local neighborhoods. "The acceptance of our office and success of daily operations depends on the degree of our ability to effectively communicate with and represent the public we serve."

Deputy Chief Ron Hickman says of Precinct 4's community policing initiative:

Changes in the community as a result of our community policing approach have manifested themselves in the expectations and demands they have on the type of services we provide. Communities now look for police agencies to provide programs that will help them protect themselves and their property. They look more to police agencies for varying solutions to all types of problems, even ones not normally police related. Our approach to handling community issues is now much wider and the days of a narrow focused approach to issues of illegality or criminal activity are gone.

Deputy Chief Ron Hickman

TRAINING AND HOW IT RELATES TO COMMUNITY POLICING

"Each of our patrol officers," Chief Hickman continues, "receives training in community policing through our Training Division. The general focus of this training is to provide to our field personnel our departmental philosophy on building and maintaining community relationships. In addition to this, we provide a brochure to our communities on this Partnership Program so that they have a better understanding of this approach and can develop a realistic set of expectations for our services and responses."

The precinct carries about 70 reserves on its personnel list. Most of them remain active and the use of that group as the training medium provides the chiefs and the officers with a first look at abilities and knowledge of the business. They are brought into the field training program as reserves and work through it until they are released to solo status and get on the hiring list for full-time employment. That minimizes the precinct's exposure and ensures a commitment to the overall program.

ASSESSMENT OF PROGRAMS

Deputy Chief Hickman has this to say about program assessment:

Our programs have been widely accepted and very popular in the community. We have reached hundreds of kids with the anti-gang message and provided "stranger danger" and gun safety information to kids through our Junior Public Safety Academies. Our focus for programs has changed from an internal in-service approach to educating our own personnel to an external outward focus on educating and reaching the community with information that is designed to prepare them to handle day-to-day threats to their personal welfare and standards of living.

Furthermore, our personnel and supervisors attend monthly meetings with each of our contract communities and work on various Chamber of Commerce committees across the precinct. We attend a large number of annual homeowner meetings and community forums. We have solicited comments via e-mail from our Internet web site. Additionally, we utilize the Citizens Police Academy and the local Chambers of Commerce as a gauge to the success of our community policing programs. Mostly, it's our drive toward a stronger customer service approach that keeps our relationship with the community strong. Working in a competitive environment with other agencies forces us to constantly review our response to the community in a variety of areas. Also, it's hard for other agencies to understand that none of our patrol personnel were provided by federal money. The only programs we have that were funded through this manner were Domestic Violence and Victims Assistance. Thus far, the county has picked up those programs to be continued as the federal money is phased out.

Deputy Chief Ron Hickman is available via e-mail at
ron_hickman@co.harris.tx.us.

Two Trainers Talk About Precinct 4

Sargent J.W. Smith says:

Community policing—fact or fiction? In law enforcement today there is a label that is frequently used by officials in policing to attach to day-to-day operations: community-oriented policing. Use of this label is a trend that has become popular in our profession today, more as a "feel-good" approach for many agencies in dealing with the public than as a true philosophy. There is more to community-based policing than just a label. Our approach is to give the community the facts, educate them, and offer support to them instead of asking for or demanding their support for the police. In today's society, we must be able to establish a solid base with the community in order to have positive interaction and avoid the "us versus them" mentality that prevails in certain law enforcement circles today. To accomplish this objective, we need to offer educational programs to the public. By offering programs such as Citizens Police Academies, we are given the opportunity to inform the public of who we are and what we do. At the same time we receive feedback from the community as to their needs and expectations for law enforcement. By giving our communities the support they need, we in turn receive support from them.

A true community policing program has to be developed through education and communication. If we are to win the hearts and minds of the community, they must first trust their law enforcement agency and police officials.

Captain Larry Shiflet, community policing instructor, says:

Community-based policing is a very positive interaction philosophy between citizens and law enforcement. The mental barriers come down, the officers are accessible, and the focus is on problem solving and preventive techniques to improve the quality of life by reducing crime or the fear of crime. Community-based policing affirms that citizens and law enforcement can work together. The law is enforced fairly, professionally, firmly, courteously, and respectfully. It creates an atmosphere of "what can we do together" rather than "what are you going to do."

Community Members Talk About Precinct 4

Larry Lipton says:

The Constable's Office of Precinct 4 has done an outstanding job of modeling its services to the community's needs. Where one usually only thinks of a Constable's Office as a process serving unit, we have an organization that is far more than that. This is a full-service governmental unit that not only serves the traditional process serving needs of our community, but is also an extremely effective law enforcement arm of the county. Some of the

biggest drug busts in our county have been handled by Precinct 4 along with a recent capture of a huge burglary ring, which cleared about 100 burglaries. Their traffic enforcement teams are out in force helping to control the enormous miles of roads in this precinct.

Family violence, bicycle patrols, youth issues, and Contract Deputy Programs for specific subdivisions are all part of the services provided. In addition, their involvement in the Chamber of Commerce both in various committees and in helping to produce the annual Salute to Law Enforcement is particularly valuable. Various ranking members of the department are regularly in the community speaking about public safety issues.

Contact Larry Lipton at Houston NW Chamber of Commerce, Crime Awareness Committee, phone: (281)580-2510.

Mike Byers says:

I have lived in Kingwood for 25 years and have been employed as president of the Humble Area Chamber of Commerce for eight years. My job as president requires continuous interface with all police agencies and other public service organizations. I am a strong supporter of community-based law enforcement. I believe community-based policing provides the most efficient and thorough law enforcement while encouraging trust, support, and respect by the citizens for the policing agency. This is not just my opinion but comes from my firsthand experience living in Kingwood.

When Kingwood was annexed, one of the major concerns from residents was the loss of constables as our primary law enforcement agency. Everyone realized that other police personnel are well trained and qualified, but for the most part, work their shift and go home. It is just a job. The constables, with community-based law enforcement, were there to support school events, community projects, help stranded motorists, or direct traffic at a congested stop sign or faulty red light. These things go beyond law enforcement; they were there to protect, serve, and participate. In my opinion, the Precinct 4 Constable's approach to community-based law enforcement should be modeled by all police agencies. Respect and trust on both sides is created by interaction. The lines of communication that are created are so critical for good law enforcement.

Contact Mike Byers, president, at Humble Area Chamber of Commerce, phone: (281)446-2128.

Anne Wallace, President of Homeowners Association, says:

With the advent of the population explosion in and around large cities, families moved out beyond the city limits into areas where county law enforcement was already stretched to the limit. Crime and gangs also moved to these new areas. Since these areas were unincorporated, it became the responsibility of the Homeowners Association not only to govern and

provide services to these families, but also to police the communities. The associations banded together and contracted for police protection around the clock.

Each association board is represented by a security coordinator who is the area contact for the Constable's Office. Incidents are reported between them, information exchanged, trends noted, and tentative solutions discussed. The security coordinator becomes the extra eyes and ears through which information is received and relayed to the community. Weekly and monthly reports are available from logged calls each deputy handles. Long-range plans can be addressed, enhancing not only the property values in the community, but the efficiency of police operations as well.

Community-based policing can only be accomplished through a close and open effort by citizens of the associations and the officers assigned to these areas. Deputies become a part of the area's family and residents there become more than just a part of the deputy's responsibility. A partnership and a bond of friendship and trust is formed. Through the years, experience in dealing with these communities and the familiarity of the area and its citizens is the valuable commodity which leads to almost effortless policing.

SUMMARY

The demographics of Precinct 4 were presented along with their mission statement and the events leading to community policing initiatives in their jurisdiction. Precinct 4's policing programs were emphasized since programs are at the core of their police service. A brief history of the Precinct is reviewed leading to a detailed discussion about Harris County's Contract Deputy Program. A description follows about Texas law enforcement and Precinct 4 including their service responses to crime. The constable and the deputy chief revealed their ideas on constable service, training, and program assessment. Several individuals offered testimony about the Precinct's efforts.

CONCLUSION

Precinct 4 has a unique method of community policing that includes public programs and the contracting of police services to communities who lack police protection due in part to the limited resources of other police agencies. Through advanced technology, highly skilled officers, and aggressive, yet, competitive police management, and due in part to the election process, Precinct 4 has a vast number of contracts to provide police service to many communities. This innovative and highly profitable venture is, of course, Precinct 4's community policing mainstay. Their detailed model might encourage other public agencies to follow in their "for hire" footsteps as the benefits for both the public and the private sectors seem satisfied and rewarded with the entrepreneurial leadership of the Constable Office. Perhaps, too, a police chief should be an elected official in order to step around one of the obstacles as demonstrated in many cities in this study—city hall!

DO YOU KNOW?

1. As a law enforcement officer, in what way does the constable's role differ from the sheriff's role in Harris County?
2. Describe the primary programs sponsored by Precinct 4. Compare and contrast some of those programs with programs from Broken Arrow, Oklahoma (Chapter 2), and Lansing, Michigan (Chapter 5).
3. What were the variables responsible for decline of the principal law enforcement agency in the county and how did those variables impact Precinct 4?
4. The number of officers in the Precinct 4 Constable's Office grew at a rapid rate through practices such as the Contract Deputy Program. Describe how those contracts were developed and their advantages and disadvantages to the communities they serve.
5. In what way is the Contract Deputy Program in Precinct 4 perceived as a community policing effort? In what way are those contracts similar/dissimilar to community policing initiatives of Broken Arrow, Oklahoma (Chapter 2), and Columbus, Ohio (Chapter 4)?
6. Describe the various units within the precinct and compare those units with Broken Arrow, Oklahoma (Chapter 2).
7. Describe the technology advantage produced through Deputy Chief Hickman's office and explain how that would have given Precinct 4 an advantage over other law enforcement agencies.
8. In the community member commentaries, describe any trends suggested concerning Precinct 4's ability to offer quality police service.

CHAPTER SEVEN

SACRAMENTO POLICE DEPARTMENT

Sacramento, California

INTRODUCTION

Sacramento is located at the confluence of two rivers, the Sacramento and the American. It is surrounded on the south by the delta, and to the east are the foothills of the Sierra Nevadas. North and west are mainly farming regions that make the outlying areas profitable to agriculture, one of the largest enterprises in the state. Yet, before Anglo invasion of this area, other people lived and toiled in the valley. They were the Maidu Indians, a branch of the Valley Nisenan group. The Maidu Indian's domain covered over 10,000 square miles, which included the Sacramento area.

Sacramento was named in 1808 by Gabriel Moraga, a Spanish explorer who named the valley for the Holy Sacrament, a Christian religious rite.

In the winter of 1848, builder John Sutter's long trusted employee James Marshall built a water-powered sawmill 45 miles up the south fork of the American River at a place called Coloma. This mill's purpose was to produce the planks and beams that growing valley towns needed for building purposes.

On the morning of January 24, 1848, James Marshall reached into the icy waters of the American River and found the first gold nugget. Needless to say, not much lumber was milled at Coloma—the announcement of gold set off a worldwide contagion known as "Gold Fever" in the foothills of the Sierra Nevada.

The discovery of gold not only changed the history of California, it was also one of the most significant events in the history of our nation. For example, the Gold Rush created the largest peacetime migration in history. People from around the globe came to California in search of their dreams. While the Gold Rush brought wealth to many of Sacramento's early citizens, it also brought problems. Brawls, gunfights, and stabbings were common characteristics of Sacramento's early days. To help curb this lawlessness, Sacramento's early citizens appointed N. C. Cunningham as its marshal. Cunningham and his two deputies dealt with the problems of this new western town of about 2,000 citizens.

Today, as the oldest incorporated city in California, its state capital, and home of California State University, Sacramento has enjoyed over 150 years of history that is rich in cultural, religious, ethnic, and economic growth. Approximately 400,000 people are living in its approximately 98 square miles who represent very diverse and cultural backgrounds much like those individuals who lived here for the preceding few hundred years.

CHAPTER OUTLINE

The Sacramento Police Department is described in detail including its divisions, responsibilities, accomplishments, and programs. An overview about their community policing initiatives is given that includes internal mobilization, a specialty versus a generalist perspective, COP as culture, training, and their methods of solidifying the commitment to COP. The department's strategic goals for 1994–2003 and its commitment to partnerships are revealed.

PROFILE OF THE DEPARTMENT

There are 654 sworn officers employed by the Sacramento Police Department[1] plus 373 full-time civilians, 129 part-time civilians, and 107 volunteers. During the calendar year of 1998 the Sacramento Police Department logged 385,085 calls for service and a total amount of all arrests including misdemeanor cites of 25,706.

New grants awarded in 1998 included these:

- $100,000 for gang violence suppression
- $100,000 for advancing community policing
- $90,000 for alcoholic beverage control
- $100,000 for community partnership for Safety II

Mission Statement

The mission of the Sacramento Police Department is to work in partnership with the community to protect life and property, solve neighborhood problems, and enhance the quality of life in Sacramento.

---

[1]See the Sacramento Police Department's web site at http://www.sacpd.org.

Divisions

The SPD is portioned into four areas, the offices of Technical Services, Investigations, Operations, and Office of the Chief.

The office of Technical Services is responsible for the auxiliary functions needed to support the line units of the department. The office is divided into three divisions: Staff Services, Personnel Services, and Communications. Also included in this office is the Regional Community Policing Institute, a grant-funded training unit. Deputy Chief Albert Najera heads this office.

The Staff Services division contains three areas: Property, Records, and Data Services. Each of these areas is headed by a civilian manager who is commanded by a captain. A few of the outstanding accomplishments of this division are:

- Destroyed nearly 1,000 pounds of narcotics and disposed of toxic chemicals from 30 clandestine laboratory cases.
- Hired 63 police officers, 22 community service officers, 30 dispatchers, and 11 civilian employees.
- Received 753,502 calls including 239,788 on the 911 lines (one call every 42 seconds).
- Trained more than 400 people from law enforcement, local governments, community organizations, businesses, and/or schools.

The office of Investigations has the responsibility of developing information leading to the arrest of criminal offenders, preparing cases, recovering stolen property, locating missing persons, and focusing attention on violence in families. This office comprises the Detective and the Special Investigations Divisions. In 1999 the office created a Family and Youth Services Division, which focuses on violence in the family. This office is directed by Deputy Chief Larry Gibbs who oversees and manages all services provided by this office.

A few of the many accomplishments of this office are:

- Homicide Department cleared 82 percent of their cases.
- Auto Theft completed four VIN verification courses and recovered 93.7 percent of stolen vehicles.
- Crime Alert located 135 wanted suspects as a direct result of information provided by citizens.
- Special Investigations Division made 996 narcotic arrests and 448 arrests for prostitution. They seized $102,305 in case assets for the fiscal year and 36 vehicles.

The office of Operations is responsible for the city's first-line response, managing approximately 750,000 annual calls for service and linking with neighborhoods and communities to cooperatively solve problems. The office is divided into the Patrol Division and Metro Division.

The Patrol Division is staffed by patrol officers, problem-oriented police officers, community service officers, and support staff. The city is divided into four geographical patrol sectors and then divided again into seven to nine patrol districts, each of which is managed by a captain.

The police department also received funding from the California Office of Criminal Justice Planning to implement a program named InfoCom (Information, Community Oriented Policing, Offender Apprehension and Management Accountability), which is an accountability tool for management similar to CompStat at NYPD. InfoCom demands continuous communication of information distribution between divisions. Once the implementation is completed, the department will become a training site for other departments interested in this strategy.

The Patrol Division has had many outstanding accomplishments. Some examples follow:

- The central sector generated 62 problem-oriented policing (POP) projects, 30 percent of which were initiated by patrol officers. The 62 projects represent a 150 percent increase from 1997.
- The east sector reduced calls for service in Oak Park project locations by 50 percent with a total of 153 arrests.
- The north sector completed a 30-hour training session for all officers, sergeants, and lieutenants on the philosophy of community-oriented policing (COP).

The Metro Division consists of three specialty units: Administrative, Traffic/Air Operations, and Strategic Operations. A captain commands the section and supervises two lieutenants and a sergeant. The Administrative Unit is headed by a sergeant and encompasses the Court Liaison, Alarm, and Licensing/Permits Units. The Traffic/Air Operations Section is supervised by a lieutenant and consists of Traffic, Air Operations, Marine/Reserve, Mounted Patrol, and Regional Transit Police Services.

A few of their many accomplishments in 1998 are as follows:

- Traffic issued 18,216 citations, a 31 percent increase over 1997 and investigated 18 fatal accidents.
- Air Operations responded to 1,973 calls for service with an average response time of 54 seconds and canceled 41 patrol calls due to helicopter assistance.
- The Marine Unit issued 180 citations of which 101 were for speeding and received $55,000 in grant funds to remove abandoned vessels.
- The Mounted Unit became a full-time unit.
- Regional Transit made 490 arrests and issued 1,890 citations and responded to 6,995 calls for service.
- SWAT participated in 12 callouts on critical incidents and coordinated and participated in 38 high-risk raids.
- K-9 conducted more than 1,400 building and field searches and located and arrested 163 felons.
- Explosives Ordinance Detail (EOD) responded to 156 incidents and recovered numerous pipe bombs and military devices.

- The bicycle unit created a chronic public intoxication and liquor merchant education program and formed a partnership with Safe Kids and Safetyville for educating children about helmet safety and bicycle laws.

The Office of the Chief plans, organizes, directs, coordinates, and administers all department activities. The office has two captains who oversee the activities of the office and report directly to the chief of police. One captain supervises Administration, Criminal Intelligence, Economic Development and Fiscal while the other captain supervises Internal Affairs and Professional Standards.

A few of the accomplishments generated from this office are:

- Administration tracked and/or took positions on 48 assembly, senate and federal legislative bills including 7 for which positions were taken citywide.
- Economic Development produced a comprehensive Family and Youth Services Action Plan and a Police Career Development Program.
- Fiscal monitored and administered a $72 million dollar budget with a year-end savings of $90,000, which was carried over to the 1999 fiscal year budget. It administered 27 grants and special programs totaling over $30 million during the term of the projects.

Sacramento Police Department Office of Operations

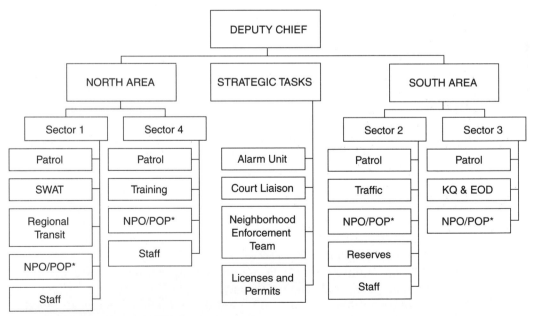

* Neighborhood Police and Problem Oriented Policing
Chart Available at: http://www.sacpd.org

Programs

- Community Chaplaincy Program
- Citizens Academy
- Expanded Problem-Oriented Policing
- Decentralization of Office of Investigations
- Safe Streets
- Departmental Volunteer Program
- Business Problem Management Program
- Partners in Prevention
- Expressions Program
- Problem Identification and Conflict Resolution
- People Reaching Out
- Police Cadet Program
- Drug Abuse Education in the Workplace
- Drug Abuse Education Program
- Neighborhood Improvement Plan
- Neighborhood Reclamation
- Apartment Problem Management Program
- Property Management Assistance
- Crime Alert Program
- Magnet School Program
- InfoCom
- Police Reserve Officer Program
- Sacramento Police Athletic League

COMMUNITY POLICING

While community-oriented policing (and problem solving) is being adopted as the appropriate form of policing throughout the country, many agencies continue to struggle with the operational dilemma of a specialty versus a generalist approach.[2] While many law enforcement agencies speak of actively practicing the principles and philosophies of COP, when they are asked who is involved internally, we hear of special designated units such as neighborhood police officers, bicycle beat officers, neighborhood policing teams, neighborhood abatement teams, crime prevention patrol units, COP officers, and so on. What we do not hear enough of is that the entire organization has a role in COP, with a specific focus on patrol for neighborhoods. For that reason the entire department's profile was presented in the preceding section because all parts of the department contribute to community policing. With the availability of COP grants and through the implementation of COP during the last six years, there exists an abundance of history related to successful problem-solving projects that have

---

[2]Written by Captain Steve Segura and Nancy Boemer-Otis of the SPD.

had a direct impact on the communities we serve. However, it is difficult to find this same history about successful implementation of COP on a department-wide basis, with a general emphasis directed toward the entire organization. Law enforcement agencies that implement COP will experience some form of success; however, the long-term transition must be carefully planned if institutionalizing COP is the goal.

We know that incident-driven policing fails to motivate line officers, in part because it lacks feedback and conclusion. Yet, personnel continue to resist the changes associated with community policing because they believe traditional methods of police work are more effective, and their time is monopolized by the increasing number of calls for service. Herein lies the dilemma. The role of COP in the organization must be clearly identified so that its overall shared value contributes toward the eventual institutionalization of COP as a department's way of doing business. While we advocate COP as the right thing to do, we must also accept that there is a transition period and that successful institutionalization will require an incremental process that is more than a specialty unit can accomplish. The process must include incorporation of COP from hiring to promotion. We have to grab the attention of personnel with the same vigor used to gain the attention of the community.

Internal Mobilization

Mobilizing the organization is as important to success as is the mobilization of the community. It is vital that leaders within the organization listen to the concerns of personnel and communicate what the organization is trying to accomplish. People desire the establishment of an end result that clearly indicates when success has been achieved. Be careful of the risk. Although we would like to project the desired outcome, we must remain flexible and understand that most progress is better than none, and that initial cooperation among your resources may be slow to come. It may be important to reward the effort given toward a complex project that may not have achieved its ultimate goal. In other words you may have to celebrate a "failure" that requires a re-think and regroup effort. However, for the employee, the vision has been established and the motivation to succeed has been rooted.

Specialty Versus Generalist

One of the common trends toward implementing COP has been the development of specialized units or programs to deliver the organization's COP strategy. While this form of operation has its positive effects and delivers quick results, there is concern that the remainder of the organization is often left on the outside looking in. The specialty units are seen as those that are provided the necessary resources to be successful, while the remainder of personnel continue to answer calls for service and see themselves as doing "real" police work versus shaking hands and organizing community events. Specifically, the line officers resist the efforts of the specialty teams if they perceive the position as glorified via good days off, preferred working hours, and not having to answer regular calls for service. In some instances, while calls for service increase and available patrol time decreases, line officers' frustration grows and they perceive that COP is "just another program." In these instances, even though the success of COP may be supported by statistical data and community satisfaction, resistance by some SPD police officers was still evident. After conducting training sessions for several California police/sheriff's departments, it is apparent that this is a common theme, and is an obstacle that contributes toward moving an organization away from institutionalization. Be careful; it is very easy to give community problems to those who are trained and have the time to problem solve. However, once the specialty theme is established, it grows, and within a short period, the only real problem solvers are the specialty units.

COP as a Culture

How many of us can remember what we told the interview panel when we tested for our law enforcement position? Does something to the effect of "I want to give back to the community" or "I want to serve the people" sound familiar? We laugh about it, but if that were our true desire, how did we lose sight of that commitment along the line? As much as we profess to hold ourselves accountable for delivery of law enforcement services, it is important that at the hiring process, we commit those who desire to be employed within our organizations be held accountable for our commitment to COP. It is imperative that the applicant's understanding of police work incorporate COP. The organization must achieve COP as a culture versus a program.

If we envision the culture of the organization as truly community and problem-solving oriented, strong creative leadership is necessary to abandon the traditional methods of running an agency and to adopt leadership flexibility to encourage change right from the beginning stages. The leadership must establish during the selection process that COP is a functional, living, working tool that is a basic requirement of the organization. Just as an applicant's acknowledgment that deadly force may be a necessary part of the job, similar recognition should be given to their understanding and willingness to incorporate and accept COP as a functional tool. The oral interview process offers an opportunity to gauge an applicant's understanding and commitment toward the organization's goals.

Training

Training is also a necessary component to move the organization toward agency-wide community policing, and it starts with the basic academy. For those agencies that have the luxury of operating their own academy, the incorporation of COP training can be mandated by the department. However, for those agencies who send their recruits to other training facilities, mandates for COP training may require a joint effort that is driven by the agency leaders. Follow-through from academy training is vital during the field training program. The expectation must be established in the form of recruit evaluations that assesses their ability to incorporate COP into their daily activities.

Opportunity

Empowerment guidelines must be developed to create consistency as to how personnel operate. Implementation is only a start, while institutionalizing COP as a way of doing business is the long-term transition. Outside the basic academy, field training program, and patrol services, the opportunity to learn and practice the principles of COP must be available. Ongoing training programs for in-service officers and civilian support staff are essential. It is short sighted to believe that only sworn personnel will deliver the institutionalization of COP for the organization. The role of support personnel in helping to solve problems offers the opportunity to understand the importance of the process. How often do we leave out the dispatcher who answers the initial call and can identify the caller when they hear the voice? How often do we not consider the clerk who answers the phones and resolves problems by providing resources that they have learned about through trial and error? Similar to our mobilization of community members, it is equally important to recognize the resources that are working and available internally. The opportunity to involve them exists if you encourage it!

Solidifying the Commitment

The transition to COP is long term. The organization will not change overnight and the resistance to change is natural. Accept it, but do not give up. Realize that your organization will have personnel who will act in various manners. There will be those who want to let things happen, those who wait and see, and those who can make it happen. Initially, use and develop the skills of those who can make it happen and let the successes speak for themselves. Encourage the easy projects that offer successful results. These type of projects offer experience, team building, and liaison with resource agencies. Once the orientation to COP has been developed in the community and within the local government, the accountability for addressing problems in the most efficient and effective manner possible will progress more broadly. Accountability for problems is not relinquished, it is enhanced. For instance, in 1998, the city council, in response to the public's request for a citizen review committee, authorized the Police Blue Ribbon Committee to investigate and recommend "changes in processing and investigating citizen complaints of police misconduct and in deployment of police vehicles in emergency response or pursuit modes."

As a result of their investigation, the Police Blue Ribbon Committee strongly endorsed civilian review of police handling of citizen complaints, and recommended the creation of a new unit headed by a senior-level appointee with broad oversight powers reporting directly to the city manager. The police monitor would have broad oversight powers to review both ongoing and completed investigations of citizen complaints and to encourage procedural and systemic reforms on behalf of the city manager. The monitor's job description was drawn from the experiences of California cities employing inspectors general, ombudsmen, and independent auditors. The committee recommended that the jurisdiction of the monitor be extended to all municipal agencies, after an initial trial period and performance evaluation.

The opportunity and demonstration of success, both professionally and organizationally, will allow for conscious decisions to get involved. There is meaning to working smarter, not harder! It goes further; some of the partnerships the SPD is experimenting with are with other agencies and organizations and that will become the rule rather than the exception.

For instance, the Regional Community Policing Institute (RCPI) is a Sacramento-formed partnership with the California Attorney General's Office, the Commission on Peace Officers Standards and Training (POST), and the Sacramento County Alliance of Neighborhoods (SCAN). Accomplishments with these partners include:

- The Attorney General's Crime and Violence Prevention Center established a statewide clearinghouse of community-oriented policing and problem solving (COPPS) information that is available to law enforcement and other government agencies, community groups, schools, and citizens through various mediums including telephone, fax, and the Internet.
- POST has certified the training provided by RCPI and is handling travel and training reimbursements for workshop attendees. POST is also collaborating on the COPPS clearinghouse.
- SCAN serves as a liaison between neighborhoods and local government. SCAN maintains communication between neighborhoods and helps to establish and monitor programs that will benefit residents. SCAN provides a link to enhance the community policing partnership throughout Sacramento. A Community Partnership for Safety Forum was cosponsored by RCPI and SCAN in 1999.

Other partnerships include other police organizations such as the California State University police and SPD. California State University–Sacramento, lies nestled among 300 acres of property in a section of our community known as East Sacramento. With a yearly school attendance of 25,000, which includes faculty, staff, and students, the campus has its share of law enforcement concerns. From live concerts and special events at Hornet Field, vehicles stolen from their parking lots, to disturbances and fights at fraternity houses, California State University Sacramento Police Department (CSUSPD) has a number of issues that can drain Sacramento Police Department resources in terms of traffic and mutual aid.

In 1995, Sacramento received funding from a COPPS More grant. Part of the funding was for a neighborhood police officer (NPO) for the East Sacramento area. This officer works to address neighborhood problems in the East Sacramento area. This was the catalyst for incorporating a partnership with CSUSPD. CSUSPD employs 15 full-time officers who provide police services to the campus. This includes the residential area that surrounds the campus, which overlaps the area targeted by the East Sacramento NPO. We began to network with CSUSPD Chief Norman Scarr. The idea was for a CSUSPD officer to become a full-time member of the Sacramento Police Department's central problem-oriented policing and NPO team. The CSUSPD officer would report to our facility, dress in our locker room, and drive one of our patrol cars. He or she would be working, at no expense to the Sacramento Police Department, with the East Sacramento NPO as well as other SPD officers.

The most important benefit to the university was that the lines of communication between the two agencies were streamlined to provide CSUSPD with an immediate response and resources to critical incidents or major events that occur on the campus. With the university officer working within our department, he knows where to go or who to contact for departmental resources. The Sacramento Police Department gained additional resources by partnering with the university. The CSUSPD officer answers calls for service in the East Sacramento area. We have been provided access to sociology students to develop community surveys and interviews; been given the opportunity to obtain discarded but usable office equipment; and also had access to meeting space for large groups and training locations for our SWAT team. These are but a few of the benefits that both agencies have realized from this ongoing relationship. Both the Sacramento Police Department NPO and the CSUSPD officer use community policing principles to guide in the identification and resolution of neighborhood problems that foster criminal activity in the East Sacramento area.

Partnerships with other police agencies and criminal justice organizations can become meaningful and productive relationships because of similar missions and experiences.

As a quick overview, SPD is preparing to celebrate its 150th anniversary and initiated the process of researching COP in 1989. In 1990, using COP as an overarching umbrella, we used problem-oriented policing as one of several components to move us forward. To make a long story short, we have implemented a variety of strategies to enhance partnerships and to instill COP as a natural way of doing business in Sacramento. To say that we are at 100 percent would be nice, however, we are still fine tuning our process every year. We have been very successful in obtaining grant funding for our efforts through the COP's office in Washington, and are very committed to institutionalizing COP in the department.

Strategic Goals for 1994–2003

After reviewing the information gathered through a planning process conducted two years ago, the police department developed the following strategic goals. Listed below the goals are the new initiatives that will be implemented to achieve them. Some of the initiatives are in the initial planning stages or early implementation phase. The strategic initiatives section of the actual plan includes a more detailed description of the programs along with potential timetables for completion. Because this plan is a living document, we anticipate new goals will be added throughout the years. Following is an abbreviated list of those goals (there were 26 of them) that apply community policing initiatives:

1. Educate Sacramento's citizens in crime prevention techniques and services that can be useful self-help crime-fighting tools.
2. Develop a Citizens Police Academy, which will increase community awareness of police policies, practices, and challenges.
3. Increase participation in Neighborhood Watch and other crime prevention efforts and establish a nonprofit corporation to coordinate Neighborhood Watch efforts throughout the city.
4. Work in partnership with the entire community to resolve crime-related problems in neighborhoods.
5. Assist the community in establishing drug-free zones in targeted areas, parks, schools, public housing developments and other areas where drug trafficking and alcohol availability problems exist.
6. Expand the use of problem-oriented policing strategies throughout the department.
7. Decentralize the current two-area command structure into a four-area command structure.
8. Encourage community mobilization efforts by coordinating with the Neighborhood Services Department.
9. Solicit total community input through the continued use of community forums.

THE COMMITMENT TO PARTNERSHIPS

Throughout the department's strategic plan document there is the mention of "partnerships." The new mission statement of the Sacramento Police Department commits it to working in partnership with the community to advance the cause of peace in the streets. Partnerships are two-way relationships, and will require a similar commitment from individuals, groups, and organizations outside of the control of the police. Everyone has a role in the pursuit of public safety.

In a very practical sense the absence, weakness, or strength of the Police Department's partnerships determines the ability of this organization to maximize its contribution to the public safety of our citizens, neighborhoods, and communities. For a myriad of reasons partnerships take a lot of hard work. The Sacramento Police Department is committed to this work and envisions that the following types of partnerships will serve Sacramento and the community well:

- Public partnerships
- Private partnerships
- Local, state, and federal justice agencies
- Concerned citizens/groups
- Crime prevention specialists
- Church or religious leaders

- Drug suppression officers
- Neighborhood Watch groups
- Educators and school administrators
- Parent groups
- PTA's
- Community-based programs
- Public housing resident associations
- Community action agencies
- Park and recreation specialists
- Youth and youth-serving organizations
- Social service organizations
- Business and professional organizations
- Mental, alcohol, and drug treatment programs

The major contributor to this chapter, Captain Steve Segura, has been employed by the SPD for 20 years. He helped the department with its development and implementation of COP and coordinated the department's establishment of collaborative working relationships with other city, county, and state resources. Segura remains actively involved in the development of COP training programs with the California Commission for Peace Officers Standards and Training and the Eastern District of the United States Attorney's Office. Captain Segura can be reached at ssegu@aol.com.

CRIME RATES

As a matter of interest, when comparing crime rates with cities similar in size to Sacramento (see Table 1), it appears that Sacramento's Total Crime Index tends to be lower than most other cities its size (source, Bureau of Justice Statistics, 1997). (Caution: Total Crime Index rates are not necessarily reliable methods when comparing various cities due to a large number of variables.)

Both Cincinnati and Tulsa had lower motor vehicle theft than Sacramento. (Cincinnati, 1,822; Sacramento, 6,260; Tulsa, 3,711). Both Cincinnati and Tulsa

TABLE 1   Comparison of Total Crime Index Among Similar Size Cities

CITY	TOTAL CRIME INDEX
Alexandria, VA	47,923
Atlanta, GA	58,591
Cincinnati, OH	27,455
Fresno, CA	37,623
Miami, FL	50,259
Oakland, CA	38,048
Sacramento, CA	34,132
Tulsa, OK	28,517

reported more rapes and more aggravated assaults than Sacramento. Last, when comparing Sacramento with other cities of similar size in California, both Fresno and Oakland reported more crime than Sacramento.

Also, as a matter of review, a year to year comparison of crime in Sacramento is compared to 1998 crime rates in Sacramento. Each index crime is compared to a national percent average as calculated by the Uniform Crime Report (see Table 2).

SUMMARY

A colorful history of Sacramento was introduced leading to a description of the agency, its mission statement was defined, and its divisions along with some of their accomplishments were identified. The SPD's programs were identified and a statement about community policing was articulated describing community policing initiatives, its culture, officer training, and agency opportunity. Solidifying a community policing commitment was revealed followed by the agency's strategic goals until 2003. The SPD's characterized their commitment to community partnership and identified groups that the department is involved with. Lastly, crime rate comparisons between Sacramento and similar size cities and comparisons in Sacramento from 1993 to 1998 were offered.

CONCLUSION

It is easy to come away from this chapter thinking the SPD has a community policing philosophy infused in each division, unit, program, and process within the department. Is the Sacramento Police Department a vision of a community policing success story? What is clear is that the SPD has many of the answers which suggest that they had to learn those answers through trial and error. Thus, they have experienced failure and apparently mastered the concepts. Or have they? Clearly, the SPD is moving in a direction of empowered partnerships, but those partnerships seem to be among other justice agencies who possess their own authority including other police departments. Is this the next step in the evolution of community policing or has the community been lost in the maze? One question is: do those justice type partnerships come at the expense of community relationships? There is evidence throughout the material in this chapter and on SPD's website that SPD delivers quality police service. There's evidence that their managers are well tutored in the art of enforcement. And there's evidence that their rank and file are hard working officers who possess integrity and honor. It is also clear that police programs exist. But, what is missing from the programs offered by the SPD is community member decision-making influence. One bit of evidence that lays the ground work for this suspicion is that SPD's community centered programs (as opposed to a philosophy) are administratively tugged neatly into incident-driven enforcement units. If it waddles like a duck but doesn't quack, is it still a duck?

TABLE 2   Uniform Crime Report
Year-to-Year Comparison

	Murder	Forcible Rape	Robbery	Aggravated Burglary	Burglary	Larceny-Vehicle	Motor Vehicle Theft
1993	85	167	2,310	2,288	8,080	18,670	7,885
1994	62	174	2,292	2,170	8,076	18,598	8,846
1995	57	158	2,129	1,936	8,003	18,538	7,982
1996	43	154	1,874	1,636	7,148	16,842	6,083
1997	41	161	1,851	1,664	6,873	17,282	6,260
Percent change from 1993 to 1997	−51.8%	−3.6%	−19.9%	−27.3%	−14.9%	−7.4%	−20.6%
National Average	−25.8%	−9.3%	−24.5%	−10.0%	−13.2%	−1.2%	−13.4%
1998	31	141	1,689	1,515	6,495	15,725	6,003
Percent change from 1997 to 1998	−24.4%	−12.4%	−8.8%	−9.0%	−5.5%	−9.0%	−4.1%
Percent change from 1993 to 1998	−63.5%	−15.6%	−26.9%	−33.8%	−19.6%	−15.8%	−23.9%

Source: http://www.sacpd.org/Annual_Reports/ftats.htm

Do You Know?

1. In what way might the history of a city help shape the influences of that city today? What examples can you give that relate directly to Sacramento's history?
2. The SPD says that patrol officers participate in community policing efforts. What evidence have they shown that supports that perspective and what evidence might suggest that patrol officers do not engage in community policing efforts as often as other officers?
3. The SPD makes a case that incident-driven policing fails to motivate line officers yet many of them resist the changes associated with community policing efforts. What recommendations does the department make to overcome this dilemma? Under what conditions might you believe that this recommendation would work? Would fail?
4. It is believed by the SPD that mobilizing the organization is as important to success in community policing as is the mobilization of the community. In what way do you think they are correct in their observation and in what way might they be wrong?
5. Why does the SPD suggest that during the interviewing process for new police personnel that community policing initiatives should be discussed? In what way do you agree with their observation?
6. Describe the concerns of the SPD about specialized units or programs (versus generalist) to deliver the organizational COP strategy. Explain the shortcomings from the perspective of the SPD. In what way do you agree with their observations concerning this perspective? Under what conditions might their recommendations be invalid?
7. It is believed that in the partnership relationship between the police department and the community, every one in the community including the groups and organizations outside the control of the police must play a vital role in community policing. Why? Do you know of some evidence outside this chapter that might support the SPD's position?
8. The primary focus of the SPD is on community policing, however, partnerships with other justice organizations including other police agencies is on the rise. Describe the advantages of those partnerships to justice agencies and the disadvantages toward community partnership initiatives.

CHAPTER EIGHT

FAYETTEVILLE POLICE DEPARTMENT

Fayetteville, North Carolina

INTRODUCTION

Fayetteville, on the banks of the Cape Fear River in southeastern North Carolina, is the heart of a metropolitan area with a population of 287,000 that includes a military presence of Pope Air Force Base and Fort Bragg, headquarters to the XVIII Airborne Corps, Army Special Operations Command, and home of the 82nd Airborne Division. They have an active duty contingent of 50,000 soldiers and airmen. These service members and their families increase the population of the greater Fayetteville area to appropriately 130,000 residents (an increase of 68 percent over 10 years). Fayetteville is North Carolina's fourth largest metropolitan area, and it can boast the highest concentration of retail sales dollars spent in the state. Although the military presence provides the bedrock for Fayetteville's economy, many nationally and internationally known businesses originated here: Putt-Putt International, System Office Automation, McClune Technology, M. J. Soffe, Stork News, and State Bank. Other major industries, including Westinghouse, Kelly-Springfield Tire Co., DuPont, and Black & Decker, are also a part of the Fayetteville community.

Fayetteville history runs long and deep. It was originally settled in 1739, and was known as Cross Creek. It grew to encompass another settlement known as Campbellton and in 1783, the community took the name of Fayetteville to honor the Revolutionary War hero, the Marquis de LaFayette. Fayetteville's central location on the old colonial North–South trade routes, as well as its situation on the Cape Fear River, helped the city to maintain steady growth during the post–Revolutionary War years. Today, Fayetteville's central location on the East Coast remains one of its strengths in attracting new industry to the region.

CHAPTER OUTLINE

This chapter presents an overview of the Fayetteville, North Carolina, experience with initiating and maintaining a police service strategy that expands a generic community policing concept. A departmental profile is outlined in addition to a description of the department and a brief history of the efforts leading to the establishment of their new policing strategy. Fayetteville Police Department's programs are emphasized, leading to the chief's philosophy about community policing initiatives and community partnerships. The legal counsel for the department addresses serious issues about Fayetteville's efforts, and its training director highlights officer training experiences. Crime rates in Fayetteville are reviewed followed by the FDP attorney's responses to the nine hard questions about community policing. Finally, a testimonial from a former Fayetteville commander is offered to help better understand Fayetteville's policing service experiences.

DEPARTMENT PROFILE

Fayetteville Police Department (FPD)[1] has 303 sworn law enforcement officers, 94 civilian employees, and the police department has been accredited by the National Association for Law Enforcement Accreditation since 1989. Its annual budget has almost doubled in 10 years (1990–1999) to $18,603,512 while calls for service have risen from 110,116 to 167,564, but its arrests and FI stops[2] have almost doubled to 8,393 and 13,221, respectively, in the same period. Its mission statement is:

> *We are committed to leading the community problem-solving efforts that improve the quality of life for all citizens of Fayetteville. We will work assertively with the community to address the underlying conditions that lead to crime and disorder.*

The FPD's value statement reads:

> *Professional service to all persons without regard to race, religion, gender, or economic status. We are committed to community partnerships that can identify and abolish barriers to community wellness.*

---

[1]Fayetteville's web site is at http://www.fayettevillenc.com.
[2]Field interview stops. Terry stops, investigative detentions. We call them FI stops because we fill out a card documenting who we stopped, where, and why.

DESCRIPTION

Responsible for enforcing the city and state criminal codes, the chief of police, who is appointed by and accountable to the city manager, directs the activities of the department through three major bureaus: Field Bureau, Investigative Bureau, and the Service Bureau. The chief's office also includes the chief's Staff Unit, Professional Standards and Inspections, and Carl Milazzo,[3] the department's legal advisor who was the primary contributor to this chapter (see the accompanying organizational chart).

- The Field Bureau is primarily responsible for enforcement activity and includes the following field divisions: North and South Uniform Division and the Patrol Support Division are responsible for 24-hour services in directed patrol, protection of life and property, apprehension of violators, investigation of accidents, special events, and neighborhood improvement teams.
- The Investigative Bureau is responsible for investigating crime against persons, crime against property, youth services, and vice and narcotic investigations.
- The Service Bureau provides general administrative and operational support emphasizing program development, operational planning, and general administrative direction. The Service Bureau has a number of components: a Service Staff Unit that includes budget control, planning and research, and personnel functions. The Service Bureau also includes the Technical Services Division, which is comprised of the Central Records Unit, the Training and Education Center, and Administrative Unit. Development and evaluation of programs, including community policing, originate from this bureau.

BRIEF HISTORY OF THE COMMUNITY POLICING EFFORTS

In the 1980s, policing nationwide was abuzz with new terms representing new policing ideas. Some of the most common terms were *community policing, community wellness,* and *problem-oriented policing.* Chief Ron Hansen and other managers of the Fayetteville Police Department studied those new ideas. The underlying belief was that in view of rising crime rates and increased police calls for service, FPD needed to devise a better way to deliver its police service. The old philosophy based on reacting to crime and disorder required an updating through a philosophy that fostered a proactive approach to delivering police service. In those days, community policing was the catch phrase for a modern philosophy. However, community policing concepts appeared to be part of the old police/community relations dogma. The department, therefore, emphasized the problem-oriented policing (POP) philosophy espoused by Herman Goldstein and pioneered by the Newport News Police Department in Virginia.

---

[3]Carl Milazzo can be reached at cmilazzo@ci.fay.nc.us.

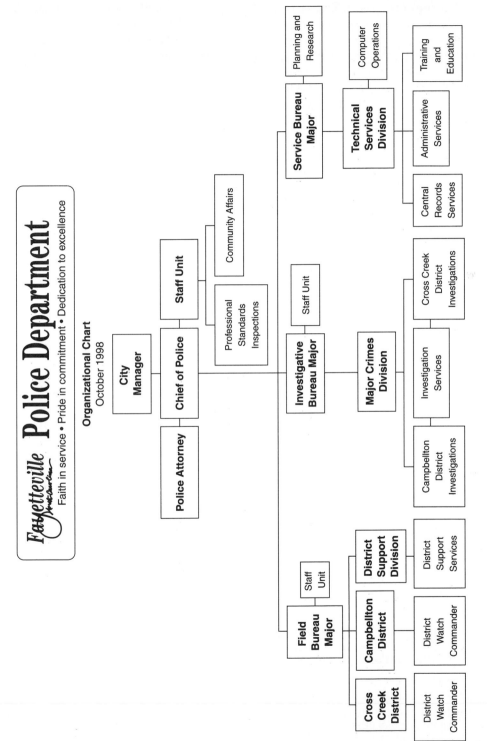

Fayetteville Police Department Organizational Chart

Problem-oriented policing is a philosophy that held realistic promise for Fayetteville. More than an ideal, it utilized the SARA (Scan, Analyze, Respond, and Assess) model. In POP, a department had a practical guide for exchanging an incident-driven, reactive service with a more proactive, preventive method of policing. By utilizing the tenets of POP, a department confronts crime and disorder in a way that requires the inclusion of neighborhoods, political leaders, outside agencies, and anyone else who might have an impact on the favorable outcome of community problems. The goal of POP includes police interaction with the community, but in a more positive manner, through the mutual efforts of all departmental personnel to solve community problems to ultimately enhance the quality of life of its residents.

In implementing this strategy, FPD made mistakes that were common to departments seeking change. Fayetteville leadership assumed veteran officers would quickly adapt to this new approach because its merits were supported by an abundance of supporting evidence in the press and justice academies across the state. However, many officers were wary of any new "program" and were content to give lip service to new changes. Apparently, they needed to be convinced that POP was more than a temporary change. Nonetheless, FPD leadership failed to recognize that the philosophical change of POP was an organizational-wide commitment. That is, the scope of police service change required a commitment from all departmental personnel as well as all constituents of the department, which included civic, business, and community members, too. This resistance is documented in the literature as being a universal problem for many departments across the United States. Therefore, top management gave its full support in order to win the confidence of all concerned. Through an evaluational process, a plan was devised to guide the organizational-wide efforts of the department through change agents.[4] It was clear to management that these change agents needed to weave the change process in each of these areas together. If the change agents became unraveled, the organization would be working at cross-purposes and therefore cripple its own ability to capitalize on the desired changes. These change agents included:

- *Technical agents of change:* These are those whose skills and activities provide the output of the organization. That is, knowledge, skills, and abilities of the officers were enhanced through training and appropriate leadership styles.
- *Political agents of change:* The public as consumers of police service and the city government that receives input from those consumers were introduced to new police strategies.
- *Cultural agents of change:* Police culture had to be guided through issues such as "real cop" identification and about their new role and its expectations in the department.

---

[4]Part of this evaluation process was guided by FPD's Training Director, Lt. Josh Phillips, whose master's thesis included a study on implementing community policing as a large-scale organizational change.

- *Administrative agents of change:* The structure and policies used to facilitate the department's output required new direction especially with
communication and directives.

In 1988, Chief Ron Hansen addressed those technical agents of change by in-
structing police trainers, in collaboration with outside professionals, to develop appropriate materials, distribution methods, and training schedules in
order to instruct all personnel of the Fayetteville Police Department in the new
police service strategies. POP requires a higher level of problem-solving and
critical thinking skills on the part of the officers than traditional policing, and
initial and continual training was necessary to develop their skills to bring the
department closer to its mission. Also, unlike community policing initiatives in
which a few designated officers carry out those initiatives, every employee of
the department, both sworn and civilian, had a responsibility toward problem
solving. Therefore, all personnel had to attend training in POP philosophy and
the application of the SARA model. In-service training was also delivered to all
investigators and supervisors of the department. Through a sound training initiative, the personnel of the FPD became familiar with the new strategies and
at the same time realized the commitment of top management toward those
strategies. Winning personnel confidence refined police service, which ultimately enhanced public safety and quality of life issues.

The chief introduced POP, the training initiative, and the department's
commitment levels to city and business leaders, community members, and
personnel at meetings and through the media including radio broadcasts.
Getting the message to the all concerned would add strength to the program.
Additionally, a police sergeant well versed in POP perspectives was assigned
to the city manager's office to facilitate the use of its principles by all city departments.

Usually, police culture and organizational structure change agents represent enormous challenges when confronted with policy change in departments
of all sizes. In terms of police culture, changing the values of individuals is a
slow process that requires time and quality leadership. Key officers of all ranks
who have excelled in the POP philosophy have become unofficial change
agents throughout the organizational structure. However, some officers continue to resist change and continue to practice traditional incident-driven
methods of police service.

The Fayetteville Police Department still utilizes the traditional line and
staff organizational structure. This mechanistic or quasi-military structure,
used by most public safety departments, is good for top-down communication,
yet it has its limitations especially when facilitating the type of communication
needed for POP. The POP concept works best with communication across divisions and individuals as opposed to top-down communication system. The
FPD operates as several different divisions addressing similar problems individually. One result is that several individuals are guiding an issue through different means at the same time, while unaware of the efforts being made by others. Therefore, cross-channel communication is instituted to bring all ends of

the department together. Some police departments have experimented changing their traditional structure to a modified matrix structure, but the success of that change was dependent on the skill of those involved because a matrix structure relies on informal leadership for success. In a quasi-military structure such as at Fayetteville, informal leadership is a difficult task, especially when many patrol officers are former military themselves and Fayetteville itself is impacted by a strong military presence.

Implementation and maintenance of FPD's POP strategy represents a challenge worth its effort because it provides an effective path to public safety for most individuals in the community. However, as many researchers argue, POP involves rendering more freedom to patrol officers to explore nontraditional approaches to enhancing public safety. Yet, in an age of guarded resources and liberal litigation many police commanders feel it inappropriate to loosen control over lower, less experienced officers (especially since departments can be held liable for the actions of their officers). Continuing along this line of reasoning, the working environment of Fayetteville may not be as conducive to the more independent, critical thinking type of officer required for POP principles. The Fayetteville Police Department, while was probably more successful than most departments in implementing quality police service strategies, is committed to this effective police initiative and is working with the strategy to modify it to the department and the community it serves.

PROGRAMS

Chief Ron Hansen arrived in Fayetteville, North Carolina, in 1985. In 1986 he attended a conference in Ft. Lauderdale, Florida, where he learned about their code enforcement team. This approach focuses on using city ordinances, often times civil in nature, to enforce quality of life types of issues. City Manager John Smith of Fayetteville approved the chief's plan to implement this type of program at FPD, and the police department started using the code enforcement program and began to promote the idea of officers using all city resources to resolve neighborhood problems. For example, officers make reports from the field on potholes, trash accumulation, broken street lights, potential fire hazards, and so on, and forward those reports to the appropriate city department such as building inspections, zoning, fire, and garbage.

There was no specific triggering event other than the arrival of a new chief that led the FPD to initiate what can be referred to as FPD's community policing initiative. The chief's approach has been more of an individual problem-solving approach rather than a blanket approach of community policing. Fayetteville still concentrates more on solving individual problems instead of treating all problems with a one-size-fits-all approach. For example, Fayetteville has never had community policing officers per se; everyone is a community officer and everyone is responsible for helping to solve community problems.

The typical methods employed to ensure that typical members of the community are represented in the community policing process began with a community watch council. This council brought in community members from all over the jurisdiction (mostly church and business, in addition to the newly forming community watches) and began extensive survey work in neighborhoods to identify problems. Fayetteville still does survey work, even in areas before they are annexed into the city (which happens often) so FPD can provide full service at the stroke of midnight once an area is annexed, instead of starting to figure it out *after* an annexed area becomes part of the city. Zone officers make personal contacts with citizens and attend every community watch meeting to receive and to report information. Zone officers maintain a zone book in the station in which every officer who works that zone keeps a log of significant activity, trends, problems, and people (both good and bad) for every other officer who works that zone. All officers are responsible for maintaining the book.

One method used to ensure that all community residents are included in the decision making is the use of two mobile substations. When fully staffed, both work different shifts and are part of Fayetteville's Neighborhood Improvement Team. These units can be deployed in any area of the city, and are used to stabilize a neighborhood with intensive foot and bike patrols, citizen contacts, and supervisory evaluation. The affected neighborhood continues to get randomly selected visits after stabilization to ensure stability continues after the NIT leaves. The mobile substations continue to serve various locations, such as hostage standoffs, working shopping areas around the holidays, and stabilizing significant crime scenes such as officer-involved shootings. Citizens can use the mobile substation to communicate with officers and supervisors instead of having to visit the station downtown. There they receive officer names and pager numbers and share information.

Fayetteville has purchased a new device (the trademark name is Reverse 911, but other programs are available) that allows officers to communicate by computer using the 911 system to neighborhoods. Fayetteville has two dedicated crime prevention officers who work out of the Community Affairs office and communicate community programs with citizens, often acting as the first means of introducing a citizen to a zone officer. Since the FPD utilizes programs as one of their primary methods of delivering police services throughout Fayetteville, the following list (with a few explanations) might help the reader to better understand their extensive delivery system.

Milazzo says that the FPD continues to work with the Community Watch Council (each Community Watch group is represented), and started the local Crimestoppers program here, which is run by the Crimestoppers Council. Our Crimestoppers line has become so successful that the schools have begun their own school Crimestoppers program. We regularly publicize the success of Crimestoppers. On one day, we inserted a flyer in the local newspaper with our ten most wanted. By the end of the next day, seven were arrested after being turned in by the community. In the early years, we used a Citizen Police Advisory Council that took on a life of its own and it was quickly scrapped. Community Watch groups have been our backbone. So far we have kept the list confidential because the politicians routinely try to get their hands on it to turn it into an election committee. Our most effective collaboration has been in public nuisance lawsuits to close problem nightclubs. Citizens and church groups have provided needed testimony on the effect on the neighborhood, while officers research the calls for service and concentrate on a problem location. Our public nuisance lawsuits require participation by church and Community Watch leaders to testify in court. We do a weekly cable television show that is produced by our community affairs sergeant, who frequently involves residents in program segments sharing their experiences on crime or victimization. Our annual awards banquet always includes citizen awards to people who intervened to prevent a crime and they get the most applause and news. Continued crime and sense of vulnerability will encourage some people to remain or become active, while others will be encouraged by seeing results. Those who live in our annexed areas tend to show the most involvement because they see a whole different type of policing than what they were used to. High visibility and actual problem solving of things like broken street lights, abandoned houses, clearing a street corner that used to operate as a 24-hour drug market, and driving off the prostitutes shows the community that it is not a waste of time to call police anymore. An often overlooked condition is political support from the city manager and other city departments and city council members. Police cannot fix a lot of problems alone; they need other city departments such as inspections, zoning, garbage, and public works to act. If the manager or other department heads do not want to give the police department that kind of support, then residents will see less problem solving and more lip service. FPD programs follow:

- *Alarm monitoring ordinance*
- *Are You OK?* A computer program automatically calls subscribers at a prearranged time to check on their safety.
- *Auto Theft Action Camp.* Two reflective decals are placed on the front and rear windshield with the ATAC logo identifying the car to police that it is registered in the program. The owner of the vehicle voluntarily signs a consent form allowing the police to stop the vehicle during the target hours of 1:00 a.m. until 5:00 a.m. Studies show that a vehicle registered in the program is 40 times less likely to be stolen.
- *Citizens Volunteer Auxiliary*
- *Civilian firearms training*
- *Code Enforcement Team.* By using the city codes effectively, the Code Enforcement Team has removed a number of potentially hazardous structures and has had other areas cleaned up.
- *Community Policing Television (CPTY).* A television show, CPTV, is aired on the commu-

SGT. STEVE MCINTOSH
COMMUNITY AFFAIRS OFFICE

nity access channel, courtesy of Cablevision of Fayetteville. The show airs Thursday nights at 7 p.m. CPTV is written, directed, and produced by members of the Fayetteville Police Department.

- *Community relations.* The community relations specialist works with neighborhood groups and individual citizens on problems that are not necessarily law enforcement related but are of great concern to the residents.
- *Community Watch coordinator*
- *Community Watch Council*
- *Crime analysis*
- *Crime prevention.* Crime prevention specialists take a proactive stand against crime by helping citizens avoid becoming victims of crime *before* it happens. The following examples of services that are offered free to the public: PR-4 Speed Screen, home/business security surveys, safety presentations, establishment of Neighborhood Watch, Operation Identification, burglar alarm information, and McGruff, the Crime Dog.
- *Crimestoppers.* Citizens receive cash rewards for convictions.
- *Family Intervention Team (FIT).* This program identifies youthful offenders at an early age as they are initially introduced into the criminal justice system via undisciplined or delinquent behavior. Youthful offenders between the ages of 6 and 12, and attending an elementary school within the city limits, will be referred to the FIT investigators.
- *Fayetteville Police Athletic League Judo Program (PAL)*
- *Gang intervention.* The Gang Intervention Unit identifies, collects, and disseminates intelligence on local gang activity to local, state, and federal law enforcement agencies.
- *Grove View Terrace Substation*
- *Homeless Project Program.* This program provides a uniform way in which to work with homeless/street person(s) as well as identify these individuals. This program assists individuals with getting shelter, clothing, food, financial assistance, returning home to their families, medical assistance, and getting jobs.
- *Juvenile Restitution Program.* A sentencing alliterative referred directly from the court. It offers a positive work experience under adult supervision through the community service component. This program aspires to enhance self-esteem and job/life skills.
- *K-9's*

OFFICER C. ROTAN AND WHISKEY

- *Mobile One.* A mobile police substation used by the Neighborhood Improvement Team. Mobile One and the Neighborhood Improvement Team are a proactive approach involving neighborhoods and the police working together to solve problems within a particular neighborhood. This innovative approach is known as community wellness and problem-oriented policing. Mobile One brings proven police and crime prevention programs into the neighborhood, thus reducing neighborhood crime.

OFFICER C. GARRISON AND DOC

- *Mobile Two.* Mobile Two is a mobile police substation used to improve the quality of life, funded by a grant from the Fayetteville Metropolitan Housing Authority.
- *Mounted Patrol*
- *Neighborhood Improvement Team.* Officers are assigned to specific troubled neighborhoods. The officers become familiar with residents and problems in the neighborhood, creating a strong bond of trust between the residents and officer.
- *Officer Blue.* A safety training advancement robot designed to educate children about personal safety, the dangers of drugs, and stranger danger.
- *Officer Friendly.* Officer Friendly is available to visit students in grades kindergarten through 3 to speak about the role of a police officer and safety.
- *Police Band "Roll'RZ"*
- *Police Reserve Program*
- *Police Surgeon Program.* The Police Surgeon Program is a program where medical personnel will provide Fayetteville Police employees with quality medical support. Volunteers are on call, subject to their schedules, for high-risk apprehensions.
- *Repeat Offenders Program.* Targets career criminals: identification, apprehension, and enhanced prosecution. Repeat offenders are selected based on intelligence information, drug use, arrest warrants that already exist, probation from previous offenses, recent prison release, and release on bail.
- *Santa Fe Substation*
- *Trading Card Program.* Cards bearing the likeness of their favorite police officer help children get to know the police officers assigned to their neighborhoods and encourage the children to interact with police officers.
- *Victim assistance*

- *Violent Crime Task Force.* Target violent offenders for federal prosecution.
- *"We Care Bear" Program.* To help relieve stress in children.
- *Problem-oriented policing.* Officers analyze crime to determine the underlying cause of repeat calls for service, officers then use whatever resources are appropriate in and out of the department, to solve or better control the problem. This program is linked to the community policing efforts in Fayetteville.

THE CHIEF

Ron Hansen is the chief of police. He is a native of Racine, Wisconsin, and served as a lieutenant in charge of their intelligence and narcotics division. He served as chief of police for Menomonie, Wisconsin, and Rock Island, Illinois, before coming to Fayetteville. The following interview was conducted with Chief Ronald Hansen on Thursday, March 25, 1999, in his office by Professor Stevens.

Chief Ronald Hansen

Community policing is a universal term often misapplied by politicians and scholars to mean whatever they think the public wants to hear. The theory of community policing as we practice it in Fayetteville is that specific problem-solving strategies are implemented at a decentralized level with an officer who is empowered to use discretion, training, and outside resources to provide a long-term solution to a community problem. Community problems tend to be neighborhood specific even if they fall into a general category, like drug activity. There are many potential solutions, and our philosophy is that every officer is responsible for analyzing the problem and implementing a solution in a way that more centralized staff is not able to do. Community policing is not a job title or a grant funded unit; it is a problem-solving philosophy embodied by all officers, regardless of rank or position. The terminology unfortunately gets hijacked by politicians, writers, or activists who misuse it as a weapon to criticize something they know nothing about but who will appear as if they do by using the popular vocabulary.

Community policing programs are ever changing and a police department has to be in balance with the community to be sure to provide quality police service. Changing community conditions might present some of those changes and so the department must be "listening" to the community. It's about developing and maintaining a trusting relationship—a partnership with community members. Building relationships aids police departments to see problems and to resolve them. A community partnership or what can be called community policing requires a different set of responsibilities for a department and a community. From the department's standpoint, community policing must be a department-wide philosophy as opposed to a police unit on an organizational chart. Community policing is an all-around plan to help a community stay safe, and it should influence every part of each individual's life. For example, officers should deal with such matters as potholes in the street. Reporting them isn't enough. They should also check to see if those potholes were filled.

Community members must be able to see that officers are working for the community relative to their quality of life issues that concern all parts of their daily life in addition to crime control matters. From the standpoint of the community members, they may have accepted a certain amount of criminality in their community, but if they see police officers effectively resolving their daily problems, the lives of the community members will be improved. They will stop tolerating crime and report it. Their satisfaction levels will rise and they'll not put up with criminals in their community. They'll seek out their partners—the police—and report the crime they once tolerated. Departments have to build trusting relationships through problem resolutions of both crime control and daily life issues of the communities they represent.

One way to listen to the community is for officers and officials to attend community meetings and to listen to what community members have to say about their lives. After all, we work for them and if our clients express a problem with something, then we must find the appropriate response, bringing them closer to their goals without sacrificing safety or bending the laws. Community policing is the link between community expectation and quality lifestyles. The police have to show that they can make it happen.

Another way to build relationships is through decentralized policing; getting the job done without relying on a chain-of-command for orders. That is, line officers have to do both: take the responsibility of listening to the problems and making decisions that get those problems resolved in a lawful way. Eventually, when the police have been successful, the community will rely on the officers and the officers will rely on the community. For example, a night shift detective notices a pattern of vehicle break-ins in a particular residential neighborhood. Traditional policing would mean the detective uses the information to help solve his cases, or maybe pass on the information to the patrol division. Community policing in its most effective form means the detective, on his own initiative and without supervisory direction, will analyze the problem with available information and implement a solution to include public education by coordinating press releases through community affairs and the community watch coordinators, using the police department's public access cable television show, briefing the patrol assemblies on information regarding suspects and patterns of activity, and setting up covert surveillance. Another example is a patrol officer who notices young kids selling drugs at the end of a cul-de-sac who run through a fence whenever police drive into the street. The officer should now use a form we call an information exchange to notify other city departments about problems. One form would go to the inspections department to enforce the city *ordinances and work with the owner of the property where the broken fence is located. Another form would go to the public works commission notifying them about any streetlights that are out. The community watch coordinators are contacted and encouraged to contact the property owners, even checking tax records to identify who owns the property.*

Assessment of community policing efforts is a major issue that takes time, professionalism, and, above all, commitment. We do it here in Fayetteville, North Carolina, community by community—neighborhood by neighborhood—program by program. What works in one community might not work in another community, and what worked once doesn't mean it will continue to work and/or that another set of solutions might bring about a more efficient outcome. One question asked about programs might be how we can enhance the quality of service of a program. Some ways might be to alter a program or to redirect the resources of a program. For instance, take our School Resource Officer program. Police presence in schools helps provide a safe environment, yet the fact remains about the impact one officer can have among two thousand high school students. An officer can't be everywhere, and when there are problems, other officers assist to resolve or neutralize the situation. So we redirected our efforts and came up with a program that better served the schools by helping them find other forms of security. Resources were put to use in areas such as a Mentoring Program, athletic league judo, and Roll'RZ, the police band. The Roll'RZ plays at community functions and is popular with most youths and their communities. Programs such as these help build relationships with kids through role models and music. Another example of redirecting resources might be found in our DARE program. What kind of an impact does DARE have on the family and the student? We redirected resources to a Family Intervention Program. This program is used to identify youthful offenders when they are very young since largely there's police intervention with those youngsters due to their inappropriate behavior. This way, community interests are better served as well as those of education and the family. Family Intervention Teams have a long lasting impact on offenders and their communities. The overall philosophy of an efficient community partnership is to reexamine programs on a regular basis. If they don't work despite what our agencies are doing across the nation, get rid of them or repackage them.

There is also another part of programs that should be addressed along with assessments. An agency has to be sure that its programs are operating in the best interests of the community. Sometimes, an agency develops a great program that works for the community and others—but sometimes policymakers might want to use a program for other interests. Take our Reverse 911 Program. Police personnel contact individuals in a community to warn them of an anticipated problem. Control of technology is important. Some officials might want to utilize those connections as a political tool I would imagine, and if they did, could that set the stage for a break in a community partnership?

Training of officers, community leaders, and city officials is vital. There are many changes within the department that must be addressed. For one, the responsibility of all members of the department change, especially with decentralization of command. Field officers and commanders must make decisions in the best interest of the community and with added decisions go added responsibility and added training. For instance, seminars with officers, educators, and policymakers on subjects such as ethics are helpful to the success of community partnership relations. Providing appropriate training requires both talent and money. Having the appropriate and ongoing funds to operate community policing programs is fundamental. Here's what could happen sometimes, say, for instance, that a community has inspired members, a good chief, good police officers, and great community programs. As a result, crime drops and with it—funding gets pulled since there are fewer problems to deal with. Then an agency must try to raise the needed funds to get the necessary equipment and payroll. Overall, an essential key to successful partnership building is to recognize and capitalize on the strengths of all the partners involved without compromising the rights of others. I hope this gives some of you a broader idea about community partnerships and how they work.

DEPARTMENT ATTORNEY

Carl Milazzo is legal counsel for the Fayetteville Police Department. He has been employed by FPD for seven years and also teaches at the Fayetteville PD's training center and at a local university. It is his opinion that one weakness of the department is it lacks the financial resources to supply more expertise and time to appropriately empirically research each program and the operational activities of the department as closely as he would like.

Carl Milazzo suggests that while DARE is extremely popular, they relied somewhat on the scholarly literature to help the Fayetteville PD managers make a decision about its success. Much of the literature was suggesting that DARE programs showed an increasing lack of validity and positive results. Carl Milazzo stated:

Police Attorney Carl Milazzo

In Fayetteville, we noticed that our juvenile crime and drug crime in particular was not decreasing, but in fact increasing. We also noticed that some of our most problematical juveniles were well known to the police or they came from dysfunctional families. Therefore, the chief made a very controversial decision to replace DARE with the Family Intervention Team (FIT), a program that would make more of a long-term impact on the community and the kids. Because of the age of the individual at the time of intervention, measurement will not come quickly. We believe that FIT as op-

posed to DARE has a greater impact on the outcome of the children who are more likely to engage in criminal activity as they get older. FIT centers around issues they don't know; DARE tells them what they already know, that is, about drugs.

Additionally, like most police departments, FPD responds to burglary and hold-up alarms, however, a high percentage of them are false alarms. This in turn causes officers to become complacent, and they are vulnerable when they finally arrive at low valid alarms. In addition, officers are wasting time responding to nonproblems instead of spending time solving community problems. Finally, the risk to public safety is increased whenever an officer responds to an emergency only to arrive at a false alarm.

Two years ago, the FPD appealed to the city council for an ordinance that would penalize alarm users for false alarms. We ended up with a limit of six false alarms per year, with increasing penalties thereafter. Unfortunately, we have not noticed a reduction in our false alarm rate. We are currently trying to get a stronger ordinance with fewer false alarms allowed, higher penalties, and a no-response provision. This is understandably meeting political resistance. This may turn out to be another concern that I attribute to community and political response.

Probably our most well known and successful program has been targeting commercial properties for public nuisance lawsuits. We have not lost one case yet, and municipalities from everywhere have called for help on our strategy. My office developed a register on our progress and presented it at the North Carolina Police Executives' conference. The city attorney, too, used it at a city attorney's conference. Each lawsuit takes a huge effort at coordination, starting with individual officers identifying problem properties, writing reports properly to associate the criminal activity with the property, trying to get the owner or manager to take proactive steps, and getting community support and city council approval. This is obviously time consuming and in some cases it can take as long as two years to build a solid case, but it has a long-range effect. It is so effective that the mere threat often has encouraged businesses to close and move. It is our hope that we can neutralize these types of nuisances in order to demonstrate to the community that the Fayetteville Police Department works for them.

TRAINING

Lt. Josh Phillips is in charge of the department's training program at its training site outside of town. Officers are trained in Fayetteville Police Department's POP philosophy during basic recruit academy training and during in-service training. On the wall in the academy classroom is a poster with the SARA model of community policing. Every class taught at the training school requires the instructor to associate the material with the four themes of the Fayetteville Police Department, one of which is community policing. "For example, when I teach law," says Carl Milazzo, "I show how suspicionless voluntary encounters that are permitted under the

Fourth Amendment can be used to develop information for use in solving a neighborhood problem. Officers learn from the start that the law is not always a restriction on good police work, but an additional tool they can use to solve problems."

Some recent in-service training to provide officers with additional methods of solving community problems included members of the inspections department to explain city ordinances, a retired FBI agent on communication and diversity, a verbal judo instructor, a fraud update on recent scams, and the usual legal updates. An advanced and extensive in-service course called the Police Law Institute, is a two-week class on law taught by the North Carolina Justice Academy covering warrantless searches, search warrants, interrogation law, and civil liability. Fayetteville has the highest number of officers in the state of North Carolina who are Police Law Institute graduates, and the department culture reinforces using the law to solve problems. For example, Fayetteville officers develop information for use in later search warrants and to conduct proper warrantless searches so that an arrest actually ends in a conviction of a repeat offender rather than a temporary interruption. Therefore, the community sees that law enforcement officers in Fayetteville have the training to help prosecutors obtain a lawful conviction.

CRIME STATISTICS

The principals at the Fayetteville Police Department believe that crime rates are only one of many indicators to gauge the quality of police service. Nonetheless, the North Carolina State Bureau of Investigation reported (online: http://sbi.jus.state.nc.us/crimstat/crimenc/profil98.pdf) that the rate per 100,000 of Crime Index offenses reported by North Carolina law enforcement agencies decreased 3 percent from 1997 to 1998. The Index Crime rate in cities over 100,000, which includes Fayetteville, dropped 6 percent, while the crime rate in cities under 100,000 decreased 2 percent. Collectively the rate of violent crimes as a group decreased 3 percent across the state.

Although the Fayetteville, North Carolina, Index Crime rate was reported at 9,038 in 1998, in 1997 there were 9,951 crimes reported. Therefore, there was a decrease in Index Crime reports of −0.09 percent. Crimes of violence for Fayetteville went from 885 to 688 per 100,000 of population; however, the number of murders climbed from 9 to 15 for 1998.

A FEW QUESTIONS ANSWERED ABOUT COMMUNITY POLICING INITIATIVES[5]

Question 1: How will your organization pick up the slack from federal money when it runs out, assuming some part of your community policing program is being funded or subsidized?

---

[5]Answers to these questions were given by Carl Milazzo.

Easy, we won't. At one time we did. This is another way that political support is needed to sustain our efforts. Without the budget commitment, we will eliminate programs. We have already done that and will continue to cut back. That is not good.

Question 2: What were the historical events that influenced organizational decisions to establish a community policing agenda at your agency?

There were no triggering events leading Fayetteville, North Carolina, to community policing initiatives other than the arrival of a new police chief in 1985. A program resembling what today might be called community policing was developed by Chief Hansen with the help of the city manager. The chief's approach is considered more a problem-solving approach as opposed to a blanket approach of community policing. Fayetteville continues to concentrate more on solving individual problems as opposed to treating all problems with a one-size-fits-all approach. For example, Fayetteville has never had individual officers designated as "community policing officers." Every officer of the department has the responsibility of determining "best solutions" for particular problems. That is a management philosophy that came with a new chief, rather than a new program.

Question 3: What methods are used to assess and/or evaluate the progress of the community policing effort?

We are weak on empirical assessment. We do measure our impact on a unit level, like the traffic unit measuring the statistical impact of the speed display or special enforcement project, or the investigative division measuring the number of crimes committed in response to a special enforcement project. Contributing to the overall lack of empirical assessment is probably our neighborhood-specific or problem-solving approach to community policing.

Question 4: Do you have false Alarm Responses?

Burglary alarm responses are a community problem that most police departments absorb onto themselves. We respond to burglary and hold-up alarms, and over 98 percent of them are false. This in turn causes officers to become complacent, and they are vulnerable when they finally arrive at one of the 2 percent of valid alarms. In addition, officers are wasting time responding to nonproblems instead of spending time trying to solve community problems. Finally, the risk to public safety is increased whenever an officer runs emergency traffic through intersections, only to arrive at a false alarm.

Question 5: How does your agency determine the success or failure of your community policing effort?

Crime rates, reported calls for service, arrest and conviction rates, and by citizen feedback. A program may work in one neighborhood, but not in another. The measurement has to be specific to a particular neighborhood or problem. Because we follow a problem-solving philosophy of community policing, we may have been successful closing down one crack house and arresting one crack dealer, which has an impact on a certain block, but not on the city as a whole. That is still a success if it encourages the people on that block to continue cooperating with us and spreading the message. This is not an overnight program, but a gradual effort.

Question 6: In what way have any community policing programs been changed or altered as a result of community policing assessments?

Most often by moving into a certain neighborhood with an enforcement plan. Problems can be identified by Community Watch leaders, city council members, zone officers, or anonymous reports. We have to plan both short-term and long-term problem-solving strategies. One weakness of community policing is that too many approaches are unbalanced, either focusing on the short term (like high visibility patrol) or long term (Community Watch groups) without blending the two strategies together in a way that will most effectively address that particular problem. We do an annual citizen satisfaction survey. We also do a Community Watch council survey. Before we annex a neighborhood, officers go door to door and conduct a survey and crime analysis before it even becomes part of the city. FIT requires proving a negative, that is that the children we are focusing on do nothing that would show up as a statistic. Because of the age at the time of our intervention, measurement will not come quickly.

Question 7: In what way has decentralization been accomplished in keeping with community policing efforts?

Just recently we have been able to move forward with our long planned district policing concept. We have decentralized property crime investigators to each geographical district captain, who now commands all patrol and property crime investigators for that district. Eventually, we will have a third district, and a substation with property crimes investigators assigned to that district instead of city-wide. Some investigative functions remain centralized, like juvenile and narcotics. In time, hopefully staffing levels will allow us to further decentralize those resources. The district concept has already shown great success, but it is anecdotal in nature because of the short time it has been in place. The property investigators do not just work on randomly assigned cases, they work on certain areas and problems with a goal of preventing as well as anticipating future trends. We have been able to clear numerous cases and conduct successful stakeouts, which we never coordinated before between two separate divisions.

A FORMER OFFICER TALKS ABOUT FPD

 I joined the Fayetteville Police Department in February 1981. I spent the next 18 years there. When I first joined under then Chief D. K. Dixon there was no such thing as community policing. Police work back then was all

reactive. Officers started their shift with the attitude that the public was the enemy instead of who they were hired to protect. The attitude of most officers was "Let's go kick some ass." New officers had to go out and prove themselves before being accepted by their peers. A new officer was judged by how much ass he could kick in an 8- or 12-hour shift. The attitude was to write and arrest as many people as you could during your shift. The Fayetteville Police Department had a detective unit, traffic unit, and a warrants section, and a one officer Internal Affairs office. I cannot remember a public relations unit. Community Watch was heard of but no one was assigned to work with the public.

In 1984 Ronald E. Hansen replaced Chief Dixon. Not long after Hansen arrived he started implementing change. He brought in the community policing and community wellness programs. Many officers did not have the first clue as to what community policing and community wellness were. Officers had to start getting out of their patrol cars and interacting with the public. Several officers resisted the change, refusing to change from a reactive force to a proactive force. No one likes change especially after doing things a certain way for so long. Several officers ended up leaving the department because they could not adapt to community policing. Those of us who accepted the change eventually caught on and did well. Chief Hansen started implementing training in community policing. He started a park and walk program. In this program an officer got out and talked to the citizens in his /her zone. The officer documented the citizens' concerns and forwarded them to whatever city department it concerned; i.e., traffic, narcotics, patrol. The program is not just for interdepartmental units but agencies like Social Services, Traffic Services, or any agency that can address the citizens' concerns.

Another highly used program within the Fayetteville Police Department is the SARA system. SARA is the acronym for Scan, Analyze, Respond, and Assess. Officers use this system when looking for problems in their zones. When the officer locates a particular problem in their patrol zone the officer uses SARA to solve the problem. His/her overall goal is to illuminate a problem or potential problem before it becomes a major concern or problem that will need more attention if left uncontrolled. It is each officer's responsibility to continuously look for problems and work the problem from start to finish. This system gives an officer a sense of satisfaction and a feeling of being important to the department and community.

Chief Ronald Hansen started a community relations and crime prevention unit. This unit's main concern is the citizen. They are responsible for Community Watch programs, crime prevention and much more. With the implementation of the Neighborhood Improvement Team, crime in Fayetteville has been reduced in all areas of the city especially in the public housing arm. When an area is annexed into the city the Neighborhood Improvement Team moves in and starts a rapport with the citizens.

The Neighborhood Improvement Team has been a great tool in community policing.

Chief Hansen has implemented so many community policing programs that I cannot mention them all. Ron Hansen has made the Fayetteville Police Department one of the leaders in community policing in the U.S. There is no doubt that the citizens in Fayetteville are very well thought of and protected.

I left the Fayetteville Police Department in January 1998 to take a position as police chief in Surf City, North Carolina. My town is different from Fayetteville. It is not as diverse a community as Fayetteville. Surf City is a coastal town and my challenges are different. My town goes from 1,800 citizens in the off-season to around 35,000 in the peak season. I, like many of my fellow chiefs throughout the state, have implemented many of Chief Hansen's programs and consult him on various questions of operation.

At Surf City, I experienced similar reluctance to change by several officers of my new department. With Chief Hansen's guidance, training programs have been established and successful policies implemented. Now, for the most part, the officers of Surf City have accepted change and are doing well in their efforts. Therefore, my point is that no matter how big or small the police department, community policing is vital to the quality of life issues. The police belong to the community and the community belongs to the police. It is important that citizens become a part of their police department and have a say in what policing is about.

—Mike Halstead, Police Chief, Surf City, North Carolina

SUMMARY

Fayetteville, North Carolina, has experienced a new chief with an efficient method of delivering police services through problem-oriented policing. One key difference between POP and other community policing strategies is that all personnel have a role to play in solving problems for the community. However, in this respect, the department met the agent-of-change challenges of technical, political, cultural, and administrative agents. Yet, it appears that resistance from veteran officers (cultural) due to traditional ideals and limitations in directives (administrative), due in part to its quasi-military structure, offered some of their largest challenges. However, planning, persistence, and sound management lent itself well to implementing quality police strategies. Training and communication appear to be key components in implementing POP in Fayetteville.

CONCLUSION

Fayetteville delivers an efficient method of problem-oriented policing as evidenced by surveys throughout the city, despite a large military presence that intensifies the city's cultural, economic, and educational gaps. One key component that works for Fayetteville is that all sworn officers have a role in community problem-solving efforts. However, in this respect, opposition due in part to misinformed or naive political figures tends to reinforce traditional ideals about policing, heightening resistance from some veteran officers. The push and pull of the political interests in Fayetteville might have more influence over police decisions than community members or its professional police management. One example relates to the PD reassigning its school resource officers to Family Intervention Teams. The local newspaper indicated that the sheriff felt the chief made a serious mistake and quickly placed deputies into those schools. However, planning, training, and stable sound management led Fayetteville to quality community policing strategies which are focused on solving problems as part of every officers' job. Fayetteville PD sets the standards for effective policing through professional police leadership.

Do You Know?

1. The demographics of Fayetteville, North Carolina, might affect its police delivery service. Identify those demographic differences as compared to the typical American city and explain in what ways those groups might require different police service. How might those differences affect other residents?

2. It certainly appears that the Fayetteville Police Department places an emphasis on programs as one of its primary methods of providing quality police service. In what way might "program policing" offer quality police service? Offer poor police service? What must be accomplished in order for those programs to operate in the best interests of meeting the mission of the department? Explain your rational.

3. Through evaluation of their early development of their POP agenda, FPD realized that there were four areas associated with change. Describe those areas of concern and discuss the area that is the most difficult to change in your opinion and why.

4. Fayetteville does not assign specific personnel as community policing officers because a POP perspective relies on all personnel to act in a capacity as problem solvers. Explain the differences between the two concepts and describe what you feel might be the advantages and disadvantages of POP versus community policing perspectives. In what way do you agree/disagree with POP's technique of solving problems?

5. Some of the methods employed by the FPD to ensure that all community residents are included in the decision making of community policing has to do with the Community Watch Council and two mobile substations. In what way might those mobile units be utilized to accomplish those ends and in what way do you agree and disagree with those methods of operation?

6. Describe the methods used by the FPD to assess the community policing initiatives. In what way might you agree with their perspective regarding this matter?

CHAPTER NINE

ST. PETERSBURG POLICE DEPARTMENT

St. Petersburg, Florida

INTRODUCTION

The annual budget for the St. Petersburg Police Department (STPPD)[1] for fiscal year 2000 is $55,440,444. The authorized strength is 538 sworn positions and 238 civilian positions serving approximately 240,000 residents or approximately 2.2 sworn officers for each 1,000 residents.[2] Under the direction of Chief Goliath J. Davis III, the department provides a full range of police services in a 60-square-mile area and also covers an additional 142 square miles of surrounding waterways. The police department is housed in one main building that is located near downtown. In addition to the main police building, since 1991 residents have been served at several community resource centers that are staffed by community policing officers. The department is nationally recognized as a leader in problem-solving policing.

CHAPTER OUTLINE

Ambiguous reports about the city are presented followed by newspaper accounts on the conditions in St. Petersburg produced, in part, by police service. Those accounts take issue with the reports and present what appears to be po-

[1]The St. Petersburg Police Department's web site is at http://www.st.pete.org
[2]The St. Petersburg Police Department has been accredited by the Commission on Accreditation for Law Enforcement Agencies since 1985.

litical and social opposition to the police department. Block organizing efforts of one opposition group are revealed. Community policing history in the city is discussed, leading into a dialogue about city-wide implementation of community policing initiatives. A shift to a problem-oriented policing strategy is examined along with a discussion about its national recognition and the failure of the strategy. The many lessons learned by the department as well as partnership recommendations for St. Petersburg and other similar cities across the United States are revealed. Their plan, emerging from a community retreat, reorganization, community oversights or influences, partnerships, and evaluations, and community policing today are highlighted. Initiatives, oversight, partnerships, evaluation, decentralization, community involvement, training, outside funding, and their observations are discussed in the close of the chapter. Finally, the chief presents his views.

REPORTS

"This city of 240,000 on Florida's Gulf Coast is a mix of retirees, service industries, tourist-related enterprises, and light industrial operations. It faces a typical array of urban problems—violence, drug abuse, shrinking resources—coupled with the problems of a state that continues to grow faster than it can develop services."[3] Also consider this report:

"Citizens of St. Petersburg are relatively satisfied with police services which compares to responses to surveys in other U.S. cities," stated prominent police researchers. These writers added the minority citizens tend to evaluate the St. Petersburg's police somewhat lower than whites, but minorities showed a stronger willingness to become involved in problem solving. Therefore, it was concluded that this in itself represents an "excellent opportunity for strengthening police–community relations and improving the quality of life in minority neighborhoods."[4]

THE PRESS

What both of the above messages ignored was that during the 1990s (including up to the time this chapter was written), St. Petersburg, Florida, was sidetracked by public disorder and suspect political leadership leading to confusion about its police department's community policing initiatives, depending on the reliability of the press.

For instance, when TyRon Lewis, 18, was shot to death by Officer James Knight during a traffic stop at 16th Street and 18th Avenue S on October 23, 1996, two nights of civil unrest existed and the prominence of the National

---

[3]Local Initiatives (1999).
[4]See Mastrofski, Parks, Reiss, and Worden (1999) for more detail.

People's Democratic Uhuru Movement (NPDUM) engulfed the city.[5] The NPDUM's web site suggests that they are a chapter of the African People's Socialist Party. Omali Yeshitela,[6] the NPDUM's founder, said the killing led to the emergence of the Uhuru movement, which in turn helped to unify the working-class community with portions of the middle-class community.[7] "As a consequence of (Lewis's death), the white power structure discovered the Uhuru movement," Yeshitela said. "I think that the most important thing that has come out—is the development of a new social contract between the members of the progressive (black) middle class and the (black) working class," he added.[8]

The political leadership in St. Petersburg recently invited Chimurenga Waller (formerly Dwight Waller and brother of Yeshitela) president of the St. Petersburg chapter of the NPDUM, to the Citizen Review Committee, which examines decisions of the St. Petersburg Police Department in internal affairs matters.[9]

In a letter to Mayor David Fischer, Jack Soule, president of the local Police Benevolent Association, called the mayor irresponsible for appointing a "vocal member of a radical organization that has publicly called for the state to execute two police officers. We strongly oppose this appointment and believe you have dishonored law-abiding citizens, the hard-working police officers and good reputation of the St. Petersburg Police Department."[10]

"If he (Soule) just wants people who agree with the police, I think they got enough of those already," responded Chimurenga (which means "revolution" in Shona, an African language) Waller.

The former chief of police of St. Petersburg commented, "I can understand where the PBA might be coming from, given some of the issues that have taken place in this city for a long time—not just in the past couple of years, but for a long time." Stephens worked as Fischer's top city administrator (currently [2000] the chief of police in Charlotte, North Carolina). "On the other hand, the citizens review process, I think, has made a positive impact on the community. One of the impacts it has had is that, for the most part, people have come away from their experience with a much greater knowledge and appreciation for the complexities of a police officer's job."[11]

Jeannie Blue, publisher of the *Heritage News*, an independent St. Petersburg newspaper, said there have been visible improvements in police relations among the black communities. She pointed to Chief Goliath Davis'

---

[5]See Quioco (1999) for more detail.
[6]See Caldwell (1998).
[7]Landry (1998).
[8]Landry (1998).
[9]Landry (1998).
[10]Landry (1998).
[11]Landry (1998).

efforts to improve how police officers address residents and to curb their use of profanity.

While the St. Petersburg Police Department continues to provide quality police service to its constituents, Uhuru engages in block-by-block organizing.

BLOCK ORGANIZING

"Currently, the crucial work of the Uhuru is block organizing," said the Uhuru organization's official web site.[12] "We've got a map of the city and we're dividing the city up into sections. We've created 30 sections now, but they're larger than I want them to be. For every section we want to have a section leader right out of that community. For this we're trying to win people who are Uhuru supporters. We want to commit them to just doing Uhuru work in the neighborhood where they stay. The solidarity forces are currently dividing up the white community into sections as well.[13]

In every section we want to have a section leader, and in every block we want to put a block captain. We will organize the entire city in that fashion so that no matter where the government attempts to go, no matter what kind of thing they want to do down the road, we will have put down Uhuru houses throughout the city. Every house becomes an Uhuru house. That way, we'll be able to maintain the high ground that we have now."

COMMUNITY POLICING HISTORY

It is against this backdrop (and suspect agendas of many individuals, a perspective observed by the principle researcher) that this chapter was developed with the assistance of Sargent Gary Dukema.[14]

Prior to the institution of community policing in 1989, which began with an experimental program in one of the city's public housing projects called Jordan Park, crime prevention programs were conducted by a separate, centralized unit that operated independently of other department operations. Beyond basic crime prevention training for recruits, the officers in this unit attended

---

[12]See African People's Socialist Party (1999) for more detail.

[13]The agenda of the Uhuru movement continues. April 5, 2000 a workshop was held in St. Petersburg, Florida for the public and members ("Uhuru movement celebrated," 2000). Workshop subjects include education in the black community, democratic rights of public housing residents, reparations for slavery, the CIA and crack cocaine, political prisoners, electoral politics and "The law: instrument of repression or liberation." The convention tried to "set the national agenda for winning economic development for the African community instead of the U.S. government policy of police containment," according to an Uhuru press release.

[14]Sgt. Gary Dukema was the primary contributor from the St. Petersburg PD for this chapter and can be reached at Uniform Services Bureau, Community Policing—District III, (727)892-5946 or via e-mail at gldukema@stpete.org

crime prevention training at the National Crime Prevention Institute and the Florida Crime Prevention Institute. Programs like Neighborhood Watch were heavily promoted and adopted; presentations were made on request to community groups and schools. But most of the programs, like those of many other crime prevention units, were standard items, pulled off the shelf like prepackaged goods in a store, rather than tailored to the specific audience or problem or for that matter, a specific city with specific needs.

In addition to "crack" cocaine hitting the streets of South Florida in the mid-1980s, this particular public housing complex was plagued with other drugs, violence, and crime. The residents of the complex cried out for police help. The program, called Jordan Park Pride Patrol, assigned a dedicated group of officers to patrol the complex. These community officers were tasked with working with the residents to rebuild their trust and confidence in the police and themselves, to identify problems, and work in partnership with the police toward resolving those problems. The Pride Patrol utilized a walking beat, police motorized carts, and introduced police mountain bikes. Within the next year or so, the concept of team policing led to other officers being assigned to neighborhoods surrounding Jordan Park, and eventually to other areas of the city.

In 1991, the department sent four members on a 10-city tour to observe other police departments who were experimenting with community policing. One of those cities was Fayetteville, North Carolina (see Chapter 8) to review Fayetteville's POP strategies. Upon returning home, those members shared their observations with senior staff personnel. Fayetteville's programs appeared to influence the evaluators and they, like many other municipalities, adapted some of Fayetteville's perspectives. A new mission statement for the department was prepared, setting forth an expanded role for the police working in partnership with the community to solve important community problems:

> *St. Petersburg Police Department is committed to establishing and maintaining a meaningful and productive partnership with the community.*

Their goal is to achieve excellence by facilitating a partnership between members and the citizens in order to mutually identify and resolve community problems. This partnership will ultimately enhance the safety and quality of life for the citizens of their community.

Following completion of this mission statement and the articulation of a set of values for community policing, the chief of police held department-wide orientation sessions about the new philosophy (pattered after Chief Hansen's experiences). At the same time, the department also formed a Steering Committee for Policing Excellence, a 35-member group including both police department and public representatives.

This group was charged with the development of a community policing implementation strategy that initially focused on selecting and training a small group of police officers to serve as community police officers (CPOs), designation of community policing areas (CPAs) throughout the city, and assignment of the CPOs to those areas. The objective of these initial efforts was to "jump-start" the process quickly so its impact could be felt throughout the neighborhoods of the city. Because national experience with community policing implementation was limited, the plan was moving into untested waters. Although the intention of the departmental leadership was virtuous, it was this rational that differed from the Fayetteville experiences and a decision that might have influenced the shortcomings of St. Petersburg's community policing initiatives. What was clear was that the department wanted to establish more productive and collaborative partnerships with its community.

Throughout the early 1990s, most of the department's community policing initiatives were focused on "high-crime" neighborhoods. The St. Petersburg Police Department embarked on a department-wide community policing philosophy. Once the CPAs were established city-wide, there would be a community policing officer assigned to every neighborhood of the city.

City-Wide Implementation

Initially there were 41 CPOs. The department went to an alternate response policy for handling routine police calls for service, including a no-report system, offense report officer program (light-duty officers who handle calls for service over the telephone), and limiting accident investigations to those involving injury/criminal charges/government vehicles/etc. This alternate response policy enabled a large number of officers to be unplugged from patrol and reassigned to community policing details. The initial CPOs were selected and attended a two-week training course on community policing and multicultural diversity. Following the training, the CPOs were deployed into the neighborhoods.

The community police officers were assigned to specific geographic areas and were liaisons between the neighborhood and the department. They are responsible for developing bonds between the community and the police department. They utilize the community policing problem-solving philosophy to achieve the highest level of quality service and citizen satisfaction. They are also responsible for identifying and resolving quality of life issues in their respective community policing areas.

Following that initial process, the implementation plan called for a series of supporting actions to be taken during the following year to strengthen organizational support for the community policing effort. Included were the development of a marketing plan, education of citizens, repeat call analysis, promotion of youth resource programs, and training dispatchers to support the problem-solving process. All of these elements reflected a national police perspective at the time.

In 1992, a comprehensive implementation plan was developed and covered a wide range of department activities. Five major goals were set:

- Partnership,
- Empowerment,
- Service,

- Problem-solving, and
- Accountability.

Each goal was linked to strategies aimed at achieving objectives reflecting these goals. The plan established specific actions on the part of the police department during the following years.

SHIFTS TO PROBLEM-ORIENTED POLICING

In 1995, a third planning document was prepared reflecting a shift in emphasis again, and conveying observations of then Chief Darrel Stephens about areas in which the community policing initiative needed to be strengthened. Recognizing the strong base for community policing that had been established in the department, this new document suggested three important shifts in emphasis:

1. Establishing a geographical base of accountability for everyone in the department;
2. Increasing the emphasis on problem-solving; and
3. Enhancing and improving the department's communications capabilities, both within the department and between the department and the community.

Chief Stephens had evaluated the implementation of community policing up to that time and observed its strengths and weaknesses. He understood the problems that had arisen that were preventing community policing from taking hold in a manner that would contribute to a more effective relationship between the police and community. The department issued a second strategic plan in 1996, entitled St. Petersburg Police Department—Strategic Plan 1996–2000, detailing steps to take to impact crime, fear, and disorder in the community. Building on the original community policing goals and objectives, this plan acknowledged that most basic support systems were in place to sustain community policing. The focus of activity shifted to problem solving and problem resolution in the neighborhoods of the city. This plan was updated in 1997 and retitled Community Policing—The Transition to the New Millennium.

NATIONAL RECOGNITION

For some years, the St. Petersburg Police Department has been nationally recognized as a forerunner in the implementation of community policing. Evidence of that can be substantiated by the Community Policing Consortium in Washington, D.C. Nonetheless, St. Petersburg was an early convert to the principles of the police partnerships and problem-oriented policing, moving police delivery from a reactive incident-driven style that emphasized rapid response to calls for service as the highest priority of policing. The transition to community policing in St. Petersburg was supported by a comprehensive planning process resulting in a strategic plan that was as detailed as any police agency had created during the period of the early 1990s. In that sense, St. Petersburg was a pioneer in the transition to community policing. It advanced the state of the art in a number of areas, detailing a massive number of organizational changes it was committed to implementing, and moving to dramatically alter how policing was done in the city.

It was, therefore, a shock to much of the nation following several years of community policing transition, that a series of civil disturbances in late 1996 raised serious questions about community partnerships and the effectiveness of the transition to community policing. From a national perspective, St. Petersburg had it all:

- A bright, articulate, and committed chief who was nationally recognized as a leader of progressive police thinking;
- A strategic community policing implementation plan that was detailed and comprehensive; substantial impact results from the community policing efforts undertaken until that time, including crime reduction in the city; and
- A host of other attributes often considered flowing from community policing implementation.

WHAT WENT WRONG?

There is no simple answer to this question. In mid-1997, Chief Stephens was promoted to the position of chief administrative officer for the city and Assistant Chief Goliath Davis became chief of police. The department was operating under a structure built on geographical deployment, community policing, and problem solving. Chief Davis stated clearly that he was committed to St. Petersburg's community policing transformation and would seek to strengthen its implementation.

LESSONS LEARNED

There are important lessons to be learned from the St. Petersburg experience, lessons that can only be learned in hindsight from understanding the strengths and weaknesses of the community policing transition.

The St. Petersburg Police Department was poised to move forward in solving important policy and strategic issues that impact the effectiveness of its community policing implementation. The department opened itself to an examination of its policies and operations to experts from several major police organizations:

- Office of Community Oriented Policing Services (COPS),
- International Association of Chiefs of Police,
- Police Executive Research Forum,
- National Organization of Black Law Enforcement Executives, and
- The Police Foundation.

Their examinations resulted in several key lessons for American policing as well as recommendations representing the best of current police thinking in the United States today. The project was funded by the Office of Community Oriented Policing Services, Training and Technical Assistance Division, and documented in a report entitled Policing St. Petersburg—Strengthening the Transition to Community Policing—June 1998. Several key concepts that flowed from the report included

1. The importance of establishing police officer accountability on a neighborhood-by-neighborhood basis,
2. The importance of making geography the basis of the organizational structure and policing strategy,
3. The need to communicate thoroughly the rationale for policy matters to all police employees and the community, and
4. The importance of holding each police supervisor accountable for the actions of the officers whom they supervise.

The report also volunteered the following recommendations for police agencies at large:

- The basic commitment to community policing must be well articulated by the city leadership to both the community and the personnel of the police department.
- Community policing is not the panacea for all of a community's problems. While substantial improvements in quality of life issues and citizen satisfaction can be achieved, it is a mistake for the government to sell community policing as the ultimate answer to all the problems found in urban neighborhoods. If citizens come to perceive that community policing has that objective, they will eventually lose faith in the initiative.
- Measurable outcome objectives must be set forth early in the strategic planning phase of program development. Measurements of achievement must occur routinely and be widely publicized.
- Implementation plans for community policing can be detailed and complex, but they cannot be so compartmentalized that they lose sight of the key elements of community policing philosophy: neighborhood responsiveness, problem solving, and partnership.
- Partnership with the community means that members of the community have to be included in substantive discussions about how policing is carried out. Likewise, police officers who have the responsibility to carry out these strategies must also be deeply involved in the discussions.
- The solutions to crime and violence in a neighborhood cannot only be police solutions. These solutions also must involve community commitment and action if they are to be effective.
- Articulating the commitment to community policing requires that police management have a comprehensive understanding of both neighborhood priorities vis-à-vis crime, disorder, and fear, and the perspectives of police employees about the police role in serving a community.

- A complex police organization should not expect to successfully implement community policing with a "split-force" patrol organization. Community policing requires that all police officers working in a neighborhood have a common focus on community problem solving and partnership.
- The key accountability within the police department must relate to "turf" or geographic area. A majority of police officers must know clearly what their area of responsibility is in geographic terms, so they will know the community they serve and the community will know which officers are to respond to their needs. Even in nonpatrol assignments, geographic responsibility must be reflected in work distribution and assignment.
- There must be a clear chain of command within the patrol function and clearly delineated accountability established within that chain of command focused on geographic areas. Every supervisor and every subordinate must know what their chain of command is and who is accountable for their work and performance.
- Policing congested neighborhoods of urban communities requires that every police officer act with a commitment to protect the dignity of every citizen, regardless, of ethnicity, criminal involvement, or appearance.

INITIAL POLICE AND COMMUNITY RETREAT

By the summer of 1998, the reports and recommendations of the Justice Department were consolidated into a single document (a synopsis of which has been stated earlier in this document). Additionally, a series of public forums was held, which allowed citizens and departmental personnel an opportunity to voice their opinions and have direct input in the reorganization of the agency. Chief Davis was committed to strengthening the internal policy-making process and to involving both the community and police officer in future policy decisions. To this end, a departmental staff retreat was held in September 1998 to discuss issues facing the department. In a very progressive and innovative move, a cross-section of department personnel, representatives from various community organizations, and members of various neighborhood associations were invited to attend and actively participate. The attendees were tasked with identifying the major issues facing the police department and discussing the Justice Department's report on community policing in St. Petersburg.

Retreat participants identified six major issues facing the department:

- Supervision,
- Accountability,
- Staffing,
- External partnerships/relationships,
- Internal communication/morale, and
- Training.

One resounding theme from both the citizens and employees was that the department and the community are interrelated, necessary, and important. Officers and employees asked for and received a return to the squad system, which should enhance supervision. This process and the ensuing improvements that were made further strengthened our commitment within the community to provide the highest standard of service to all citizens. By conducting the retreat in this fashion, Chief Davis demonstrated his commitment to furthering the partnership between the police and the community.

Following the retreat, Chief Davis gathered his staff, committees were formed to address the major issues, and subcommittees were formed as needed to address specific issues or research information. Each major committee had representation from across the department.

During 1998, the total number of complaints against employees decreased 10.2 percent. Significant reductions were seen in the number of unnecessary force complaints (54.3 percent), harassment (66.6 percent) and improper conduct allegations (25.8 percent). Further, there was a 25.8 percent reduction in formal discipline. This reduction is notable, considering increased public concern with police misconduct.

The area of supervision was one of the prominent issues brought up during the initial retreat. Prior to the retreat, the department was operating under a geographically based system. The supervision of the CPOs was through a chain-of-command that was also geographically deployed. The sergeants, who were the first-line supervisors for the CPOs, also had shift assignment responsibilities. Their shift assignments with the 911 responders quite often conflicted with their ability to work with or supervise the CPOs. Lieutenants had geographic responsibility for sectors on a 24-hour basis. The lieutenants were responsible for all the CPOs and 911 responders who worked within their sector. They also shared shift responsibilities, covering city-wide street activity as the watch commander. Each major had three sectors within their district and was responsible for all the personnel working in their district. The three district majors report to the assistant chief of the Uniform Services Bureau who reports directly to the chief of police. Communication and supervision quite often broke down at the first level with the sergeants split between shift assignments and geographic responsibilities.

REORGANIZATION

As a result of the retreat, majors remained in charge of all personnel within their district. They continued to report to the assistant chief of the Uniform Services Bureau. Lieutenants had the primary responsibility for a shift and all the 911 responders assigned to that shift within their district. They reported directly to the district major. Most sergeants supervised 911 responders assigned as a squad by shift. They worked the same hours and had the same days off as the officers on their squad. These sergeants reported to their shift lieutenant. One sergeant assigned in each district was the community policing sergeant. They had shift assignments and would not directly supervise 911 responders. They were committed to the goals and objectives of the community policing philosophy. They were first-line supervisors for the CPOs within their district and reported directly to the district major. Community police officers reported to the community policing sergeant in their district and had a first-line supervisor who was free from other commitments.

Since the reorganization in early 1999, Chief Davis conducted two public forums to not only keep the community updated on the department's community policing efforts, but also to promote community policing and introduce the CPOs.

COMMUNITY OVERSIGHT

The oversight of police operations is primarily the responsibility of the department's Internal Affairs Unit. There are a number of additional means of oversight. The first is through the elected mayor and city council. The chief of police reports directly to the mayor of the city. Police department policy and issues are regularly reviewed by the mayor and council through the budgetary process, special reports that are prepared on department operations, and routine administrative oversight procedures. Citizens can raise concerns directly with the mayor and members of council. A second means of community oversight is through the news media. A third means of community oversight is the police department's Crime Watch program and regular participation in the meetings of the city's neighborhood associations. The department's commitment to community policing places employees in regular contact with citizens throughout the community who have an interest in police performance.

Three different organizations have also been established over the years that have input and provide some measure of oversight into police operations. They are the Civilian Review Committee (established in 1991), the Community/Police Council (established in 1978), and the Community Alliance (established in 1968). The Civilian Review Committee reviews completed Internal Affairs and bureau investigations to help ensure they are complete and unbiased. The committee is also charged with the responsibility of monitoring disciplinary action in the cases reviewed for consistency and fairness. The information is passed along to the mayor, who in turn passes the information to the chief of police.

Membership in the Civilian Review Committee is voluntary and is made up of 25 multicultural community members. It is an example of how the community can become involved with its police department.

The Community Alliance is another community group that has regular interaction with the police department. The Community Alliance is a multicultural citizen committee of the chamber of commerce that has served the community since 1968. The chief of police is a member of the committee and routinely reports to the Government Committee and the full Community Alliance on department activities.

The Community/Police Council is a multicultural committee comprised of 19 city residents. Established by the chief of police and the Community Alliance, it functions as an information resource for the chief of police and the St. Petersburg Police Department to provide a greater level of understanding and respect between the community and its police department. The council serves as a forum for initiating, discussing, and evaluating the philosophies and policies of the police department as they relate directly to the interaction with the community.

PARTNERSHIPS

At present, there are close to 100 neighborhood associations in the city of St. Petersburg. From the mayor, to city managers, to the various department executives, there is a great emphasis on neighborhoods. The community police officers frequently interact with the neighborhood associations. They attend their monthly meetings, as well as keep in close contact with the presidents of the associations. Within the past year, the department has developed a Community and Police Problem-Solving Strategy document, whereby the CPO works with the association to mutually identify problems, prioritize the problems, then develop responses for resolving them. There are responses by both the officer and community, and the status is assessed each month at the neighborhood association meeting. The CPOs are also instrumental in establishing and maintaining active crime watches (both residential and commercial).

Many partnerships have been and continue to be formed by the CPOs. In addition to those partnerships formed with the many neighborhood associations, partnerships were formed with the Center Against Spouse Abuse, Neighborhood & Business Crime Watches, AmeriCorps Pinellas, City Housing Authority, Congregations United for Community Action, the Council of Neighborhood Associations, and many more. Partnerships were also formed with other city departments including code enforcement, traffic and engineering, sanitation, parks and recreation, the fire department, and more. The CPOs have formed many partnerships with other law enforcement/regulatory agencies such as the Pinellas County Sheriff's Office, State Hotel/Motel Inspectors, Department of Agriculture, and Probation and Parole.

As mentioned earlier, the department is committed to strengthening the transition to community policing. The department had opened itself up to the Justice Department's study in 1998, and it took the recommendations from the study back to a department/community retreat. Some need for change was realized, hence the reorganization of the department in 1999. Again the department assessed its progress by convening a second department/community retreat in January 2000. Most of the changes implemented as a result of the first retreat attained the desired effects. However, there were still some areas where improvement could be made. The administration will be reviewing the data from the retreat, and Chief Davis has committed to conducting additional retreats to further improve and strengthen the department's transition to community policing.

EVALUATION

The department also relies on community surveys for input and evaluation on the effectiveness of community policing. Surveys were conducted prior to the retreat, and the data collected were presented during the retreat. The department also keeps an open line of communication with neighborhood leaders, and encourages community involvement at all levels, from day-to-day interaction with the CPO, to department volunteer programs (such as Crime Watch and Road Patrol), to departmental retreats where department policies and procedures are reviewed.

The progress of community policing is also evaluated by the quality of police/community partnerships, successful problem-solving initiatives, community satisfaction, and also by traditional means such as looking at crime rate and number of calls for police service. Community policing has proven to be successful in St. Petersburg. The community has embraced it, the administration supports it, hence, the philosophy is here to stay. The STPPD does however recognize that, as with the problem-solving process, they must continue to assess their program and make the necessary changes in order to continually evolve as society does. They celebrate their successes and learn from their mistakes. Overall, their community policing effort has been remarkable. It has been 11 years since the Jordan Park Pride Patrol ventured into these unchartered waters.

FOLLOW-UP RETREAT II

In January 2000, a cross section of department employees and community representatives met to review STPPD progress in addressing the issues identified in the 1998 retreats: internal communication, external communication, staffing, supervision, accountability, and training. More than 80 attendees participated in the presentations, group discussions, and question-and-answer sessions. Reports were presented describing decreases in UCR Total Index Crime, decrease in complaints against department personnel, and increase in drug and prostitution arrests, search warrants, undercover traffic operations, and traffic citations. Response times and other performance measures were discussed. In addition, the results of the recent survey of the department and community members were distributed. Based on a review and discussion of the data, participants concluded the following:

- Both internal and external communication has improved.
- CPOs should continue their duty in the neighborhoods.
- The appointment of CPO sergeants has had a positive impact on the supervision and teamwork.
- Citizens acknowledge that the community can be of greater assistance.
- Supervision improved with the return to a squad system and reorganization of the Criminal Investigation Division.

- Accountability improvements are attributed to the development of role and responsibilities and return to the squad system.
- Finally, the number of training hours has increased for both civilian and sworn personnel.

The participants focused on other opportunities for improvement. Patrol allocation (patrol plan), the alternate response policy, and reducing citizen complaints were identified as important to increasing citizen satisfaction. In 1999 and beyond, the organization will be committed to developing strategies to address these opportunities.

COMMUNITY POLICING TODAY

Community policing today in St. Petersburg is still a department-wide philosophy (split-force model), with a city-wide approach. The entire city is still covered by a CPA, and each CPA has a CPO responsible for that area theoretically 24 hours a day, seven days a week. Currently there are 55 CPOs, including 11 officers assigned to the downtown deployment squad, two officers assigned to the largest shopping mall, and two officers assigned to the city's public housing department. There are three community policing sergeants (two more positions were approved for fiscal year 2000), and one sergeant supervising the downtown deployment squad. These sergeants report directly to the district majors (unlike the other sergeants in the department who report to a lieutenant), therefore streamlining the CPO chain-of-command in the hopes of providing more support for their initiatives. The 911 responders (call-driven officers) have geographic responsibility for their zone (same as a CPA) during their shift. Squad sergeants and lieutenants have geographic responsibility for their district during their shift.

As a result of outside studies of the department, coupled with the retreat held in 1998, the department decided it required more changes. The department recognized that they had "oversold" community policing to the community. This led to the expectation that the CPOs could fix everything, and when they couldn't solve all the problems, the citizens got frustrated with the officers. Geographic deployment led to problems of supervision and accountability, and the department had shifted to such an emphasis on problem solving that it was not really hearing what the concerns of the citizens were. The officers were busy problem solving what they perceived to be the priority issues. The department reorganized in early 1999, with a goal of enhancing the community policing initiative and improving accountability.

The patrol division returned to a squad system, typically consisting of a sergeant and approximately eight officers. The position of community policing sergeant was created (which hadn't existed in several years), and three veteran community police officers were promoted to the rank of sergeant and assigned as the three new community policing sergeants. The individual CPAs were again analyzed and it was determined that to better align the CPAs with the defined neighborhoods, several had to be merged. This reduced the overall number of CPAs by seven.

The department continues a split-force model for the deployment of its community police officers. There is still the basic structure in the patrol division, of 911 call responders, who work eight-hour shifts, five days a week, providing around-the-clock coverage. Their duty is to respond to calls for police service. In addition to the 911 responders, there are the designated CPOs. The burden remains to continue bridging the gap between the 911 responders and CPOs. As often as possible, 911 responders are teamed up with CPOs to work on problems such as prostitution, drugs, or traffic issues. The CPOs are encouraged to attend the shift read-off sessions with the 911 responders. The 911 responders are encouraged to partner with the CPOs for their assigned area, as well as offer "directed patrols" during uncommitted time. These directed patrols are a means for the 911 responder to be a part of the problem-solving process, such as providing additional patrols at a problem location or by assisting with a traffic enforcement detail.

The 911 responders are assigned zones to patrol. These zones mirror the CPAs to which the CPOs are assigned. This creates a "team" of a CPO and at least one 911 responder for each of the shifts (days, evenings, and midnights.) Furthermore, most of the Criminal Investigative Division also has geographical responsibilities, thus bringing them into the "team."

Additionally, the department established roles and responsibilities for both the 911 responders and the CPOs (and the sergeants for each), and documented these for accountability. The CPO is directly responsible for the community-oriented problem-solving efforts in their CPA. They will work a flexible schedule in order to meet the needs of the community based on meetings (neighborhood association, Crime Watch, etc.), events, and problem-solving initiatives. The flexible schedule also facilitates more effective problem solving. The CPOs will also foster a partnership with the community in order to mutually identify and resolve neighborhood problems and concerns. They will identify repeat calls for service and implement problem-solving strategies to resolve them. They will review problem-solving progress with coworkers, supervisors, and the community.

The major changes in the community policing implementation have been that of transition from a pilot program in one neighborhood, to "team policing" in a few neighborhoods, to a department-wide/city-wide implementation of community policing, to a geographical-based deployment with an emphasis on problem-oriented policing (POP), and now back to community policing. In 1999, the Uniform Service Bureau returned to a squad system, the position of community policing sergeant was created again, and the CPA boundaries were reviewed and some modified. All in all, the CPOs continue in their partnership and problem-solving efforts much the same as they did in the early 1990s.

INITIATIVES

The department has a strong commitment to the youth of the community. In addition to Drug Abuse Resistance and Education (DARE) for fifth graders, Gang Resistance and Training (GREAT) for seventh graders, school resource officers (SROs) in every public middle school and high school, and strong support for the Police Athletic League, officers are also serving as mentors for at-risk students, Boy Scout and Girl Scout leaders, and Exploring Advisors. CPOs actively worked with the Drug Education for Youth (DEFY) program, AmeriKids program, and Say No to Drugs Club, as well as participated in neighborhood block parties, neighborhood Halloween carnivals, holiday food and toy drives, and bicycle safety rodeos for children.

DECENTRALIZATION

The department decentralized in many areas to benefit the efforts of the CPO. Many units are now deployed to complement the CPAs, such as detective units assigned geographically. The 911 responders are assigned specific CPAs to patrol and assist in problem solving during uncommitted time. The CPO became the "chief of police" in his/her area. They liaison with both department personnel as well as with other city departments. They coordinate the long-term problem-solving efforts occurring in their area, and they serve as a wealth of information about the persons and activities occurring within their CPAs. Their assignment to the CPA is intended to be a long-term assignment, often for several years or more. In fact, there are still more than a handful of the "original CPOs" from the city-wide implementation in 1991. The CPO chain of command has been streamlined to facilitate more efficient problem solving as well as to give CPOs the necessary administrative support.

Initially, the CPAs were drawn up according to crime rates, calls for service, natural boundaries, neighborhood association boundaries, and so on. These boundaries have been evaluated several times since 1991, and some CPAs have had boundary adjustments. Some have even been consolidated. The most recent adjustments came as a result of the department retreats. Taken into account again were increases/decreases in crime rates and calls for service in the CPAs, neighborhood association boundaries, and the number of active problem-solving projects occurring within the CPA.

Additionally, the community has offered up various locations for police offices and resource centers. Police offices are now scattered throughout the city. There are also several community resource centers, often located in strip malls, staffed by citizen volunteers. Other city services are also offered at these centers, and they act as police "substations" located out in the community.

COMMUNITY INVOLVEMENT

The community has been involved in the implementation of community policing since its inception in St. Petersburg. This includes everything from having community representation on the initial steering committee to community involvement at the departmental retreats; and from community involvement during training to community involvement during the problem-solving process. Community representation and involvement has been significant. Chief Davis has committed to continuing to hold periodic department retreats, in which the associations will undoubtedly continue to be represented.

The community will continually be involved, as the neighborhood associations continue to strengthen and actively work with the CPOs to problem solve concerns in their CPAs. The CPOs will continue to attend the association meetings and interact with the residents. It is at these meetings that the CPO learns of the residents concerns. This is where the problem-solving begins. Problems are identified and prioritized, then responses are developed and implemented. Community responses can include any number of actions such as the formation of a crime watch, a drug march with citizens and police officers, the issuing of a blanket trespass on a vacant property, and pressuring landlords and property owners for tenant compliance with the law.

In determining a response to a problem, the CPO can utilize any number of tools. All the CPOs are encouraged to attend Police Mountain Bike Training, after which they can get a bike assigned to them. Currently the department has close to 80 police mountain bikes. The department does not have a dedicated police bike unit, rather the CPOs (once trained) can utilize the bike as a tool in their neighborhood. The police mountain bike is a very effective public relations tool as well as an excellent means to conduct burglary surveillance and street-level narcotics enforcement. Early on, the community purchased a significant number of the police mountain bikes. Another 21 were purchased through a COPS grant.

The CPO can conduct foot patrols of the area and police package motorized carts are available for their use. If the response necessitates a surveillance or covert tactic, undercover and low-profile vehicles are available. The CPOs have also utilized other city vehicles in order to be creative in their problem-solving efforts.

TRAINING

Training for the CPO initially consisted of a 40-hour Community Policing School and a 40-hour Multicultural Diversity Course, sponsored by the department. Additional in-service courses were offered to train the officers in police mountain bikes, surveillance techniques, problem solving (using the SARA method), and so on. At that time the area police academies were not teaching community policing. Over the years the state Basic Recruit Curriculum for Law Enforcement began to offer community policing classes. In 1999, the Florida Criminal Justice Standards and Training Commission embarked on a curriculum review, with the goal of updating the curriculum by interweaving community policing throughout the entire curriculum.

Once cadets complete academy training, they return to the department for postacademy training prior to entering the Field Training Program. During this postacademy training, the St. Petersburg Police Department instituted a block of instruction on community policing, in order to help the cadets relate to the specific department's community policing philosophy and expectations.

In addition to the basic instruction provided at the police academy and postacademy, officers today are being trained by the Regional Community Policing Institute (RCPI) of Florida, located at the St. Petersburg Junior College. The RCPI operates under a cooperative agreement from the Department of Justice, Office of Community Oriented Policing Services (COPS). RCPI provides free community policing training to law enforcement officers, community residents, city employees, social service agencies, and private sector representatives throughout Florida. The core courses consist of a two-day Introduction to Community Policing, a two-day Problem Solving for the Police Officer and Citizen (which encourages citizen attendance at the course), and a two-day Bridging the Gap: Police–Community Partnerships. The RCPI also offers a host of other one- and two-day courses such as Ethical Considerations in Community Policing, Crime Prevention/CPTED, Survival Skills for the Community Police Officer, and a three-part managerial course.

Training Director's Comments

Mary E. Peters, a major in the Training Division of the St. Petersburg Police Department, had these comments.

The St. Petersburg Police Department trains officers in several ways in community policing. When the philosophy first took hold in our agency several years ago, the original community police officers went through several days of intense training on the philosophy. The remainder of the department had briefings with the chief on the basics of community policing.

We have utilized community police officers for training officers for probationary officers who have completed their Field Training Program. This training was an "on-the-job" view of what community policing was about. Additionally, most sworn employees went through problem-solving training with the SARA model.

It is our great fortune that the Regional Community Policing Institute was started in our area. We have been using the institute to train our new community police officers and to further educate our current community police officers. The communication link with the institute is continuous, and training opportunities there are numerous.

The training we offer now, for the past several years, differs from previous training in that it is community and problem-solving focused. Much of the pre-community policing training was geared to tactical applications toward training; now much of our focus is on rapport building and problem-solving applications. The Training Division of the St. Petersburg Police Department is committed to serving our community and our officers. It is our firm belief that well-informed officers and citizens will enable us to have a stronger communication bond. Education is critical in accomplishing this and having the RCPI has helped us greatly.

FUNDING

St. Petersburg Police Department has availed itself of several grants by the U.S. Department of Justice, Office of Community Oriented Policing Services (COPS). In 1994, the department was awarded a COPS Phase 1 grant. The grant covered a three-year period, 1994, 1995, and 1996. It was the original COPS grant, and provided for 18 officers to be dedicated to street-level drug interdiction. The grant covered salary and benefits for the officers. In addition to the 18 officers, the department assigned three sergeants to supervise to the unit.

In 1995, the department was awarded the COPS MORE Grant. This provided additional funding for overtime and technology (MDTs) to enhance the current level of community policing problem solving capabilities.

In fiscal year 1998, the department was awarded the Community Policing to Combat Domestic Violence Grant. This grant provided for overtime and equipment (such as photography equipment) for the Domestic Violence Unit to document incidents of domestic violence and to collect evidence for the successful prosecution of the offenders.

In fiscal year 1999, the department was awarded the Problem-Solving Partnership Grant. This grant provided for overtime and personnel costs to conduct an auto theft case study and fieldwork. The case study was designed to collect and analyze data about auto thefts occurring within the city. Information was collected on the number of auto thefts, kind of vehicles being stolen, the average profile of the offender, and what makes the particular vehicles easy to steal.

In fiscal year 1999, the department also received a Universal Hiring Program Grant (UHP-21), covering three years (1998–2000), consisting of 21 officers. The purpose of this grant was to increase the number of officers at the street level, in order to further enhance community policing initiatives with the city of St. Petersburg.

For the City of St. Petersburg, part of accepting a grant is the pledge of intent to retain the officers, by local funding, when the grant is phased out. This pledge is a city generated "letter of intent" signed by the mayor and city manager. At the end of a grant program, each grant program is assessed to determine if the need remains for the program. If there is an essential need to retain the program, the chief of police will then have to go to the mayor and city council for funding.

Comments from Chief of Police Goliath J. Davis III, Ph.D., on March 9, 2000:

Perhaps there is no greater challenge facing law enforcement today than adapting to the ever-changing complexity of our society. As an agency, the St. Petersburg Police Department has faced this endeavor head on, embracing the opportunity to improve service to the citizens of our community. Beginning in the late 1980s, we were assigning community officers to specific areas of the city in order to form partnerships with the community as well as work to solve specific problems with and within the community. Then in the early 1990s we expanded our community policing efforts by assigning a community police officer to every area of the city and establishing a department-wide community policing philosophy. Thus it is also true today, every neighborhood in the city is represented by a community police officer.

Over the years community policing in St. Petersburg has continued to evolve. As a department, we sought to improve the manner in which we served the citizens of our community. We've continued the process of change with a series of public forums that allow citizens and departmental personnel an opportunity to voice their opinions and have direct input in the reorganization of the agency.

To this end, a departmental retreat was held in September 1998 to review the Department of Justice's report entitled Policing St. Petersburg— Strengthening the Transition to Community Policing, and to discuss issues facing the department. A cross section of the community and police department attended and actively participated. One resounding theme from both citizens and employees was that the department and the community are interrelated, necessary, and important. Several recommendations arose from the retreat, including the desire to retain a split-force model of community policing. The retreat process and the ensuing improvements that were made further strengthened our commitment within the community to provide the highest standard of service to all citizens.

In January 2000, a second departmental retreat was held. Again representation from across the department, as well as across the community, met to review the department's progress since implementing the changes initiated as a result of the previous retreat. Survey data indicated the return to the squad system for 911 responders, as well as the addition of community policing sergeants, enhanced internal communication, and improved supervision. Most community members surveyed commented that police service to their neighborhood has improved since the reorganization, the community police officers are more attentive to neighborhood problems, and these officers are doing a better job of identifying neighborhood priorities. The data also indicated the police department is open to community input.

During the past year, the St. Petersburg Police Department has continually strived to improve its service to our community, and I am pleased to report that data from the Uniform Crime Report (UCR) indicates reported crime in St. Petersburg decreased 7.7 percent overall in 1999 when compared with 1998. Response times for priority one calls for service decreased from 7.1 minutes in 1998 to 5.5 minutes in 1999. Citizen-initiated complaints decreased 12 percent in 1999 when compared with 1998. The number of drug arrests, search warrants, and prostitution arrests all increased in 1999.

Finally, we look forward to the opening of the Family Substance Abuse Service Center in St. Petersburg. Surrounding neighborhood associations have assisted with its acquisition, and are making this long-awaited dream become reality. The center will address the demand side of the substance abuse problem by providing services to chemically dependent individuals and their families.

As we continue the process of change, this agency will remain responsive to the needs and concerns of each citizen. We will continue to hold ourselves to the high standards we have set and provide the public with a means of expressing their concerns. As we move forward in this new millennium, I want to assure you the St. Petersburg Police Department will continue its efforts to work in partnership with all segments of the community, to reduce both violent and property crime, and to enhance the quality of life for all who call St. Petersburg home, including all those who visit and work in our beautiful city.

SUMMARY

Policing strategies are reported under way despite unfavorable press, political opposition, suspect leadership, and/or some community leaders with alternative agendas. The major changes in the community policing initiatives were developed through numerous meetings, retreats, visits with other police agencies, and assessments by outside organizations. As a result, there were numerous transitional periods that ranged from a pilot program in one neighborhood, to "team policing" in a few neighborhoods, to a city-wide implementation of community policing, to a geographical-based deployment with an emphasis on POP, and back to their preference of community policing. That is, police officer accountability was assigned on a neighborhood-by-neighborhood basis; geography became the basis of the organizational structure and policing strategy; police leadership communicated the rationale for policy matters to all police personnel and the community; and finally each supervisor was accountable for the actions of the officers whom they supervised.

The chain of command was altered several times to accommodate community policing initiatives and numerous substations are presently scattered through the city. Numerous changes produced many organizational, community, and political contingencies, some of which are still unchecked. Evaluations of citizen satisfaction, in part, were made on the bases of patrol allocation, formal officer discipline, citizen complaints, and response times. The department also relies on community surveys for input.

CONCLUSION

In an attempt to bridge their constituency's cultural, political, and economic gaps, the St. Petersburg Police Department ignored (or was pressured to ignore) their history of perceived exploitation, an impatient citizenry, and unsettled civic and community leadership. It is no wonder their genuine, but constantly changing, efforts to enhance police services through community policing initiatives met with difficulties from time to time. It is clear that when rank-and-file members of the department support departmental policy, even when the department tries to be all things to all people, the likelihood is better that obstacles (real or imagined) can be minimized. With that said, nowhere is it clearer that with community empowerment comes community responsibility. Are St. Petersburg's community members accepting their responsibilities as partners with the police to enhance their quality of life standards?

DO YOU KNOW?

1. The political leadership in St. Petersburg invited the president of an organization who holds a contradictory perspective to the department to sit on its Citizen Review Committee. This committee examines the decisions of the department's internal affairs investigation. In what way might you agree or disagree with this invitation?

2. Uhuru's block organizing strategy sounds like an excellent plan. How might their model be emulated by other entities that wish to develop strong grassroot support? What opportunities might the police department consider to partner with Uhuru in order to enhance public safety and improve the quality of life issues in that city?

3. In what way might the early failure of St. Petersburg's community policing initiative be avoided? That is, their implementation strategy focused initially on selecting and training a small group of police officers to serve as community police officers and they designated specific areas throughout the city to become community policing sites. They called it a "jump-start" process.

4. Realizing their earlier mistakes, the administration suggested three important shifts in emphasis. Describe those shifts and explain why those suggestions helped shape the community policing strategy.

5. The St. Petersburg Police Department opened itself to an examination of its policies and operations by experts from several major police organizations. Describe those recommendations and explain how the St. Petersburg police might improve their implementation process by following those suggestions.

6. The department decentralized in many areas to benefit the efforts of community policing initiatives. Explain how this was done, and explain why you agree or disagree with this method of decentralization.

7. In early 2000, a cross section of department employees and community representatives met to review the department's community policing progress. Describe their findings and explain why you agree or disagree with any of the findings listed.

REFERENCES

African People's Socialist Party. (1999).
Available online: http://www.uhurumovement.org/bosp9.htm
Caldwell, A. (1998, July 18). Mural to grace City Hall's blank wall again. *St. Petersburg Times.* Available online: http://www.sptimes.com
Landry, S. (1998, May 30). Police decry naming of Uhuru activist to panel. *St. Petersburg Times.* Available online: http:www.sptimes.com/
Local Initiatives (1999). Crime prevention and community policing in St. Petersburg, FL. Available online: http://www.ncpc.org/5pol1g.htm
Mastrofski, S. D., Parks, R. B., Reiss, A. J., Jr., & Worden, R. E. (1999). Policing neighborhoods: A report from St. Petersburg. National Institute of Justice. Available online: http://ncjrs.org/txtfiles1/fs000245.txt
Quioco, E. (1999, October 25). Vigil reflects on past, future of race issues. *St. Petersburg Times.* Available online: http://www.sptimes.com
Regional Community Policing Institute of Florida. St. Petersburg Junior College Eileen LaHaie—RCPI Project Director.
E-mail: lahaiee@email.spjc.cc.fl.us; web site:
http://cop.spjc.cc.fl.us/cop/index.htm
St. Petersburg Police Department Internal Affairs Unit—Annual Report 1998.
"Uhuru movement celebrated." (2000, April 5). St. Petersburg Times. Available online http://www.sptimes.com/

CHAPTER TEN

CAMDEN POLICE DEPARTMENT

Camden, New Jersey

INTRODUCTION

This is a 10-year account (1989–1999) of the experiences of the Camden Police Department to implement community policing initiatives, which ultimately failed. There are many reasons for those failures, some of which include general assumptions held by the four men who headed the department during that period of time. Although they were capable and experienced police leaders, command has limitations especially when city leadership is divisive, officer resistance is pervasive, crime is rampant, police policy is suspicious, and poverty is devastating. Other problems included receiving misinformation from professional journals and other resources on community policing practices and strategies. In Camden, the ideals of community policing were more academic rhetoric than reality. It was hard enough to find a reasonable definition of community policing let alone a plan or a practical guide that fit Camden, New Jersey. Everybody, from city hall to the community, had answers and agendas. But the police would have to control the streets before gaining the confidence of a battered community, an essential part of policing partnerships. For instance, Mischief Night in Camden was a traditional activity conducted by enthusiasts who traveled from as far as New Orleans to participate in a night of destruction and terror. It took over a decade to bring some form of order to that one evening alone, yet many of the previous dilemmas of the city remain intact. The following is an account of the Camden Police Department (CPD) experiences during that decade as provided primarily by former captain Charles J. Kocher of the CPD.*

---

*Captain Kocher retired after 27 years with the department and currently teaches at Temple University.

CHAPTER OUTLINE

The problems faced by Camden police officials are described before providing an outline of city history, city demographics, and the reputation of the police department, all of which are components that influenced the outcomes of policing strategies. A profile of the Camden Police Department and crime is given and Camden's attempts at implementing community policing initiatives are highlighted including critical decisions, their philosophy, and comments from the two police chiefs who instituted those initiatives. Mischief Night is detailed because it was the most salient obstacle to a partnership with the community. Camden's problem-oriented policing plan, programs, and implementation are discussed, followed by deployment directives of tactical units and patrol roles. A plan to control Mischief Night in its entirety is revealed. A little about community policing today is offered. Last, Camden's commanders, including the current and former chiefs, comment about Camden's community policing initiatives followed by comments from several other members of the community.

THE PROBLEM

Camden, New Jersey, has gained prominence for serious fires that occur annually on Mischief Night (Halloween, October 30). The process of convincing police commanders and officers to "buy in" to community policing and actively maintain a philosophical city-wide approach to community partnership was never really accomplished in Camden. Additionally, the attempt of the police department to identify grassroots community leaders was peppered with distrust by both the community and the department. This was largely due in part to the police department's lack of serious community commitment. City residents were accustomed to the police department trying new approaches and then after a short time abandoning those approaches, leaving residents with uncertainty. "If I cooperate with the police today, and they take a new position on crime tomorrow, will the gangs love me or kill me?" one resident volunteered.

Likewise, the department's officers sometimes learned of the department's intentions to implement community policing from individuals outside of the department rather than through their supervisors, departmental training programs, or police newsletters. A total commitment to embrace community policing may have permitted the police department early in the game to curtail the activities of Mischief Night more expeditiously, but it took over 10 years to bring that one night under control. One lesson learned in Camden about the implementation process of community policing is that it requires a great deal of time for the internal acceptance processes to occur. That is, police officers need time, training, support, and supervision before they accept and operate within the philosophy of community policing. Then, too, there are the civic leaders, community leaders, and members who need to be recruited and guided through the process, but they must trust the police department first.

HISTORY AND DEMOGRAPHICS

To get a real picture of the problems confronting new police strategies, knowing Camden's history and demographics might help. Camden's origins go back to 1764, when Philadelphia merchant Jacob Cooper became convinced that the area offered an excellent site for a town. The site was named Camden in honor of a British friend of the American colonies, Charles Pratt, Earl of Camden. In fact, the Camden Police Department's official police patch worn today by its officers displays the official Camden City Coat of Arms of Charles Pratt. The naval coronet, which forms a portion of the crest, sets forth the fact that the city is a seaport, and the pine tree rising from it suggests the origin of "Pyne Point," Camden's original name. The supporters on either side of the arms represent Education and Industry. The locomotive train engine represents the famous engine of the Camden and Amboy Railroad Line.

Camden is located adjacent to Philadelphia, Pennsylvania. A former industrial working-class city, Camden has experienced serious economic and crime problems during the past three decades. Camden encompasses 8.68 square miles and had an estimated 1998 population of 83,546, down from 87,492 in 1990. However, Camden County shows a population of 505,204 compared to 502,824 for 1990. Approximately 35 percent of the population in the city are under the age of 18. Older people are leaving the city for the suburbs.

Camden is the seventh largest city in the state and the largest city in Camden County. The city is divided into 20 census tracts. Camden's population is relatively diverse with all populations, other than whites, growing. The city's racial composition is African-Americans, 54% (14,414); Hispanics, 24% (6,374); whites, 20% (5,331); Asian and Pacific Islanders, 1% (285); and Native

Americans, less than 1% (70). Whites represent the only decreasing population; all other populations are increasing with the Asian/Pacific Islander population growing the fastest. The city population as a whole has seen a 3% increase since the 1980 census. Camden, a city with 12.3% more children than the state percentage and 9.1% more than the county percentage, is a "city of children." Also, 32 percent of all births were to individuals under the age of 17. *Time* magazine's article "The Other America, Who Could Live Here?" painted a desperate picture: "Camden is a City of broken wings . . . those with the initiative and the strength leave. Those without it, die young."

Camden is the poorest city in the state of New Jersey and the fifth poorest city in the United States. In fact, more than one-third of residents live below the poverty line. Almost 82 percent of the city's population are dependent on some form of public assistance, and 69 percent of the city's households receive Aid to Families with Dependent Children (AFDC). More than 12 percent of Camden's housing units are vacant, creating a rather dismal atmosphere in certain areas where abandoned houses have caught fire, leaving piles of ruble in their wake. Recently, Camden experienced a record number of homicides, increasing 88 percent between 1988 and 1992, many of them drug related. With these deep-seated economic and social problems and the negative image surrounding the city, it will take more than a few construction projects to bring Camden back to the thriving city it once was. However, despite undeniable truths about the depth of poverty throughout the city, neighbors understand and accept the challenge.

Mayor Arnold W. Webster summarizes socioeconomic realities affecting the city: "The city of Camden is now in the process of rebuilding itself after four decades of national economic downturns, the departure of residents and businesses who had provided the city with a sustainable tax base, and surging unemployment, which has caused increased crime and drug trafficking. The end result has been to create a destitute city filled with decaying streets, crumbling and abandoned houses, and a generation of marginalized youth without hope."

Federal programs such as the Empowerment Zone (EZ) are supplying millions of dollars for housing and human development; state programs are supplying funds to rehabilitate and revitalize neighborhoods; and private resources such as the New Jersey Housing Financing Agency, consisting of businesses such as Mid-Atlantic Bank and individuals such as Martin Marietta, are pouring million of dollars into Camden communities to help the city. This is an ongoing enterprise that will have its rewards shared by all including the police department, it is hoped.

DEPARTMENT PROFILE

The Camden Police Department (CPD) came into being in 1871, filling the gap of city marshals.[1] It had a chief and 25 full-time police officers. It established

---

[1] The Camden Police Department's web site is http://www.camdenpd.com.

two-way communication methods as early as 1877, automobile patrols in 1910, and the first K-9 patrol within the state of New Jersey in 1960. A mobile crime detection van was instituted in 1961, as well as the first police academy. A computer-aided dispatch system has operated since 1973. The department is completely computerized with over 50 terminals available to assist officers with daily information requirements.

The Camden Police Department has an authorized strength of 386 police officers (343 males, 43 females) in a patrolled area of just under 10 square miles consisting of 145 miles of city streets. CPD serves a population of approximately 84,000 residents who made 102,979 calls for service in 1998 (down from 107,074 in 1997; 111,104 in 1996; 123,689 in 1996). Camden has approximately 1 officer for each 218 residents, far lower than the national average (although its violent crime rates are proportionately higher, too). For instance, 12,126 Index Crimes were reported in 1998 including 31 homicides (homicides were as high as 58 in 1995), which rivals cities over twice the size of Camden. Of the 386 sworn officers in the department, there is 1 chief, 1 deputy chief, 5 captains, 15 lieutenants, 45 sergeants, 40 detectives, and the remainder are uniformed patrol officers. Specialized forms of patrol include canine, motorcycle, horse, boat, and bicycle.

COMMUNITY POLICING

During implementation of different community policing strategies over a 10-year period, four chiefs of police held office. Police Chief George "Bobby" Pugh began several community programs during the late 1980s that were designed to introduce community policing to both traditional police officers and the community. Aspiring police supervisors were assigned to orientation seminars at Rutgers University to learn community policing philosophy. Those officers also attended seminars in Newport News, Virginia, and Washington, D.C. They met Robert Trojanowicz and furthered their knowledge about community policing (CP).

It was Chief Pugh's belief that programs designed to help inner city youths would best serve public safety. The chief drew on his own individual experiences as a youth to formulate policy. The initial phases of CP implementation included exposure to CP concepts through education and expansion of community base programs. Programs such as the Police Athletic League (PAL) and crime prevention programs were crucial to his concept of community policing. Other programs included the formal organization of churches throughout the city and formal meetings with city business owners. Those new contacts would play an even greater role, the chief felt, in controlling Mischief Night, which was more out of control than ever.

Chief Pugh felt that dramatic results could be achieved through an open system, allowing feedback from the community. It was important to be alert to special interest groups whose purpose and objectives were antagonistic toward public safety, the chief told his commanders. Administrative battles were waged among other city departments and with city council members. Despite the success of many of the CP initiatives, elected officials, city managers, and police supervisors were inspired by traditional police assessment tools such as responses to calls for service, response time, and arrest statistics. Trying to convince city hall that CP success was not necessarily reflective of those measurements was a task in itself, the chief revealed.

Decentralization

In 1994, the Planning and Development Unit of the CPD presented a proposal to decentralize the department into two police districts. Traditional workload analyses and calls for services suggested that two divisions, each consisting of two districts, would better serve the community and the department. Chief Pugh accepted the proposal with the intention of furthering community policing in Camden and considered workload analysis a second priority. However, Investigations, Records Bureau, Vice, Juvenile, and Internal Affairs would remain centralized at the police administration building located in the center of the city. Uniformed divisions were divided into four district stations each manned with a police captain and sergeant. Their primary task was to establish grassroots partnerships with community organizations that could be mobilized to assist the police in a number of programs. Those officers were given decision-making authority, which set a precedent in the CPD. The officers changed their schedules to day hours and received a limited number of overtime hours to attend community meetings in the evening.

Reality Sets In

Mini stations and storefronts were easily opened, but not easily operated. Other unexpected issues with the decentralization process arose quickly as resource allocations were demanded elsewhere. Sworn officers were required at all four substations. Approximately 16 officers were lost to "inside duty" in staffing those substations. (Inside duty meant that those officers would respond to fewer calls, have few response times to measure, and make fewer arrests—thus some people considered those officers to be unproductive.) The use of equipment, including computers, special weapons, police cars, two-way radios, was also of concern since it was in demand in other areas of the department. To complicate matters, several high-ranking officers retired, however, many of those who retired had held traditional perspectives about policing and were replaced with CP skilled officers. Nonetheless, these new high-ranking officers lacked the experience of those retiring.

A critical decision had to be made. It was made at the command level as were most of the decisions of the day. The issues were to operate CP as a program and concentrate its efforts in a single at-risk neighborhood or to adapt the philosophy of community policing department-wide, which meant citywide, too. Police leadership decided to expand CP prerogatives at the expense of traditional programs and traditional responses to crime. One of the influencing factors in favor of this decision was based on avoiding the situation in which one neighborhood might ask for something another neighborhood might have in the way of police amenities or services. Equity police service throughout each neighborhood was one goal of police leadership.

Some commanders excelled and others were not interested and turned their efforts to personal agendas. In a move surprising to rank-and-file officers and city hall, the chief restructured the department with numerous promotions, demotions, and transfers. His intention was to solve departmental bickering and to accommodate a high number of retirements. Some of the promotions included the CP initiative which produced an unexpected change in personnel. Four police sergeants replaced each of the four captains in the substations. Four additional police officers were assigned to CP duties along with the sergeants. The sergeants, in turn, reported to a lieutenant assigned to the Office of the Chief of Police. One of the few responses from the community was that they requested more officers to be assigned to their neighborhood.

Chief Pugh's Phase II

During phase II of the chief's plan, the earlier issues of scarce resources at the mini stations especially among CP officers continued. For instance, patrol vehicles that often required repairs and the oldest two-way radios were given to the CP officers. At times, patrol officers actually hid keys to specific vehicles or "tagged" vehicles as "in need of repair" to ensure that transportation would be available for their assignments the following day. The sergeants faced with shortages of equipment seemed to have little regard for CP, and most continued a traditional patrol response. Their point of view centered solely on their objective of placing a specific number of patrol vehicles and officers on patrol duties to answer 911 emergency calls despite directives that CP initiatives should also receive some priorities. Understaffing and overdemand for police services influenced the decisions of those new mini station commanders.

Also, only officers assigned to rotating shifts received additional salary incentives and, therefore, their steady tour of duty resulted in lost pay. CP officers worked 10:00 a.m. until 6:00 p.m., Monday through Friday, with no overtime allocations. The officers were labeled as working "banking hours" by officials and other patrol officers. They were not available when they were needed most, such as to attend community meetings during the early evenings and weekends. Police officers assigned to patrol duties were separating themselves from CP officers. A new labor contract changed the work schedule to a new 10-hour workday, which resulted in additional time off for officers assigned to rotating shifts. There were no incentives for officers assigned to CP duties.

CP efforts were most successful when officers assigned to serve in CP capacities possessed the characteristic traits associated with nontraditional police responses. Officers who listened to children and had a positive attitude toward community members and business owners, for instance, were vital to the success of the initiative. From the command perspective, the most difficult task was acquiring consistency from all four districts. Assignments, reports, and allocations varied. And the traditional methods of evaluation and assessment, such as the number of car stops, radio calls handled, and tickets issued, remained a requirement by CP officers as well as the traditional police officers assigned to answer 911 emergency calls. Several attempts to change the assessment process were made by the chief. But change was slow and inconsistent due to understaffing, overwork, and interference from city managers, elected officials, and traditional values. Another factor that influenced directives was a constant "need" to transfer personnel for a number of different reasons.

Chief Pugh developed four community partnership councils in each of the police districts. They would meet with the assigned community policing officers to discuss problems occurring within their district. Two members of each partnership council were appointed to serve as ambassadors to a city-wide advisory council chaired by the chief. This was done to enhance communications among each of the districts. The groups grew in membership and some became more organized than others. The groups continued until the retirement of Chief Pugh. After his retirement, the less organized partnerships existed in name only. Some of the city's governing fathers recognized the early success of the partnerships and eventually passed a city council resolution creating a police advisory board chaired by both an appointed city council member and the chief of police. This system remains in place and functions well. However, it should be noted that during Chief Pugh's administration as well as the current administration, issues such as police strategies and personnel assignment remain the sole responsibility of the chief.

Those experiences and many unmentioned experiences continued through the remaining years of Chief Pugh's administration. As expected, those issues involving outside interference required diligent and patient leadership by the next three chiefs: Chief Albert Handy, Chief William Hill, and Chief Robert Allenbach. Finally, with Chief Allenbach's appointment, a new organizational system was initiated that placed both patrol officers and community policing officers on rotating shifts. This change of management practice eliminated the equity issue among the two groups of officers and permitted community policing functions to continue and expand. Under the new system, all officers assigned to patrol and community policing rotated together as one group. The groups would split into their assigned roles during the first shift (7–5) and second shift (2–12). Later, Chief Allenbach recognized a need to have a limited number of officers assigned to steady tours. The merchants felt well served if the same officers were assigned to their business districts.

However, community residents protested the loss of "their officer." They wanted the officer to remain assigned to their neighborhood. Departmental priorities were secondary even if those priorities included training for the officer or a special assignment. Maybe community members were uncertain whether or not the officer would return. Also, some officers resorted to contacting community leaders for help to prevent their transfers, claiming crime would increase and that no one would do for them the same things that were currently accomplished. This phenomenon of swaying the potential viewpoint of an entire neighborhood or business community was a new wrinkle for police leadership to address. The more organized community groups mustered large petition drives to keep "their officer" in their area.

One observation about Camden's difficulties with implementation of their CP initiative is that the complexities associated with CP have some basis in managerial theory as practiced by private organizations. Yet, it appears that few chiefs anywhere have managerial expertise since rising through the ranks is one common path to upper police management. The transitional process of moving from an incident-driven, reactive agency to a proactive preventive one takes a commitment of approximately 20 years in Camden time. The tenure of Camden's chiefs was significantly less than a private sector leader.

Chief George D. Pugh: Chief Pugh had these thoughts:

> *If implementation of community policing is to be successful, management has to embrace the concept and design a training strategy which ensures that the philosophy is a concept that requires a detailed, well-thought-out process by the management team of a police department. Time lines are an additional major factor.*
>
> *If community policing is to be successful, management has to embrace the concept and design a training strategy which ensures that the philosophy permeates the entire organization.*
>
> *The chief of police is key to the overall success of the endeavor and must exercise a firm commitment to change. Our success with community policing was tied closely to the problem policing methods designed for reducing various forms of deviant behavior surrounding Halloween's Eve activities. Educating city officials, civic and religious leaders, our citizen customers, members of the Asian business communities, and the news media was a huge project. The most difficult tasks involved the development of mutual respect and trust among all of the stakeholders. We had to assure everyone that this co-active response was not another cyclical program; positive results were not only possible, they were achievable!*
>
> *Normal attrition of command personnel and ongoing change among city officials required constant meetings to keep everyone informed of the philosophical changes we were attempting to implement.*
>
> *I am pleased that the Camden Police Department has continued the process of implementing the philosophical viewpoint of community policing. To change police culture from a traditional policing response to a community-based orientation requires commitment, consistency, and dedication. The success of our Mischief Night effort proves the process works. Halloween's Eve is now just that, the night before Halloween. The monumental psychological organizational change that put the police officer closer to the neighborhoods and the customers we served proved successful. The police officers involved were exemplary and should be congratulated for their acceptance and dedication to the new frontier of community policing.*

> *The lessons learned from the Camden Police Department demonstrated to me the importance of brainstorming new ideas along with community input. I am elated that Camden has continued the community policing philosophy. It is my goal to instill the same philosophy with the Atlantic City Police Department.*

Chief William Hill

Chief William Hill served two years after Chief Pugh. During Hill's administration, CP priorities and objectives resembled a program rather than a city-wide philosophy. Chief Hill was faced with a myriad of administrative matters associated with the decentralized policing concept. His superiors (mayor and city council) were calling for more efficient and effective measures of operations. Chief Hill had served as one of the first assigned captains to community policing and understood the value and advantages of community policing. Although community policing manpower allocations were reduced, community-based programs continued to operate during his two years as police chief. He experienced one of the most successful control of Mischief Night operations, which is attributed to community networking established during the preceding eight years of efforts by community policing officers under Chief Pugh's administration.

Chief Hill Says: Chief Hill has this to say about Camden:

> *Community intervention is essential to the success of our services. Wherever I travel throughout the city, people respond that we are doing a good job. Community policing is imbedded in all that we do. The newly appointed officers must realize our goals and objectives to provide the finest police service possible and protect everyone in the process.*
>
> *The commitment to community policing continues with several meetings per week. The key is certainly to intermingle with the citizens to show our commitment to fighting crime as well as the fear of crime. The future is bright for quality programs that have their basis in community policing.*

Chief Robert Allenbach succeeded Chief Hill. Chief Allenbach decided to continue community policing as a program. It was now 10 years since Chief Pugh began the series of community policing programs that would take the department through the 1990s and halfway through a major change of operations. Chief Allenbach coordinates the community policing program through his office, and most of the programs continue to varying degrees.

Many officers who had been early participants of the CP initiatives during Chief Pugh's administration are now serving the department as supervisors and midlevel managers. The officers had participated in and witnessed the success of community policing, but the order of the day appears to be a return to a traditional service agency. The probability that a senior officer whose career was influenced by the philosophy of community policing may one day serve as police chief exists, and at that time, the department may again try to implement community policing as a city-wide philosophy. Although one observation is that success for community policing in Camden has less to do with police leadership than city politics, crime, poverty, and community trust.

Mischief Night

For years, Halloween was preceded the night before by Mischief Night pranks. Vehicles would be pelted with eggs and have their windows "soaped." For the police department, this was always a night to avoid work if possible and those unfortunate officers assigned to work the 4:00 p.m. to 12:00 a.m. tour of duty could expect to be held over to aid and assist the oncoming troops. Each year throughout the 1980s, incidents became more violent and disruptive. Trash bins would be positioned in intersections and set ablaze. This required additional efforts in extinguishing the fire and also removing the debris from the path of traffic.

Each year, police commanders attempted to offset the anticipated long evening by requesting overtime expenditures and placing additional officers on patrol duties. The solutions were to no avail. The problems worsened and media coverage exploited the acts of vandalism, reporting on the incidents and thus creating copycat situations throughout the city.

The early 1990s took Mischief Night to a higher level of concern. Abandoned homes were set on fire by arsonists. The fire department was overwhelmed and handled an unprecedented number of fires requiring outside mutual aid assistance to help fight the fires and prevent further damage to property. Traditional fire fighting tactics were not working. The age of the dwellings and the fact that they were mostly wood structures provided spectacular views for onlookers and warranted special attention. The police department was limited to crowd control duties and peripheral incidents brought about by the late-night fires. Again, traditional policing methods were utilized to cordon off citizens and prevent further danger to vehicle traffic. While performing such tasks, the patrol vehicles were stationary and not available to patrol neighborhoods and business districts. Soon, residents began calling 911, for police assistance to break up large roving gangs that were throwing eggs and rocks at passing vehicles as well as at houses. October 30 was becoming a traditional "Hell Night" that police officers and fire fighters could count on to keep them busy all evening. Daylight Savings Time reverted to Eastern Standard Time at the appropriate period to allow darkness to convene earlier, providing easy cover for those who were serious about causing serious harm and havoc for residents and government officials.

By 1991, fire enthusiasts traveled from New York State and New Orleans to Camden, New Jersey, anticipating a night of terror and blazes that would provide more excitement than could be found in their own hometowns. The overwhelmed dispatchers were sending fire apparatus from one end of the city to the other. Traditional responses of a ladder company, engine, and battalion chief for each alarm were met with serious interruptions by police officers and/or residents redirecting fire equipment to other locations. Outside fire companies not familiar with city demographics could be seen throughout the city trying to locate a particular area. As a result, a fire battalion chief might arrive at the dispatched location, but the engine company wouldn't arrive at the scene for some time later—if at all. Ladder and rescue duties were also subject to disoriented rather than oriented duties. The Philadelphia Fire Department offered assistance, but their equipment was not compatible with Camden hydrants so they could not pump water. City police vehicles became excellent "targets" for mischievous kids. Police officers failing to keep their windows closed might also find fruits and other unknown objects thrown inside the vehicles.

Detroit, Michigan, has a similar experience known as "Hell Night," which also occurred on October 30. Detroit had developed a plan to eradicate Hell Night fires in five to seven years. The Detroit presentation given at FLETC's Partnership Seminar inspired Camden's observers. However, the Detroit plan was unsuitable for Camden since it was designed around Detroit's resources, demographics, and political influences. For example, all 1,000 of Detroit's city workforce reported for work that evening and were assigned a straight line block watch. This was in addition to the police and fire personnel who were assigned to duties and tasks that complemented the block watchers' duties. Volunteers were encouraged as well. A task force of city officials was invited to Detroit to hear presentations in detail of the "what" and "how" of their successful plan. One of those individuals who attended that meeting at FLETC was Camden Police Lieutenant Gilbert "Whip" Wilson.

Lt. Wilson was an early pioneer of the CP initiatives under Chief Pugh. He was one of the chief's project directors. The lieutenant was sent to Detroit as part of the contingent of city officials to study their Hell Night. Lt. Wilson selected certain programs that he thought would be applicable to Camden. Of course, all of them had to be modified to Camden. The programs served as the foundation for an army of programs that would help combat the serious fires and acts of vandalism on Mischief Night.

Gilbert "Whip" Wilson, Commander, Camden Police Department:

I was fortunate to be part of the management team as we began linking the community to the department. This was a long process. It takes time to develop a real bond, a real trust with grassroots residents. The community leaders and church leaders such as Reverend Jones, Monsignor Doyle, Father Sal, and Monsignor McDermott all played major positive roles. Any police department attempting to find a starting point should and must look to their religious leaders for assistance and participation. Moreover, I think the real test was Mischief Night. We proved that community policing and the strategies of problem-oriented policing can work as a united front. Make no mistake about it, it takes time to get this thing rolling. And Camden took the approach of a city-wide philosophy. That means we had ten square miles to indoctrinate!

Chief Pugh sent me to Detroit as a representative to see what we could find that might apply to the city of Camden. Detroit put together a program designed for my visit. Although we were unable to utilize everything, we learned an awful lot! As the coordinator for community policing, we were able to manage our growth and ensured that we were not spread too thin. The officers really wanted to help, and I had probably one of the best groups a commander could ever want. As a councilman, I am proud every time I see those officers I worked with, now, continuing the tradition. The fire department changed to a task force approach, community groups were organized, and the rest is history. The future is bright. Education of city officials, and continuance of the philosophical growth are essential for future success.

After commanding the Vice Unit for Chief Pugh, Wilson became the lieutenant whom the sergeants from the four mini stations reported to and he, in turn, reported to the deputy chief. Lt. Wilson retired and successfully ran for city council of Camden. He now serves the city in that capacity. His community policing experience serves him well in his civic duties.

COMMUNITY POLICING IN THE YEAR 2000

A city-wide, department-wide community policing philosophy died. Attention shifted to CP programs providing alternative activities to the children. Movie outings, skating activities, all-night parties at area school cafeterias, and pumpkin hunts replaced roving gangs of kids walking through neighborhoods on Mischief Night. Mayor Arnold Webster appointed a city director to oversee all community programs. The department's role changed from a CP-oriented philosophy to an assisted role, helping the community accomplish their social goals through leadership and partnerships. This surviving service is referred to as problem-oriented policing and partnerships (POPP) by many Camden police officials.

PROBLEM-ORIENTED POLICING AND PARTNERSHIPS:
THE CAMDEN PLAN

Although POPP might appear to be a contemporary movement for Camden, its conceptual origins were well grounded in Camden police service. That is, POPP is linked with the plans of the Camden police in partnership with other public agencies through community initiatives to bring Mischief Night under control. Thus, POPP is linked specifically to a single goal and was somewhat under way after Chief Pugh established the four police substations throughout Camden. But, recently POPP has developed into numerous projects. It is too soon to determine if POPP will survive or, like community policing initiatives, evolve into some other movement because only recently (1999) did Mischief Night appear to be conquered.

The early stages of controlling Mischief Night called for identifying real grassroots organizations that had a stake in their neighborhoods. The best starting points were churches of all denominations. Religious leaders needed to take a hand in putting an end to Mischief Night. Several programs were brainstormed among those leaders and specific police representatives. Because many church leaders felt uncomfortable or threatened in brainstorming with other church leaders, it became a longer process than expected. Each leader had to be met with individually many times. Sometimes, several leaders were able to meet together but then individual meetings were called after the larger meetings. Those religious leaders and their influence and the department's grassroots organizational skills would prove to be productive for the people of Camden. But in the final analysis, community members would eventually accept the leadership of this new associational venture. Finally, compromises and decisions were reached. Those first programs included:

1. **Adopt-a-House Program** required an area resident to agree to adopt a vacant house adjacent to their own and immediately report any activity in or around the premises. A large sign, about the size of a "FOR SALE" sign, was placed in a conspicuous spot within the vacant home that indicated to everyone that this property was adopted and being watched closely by neighbors. The neighbors became the "eyes and ears" for the police department.
2. **Neighborhood Watch** groups were encouraged. Walking throughout their neighborhood together with police officers the neighbors exemplified the successful crime prevention program of National Night Out. Officers walked along with a patrol cruiser not far behind in case an emergent situation required assistance.
3. **Awareness meetings** were held with corporations, apartment complexes, and housing developments. The city of Camden has seven housing communities that utilized large trash bins at each building. The police officers attending the meetings as management officials emptied the trash bins the day before Mischief Night, even if it was an added day for trash pickup.
4. **Police presentations** were conducted two weeks before Mischief Night at all city schools. Police officers and firefighters attended all city school assemblies talking about the dangers associated with deadly fires.

Mischief Night Plan

There were many plans. This one was called Operation Pride and was created by Sergeant John Bach of the Planning and Development Unit. The acronym represented a Police Response to Incident Directed Enforcement. Operation Pride encouraged one chief to make a decision that it was not in the best interests of the CPD to appear as if it were a military operation on Mischief Night. The earlier riots experienced during the late 1960s and mid 1970s were still vivid among many citizens. Class A uniforms were the "order of the day." Soft hats were the regular uniform worn by the officers every day. Commanders were told their officers should wear "soft hats" for phase 1, however, have your helmets in the vehicles in case the situation called for safety measures. Outside agencies were also asked to wear Class A uniforms. If the officers presented a professional appearance it was felt the psychological effect might be effective. All of the agencies complied with the request. Operation Pride lasted three years.

This plan permitted diversity among city departments. Fire officials coordinated plans for the advent of fires. The city government appointed the police chief as the official coordinator for all activities during the initial stages of the plan.

Tactical police questions also needed to be addressed. What was the objective? Priorities? Where would we house all those we arrest? Should a curfew be put into effect? What if they decide to start the fires on other nights? What are the union requirements for working conditions? The tactical problems included ensuring adequate equipment such as radios and vehicles was available.

Implementation of Mischief Night Plan: Tactical operations were assigned to the patrol commander. His staff would assemble the intelligence and develop a tactical operation plan to address arson, and other acts of deviant behavior. First base was intelligence. A listing of all vacant homes was assembled by investigators. Large businesses were identified that had delinquent taxes or had filed bankruptcy and could become a potential target for arsonists taking advantage of a situation to commit and cover up their crime. Investigators compiled a list of all known area arsonists including pictures for officers to recognize. Vacant homes were inspected and where possible boarded up to prevent entry. Overpasses were inspected for potential items that could be thrown at vehicles. Potential hazardous material locations were pinpointed for possible targets by arsonists.

While many prayed for rain, Lieutenant Wilson wanted a warm night to permit the plan to be implemented. The first phases began weeks before Mischief Night by soliciting community support, keeping large corporations and hospitals informed, and establishing "muster points" for citizens to sign up. Ideas were continuous and spontaneous. Many were implemented if time permitted. Such items as T-shirts and baseball caps were given away free to entice residents to participate. Each neighborhood had a different colored shirt and cap.

Tactical operations called for a police presence to supplement the regular patrol force responsible for emergency calls for services. All vehicles were fueled by noon. It was essential to identify where the officers were to report and to ensure that all the equipment would be available in an efficient and effective manner. Outside agencies enhanced operations by providing additional manpower and vehicles. How would the police department maintain contact with everyone? The chief listened to suggestions and arrived at the decision to place a minimum of one Camden police officer with each outside agency team. This officer would have radio communications with the Camden Police Department. Primary muster points and secondary points were established should a need arise to "regroup" or change plans.

Control and accountability were early concerns of the ranking officials. Detectives were assigned to stakeout duties at potentially high-risk locations along with detectives from the Camden County Prosecutor's Office and Sheriff's Department. Tactical operations included patrol of gas stations for anyone purchasing containers of gasoline, while community police officers requested inner city markets to curtail purchases of eggs.

The fire department was active as well. Traditional fire fighting methods were modified. Task forces of engine companies and rescue/ladders companies were strategically placed to respond as a team to ensure everyone arrived at a potential fire scene with the required equipment to safely extinguished the fire. Fire companies from adjacent communities were placed in position with a "pilot." Fire Chief Kenneth Penn made sure every outside fire department was accompanied by a city firefighter to get the emergency equipment there safely and effectively. The partnership among the police department and the fire department was strong and very cooperative. Problems experienced with improper valves and water pressure were corrected. Separate command posts were permitted for police and fire operations. A joint command center proved ineffective because priorities and needs were different for each entity. One officer from each department was assigned to each of the two command posts to provide technical assistance and make their agencies aware of impending changes or situation changes.

Helicopter patrols were arranged through the U.S. army and the New Jersey State Police. One Camden police officer was assigned to identify areas for the pilots and to provide communications with ground operations. This sounds easy enough, however, it took several years to develop a flight plan with effective radio communications and proper lighting equipment. The learning experience among the tactical officers and pilots proved to be a partnership that continued through the year.

Operational plans were developed and modified as required. Community members took some control of the situation and helped decide what types of efforts would be made and the police would assist in any way possible. This was a dramatic change of posture for the police department. The use of crime forecasting techniques, such as computer mapping, provided analyses that could actually predict where activity might take place. Sign-up sheets were systematically issued each August on National Night Out. Practice sessions with residents before Mischief Night were held by CP officers.

Everyone, regardless of assignment, was "on-post" by 6:00 p.m. The volunteer groups assembled after work and by 6:00 p.m. were in pairs of four or more and ready to watch their neighborhoods. The volunteers walked until about 9:00 p.m. Curfew during the week was 10:00 p.m. and for Friday and Saturday 1:00 p.m. To curtail curious outside observers, informational points were established at strategic locations throughout the city. As the traffic light turned red, police officers walked along the stopped vehicles and provided the drivers with informational pamphlets to drive safely on Halloween. The locations selected included area mini stores where large quantities of eggs had been sold in the past.

Probably the most time spent on all planning involved meals for approximately 300 police officers and another 200 outside police agency personnel. The current labor contract agreements for the police officers and the city government required a "hot meal" after eight hours. This became one of the monumental tasks of the entire operation. For accountability, the police chief could not allow the regular method of a half hour meal break to be granted to each officer and expect total saturation of all city streets during the times stipulated for the operations. Likewise, because Camden Police Officers were assigned to each team, it was necessary to ensure all agencies were provided with a hot meal before 6:00 p.m. Four meal times were established for both operations and police officers.

An interesting phenomenon occurred in 1997 and 1998. The partnership bond with the community was so strong that officers assigned to walk with those groups were provided with meals from the citizens. This provided some relief for the police department responsibility. Labor agreements among outside agencies also varied. A point officer for each outside agency was asked to be assigned to the command post to coordinate all internal regulations governing their agency. For example, the Sheriff's Department personnel met at their headquarters for briefing and assignments before reporting and were relieved to return the following day at their regular time. The middle shift remained, on an average, four hours into the graveyard shift. The midnight tour was ordered to report four hours early providing maximum manpower availability between 8:00 p.m. and 12:00 a.m. This system permitted 24-hour coverage following the Mischief Night operations. Throughout the evening, Planning and Research officers reviewed operations and suggested cutbacks where possible to minimize overtime expenditures. Officers assigned to walk with the volunteers experienced the longest day.

Modifications took place every year with the emphasis on efficiency and cost-saving measures. One ingenious idea was car wash setups for egg throwing incidents. Two locations were established for all departments to have their vehicles cleaned without leaving the area of patrol responsibility. The Public Works Department provided heavy equipment to remove dumpsters immediately upon finding out that a street was obstructed. The Water and Utilities director ensured that hydrants were closed and that water pressure was adequate for fire fighting purposes. The fire department was prepared with the assistance of mutual aid from neighboring municipalities. Rather than fight fire in the conventional manner, teams were formed to extinguish the fire and move to the next emergency. A volunteer fire company would then stand-by the fire scene to place additional water on the fire. This system worked and permitted the fire department to provide rapid responses to all situations. The plan worked so well, police officers were sent home early, saving the city expenditures and permitting the police department to return to normal operations.

The results showed that from 1991 through 1994, 225 fires were reported in the city. Of that number, 26 percent were classified as dwellings and 60 percent were rubbish or grass fires. The majority of the fires began to surface at 6:00 p.m. and continued through 1:00 a.m. The highest number of fires occurred between 10:00 p.m. and 12 midnight. The number of fires declined approximately 50 percent each year until 1997 and again in 1998.

In a way, the Camden Police Department successfully demonstrated proactive policing designed for a specific purpose; those partnerships that were formed were more between officers and other public personnel to solve a specific situation. However, without community support Mischief Night would never be controlled. Community policing concepts evolved into programs that are presently called POPP, however, many individuals in Camden refer to POPP as community policing initiatives.

■ COMMENTS FROM CAMDEN COMMANDERS AND OFFICERS

I was fortunate to be part of the training of managers before we implemented community policing. It was clear there was a need to improve communications with the citizens, and Chief Pugh put together a sophisticated plan for implementation.

The biggest objective looking back was overcoming the subtle resistance to change. Police officers had grown accustomed to traditional police emergency response. The philosophy of community policing requires a change of operations.

Our department has continued to try to implement the goals and the objectives associated with Community Policing.

Deputy Chief Edwin Figueroa.
Camden Police Department

The ideas of community policing have encouraged Chief George Pugh, Chief Robert Allenbach, and myself to believe in our commitment. The critical element I think lies with "commitment." If a police department hopes to be successful, a long substantial commitment will be necessary. As we bring on board new officers we can teach them our Mission Statement. But for the midcareer officers we must continue to instill the philosophical principles through a combination of commitment, education, and training. The first ten years might actually turn out to be the hardest. What is most important is that we display our commitment to our citizens we so proudly serve.

—Edwin Figueroa, Deputy Chief, Camden Police Department

I have served as the media relations officer during Operation Pride and later when the operation was called Halloween Eve. Media coverage was critical and we paid special attention to their needs. Hourly press releases were provided and when requested some interviews were permitted. I was amazed each passing year as the number of fires dropped dramatically. As a result, the media continued to show clippings of Detroit or the one bad year in 1991. We continued to stress community involvement and each year the number of volunteers grew and grew.

The police department displayed a very professional and methodical approach for implementing a new trend in law enforcement that is here for the foreseeable future. Community policing should work in Camden. Most amazing was the ability to open a series of district stations and mini stations that served the public from within their neighborhoods. If residents knew the police were in it for the long haul, information on drug dealers and possible arsonists should roll in. I guess the most difficult task for the police chief was making sure Camden police had not gone soft on crime. Anyone involved with the different programs knew this was not the case. The reporters could only restate the occurrences from the worst year utilizing file film for their news broadcasts. My job was easy. Chief Pugh was ahead of his time, and we trusted him for his foresight and guidance.

Joe Richardson, Camden Police Lieutenant

—*Joseph Richardson, Captain, Camden Police Department*

It's important that a department committed to community policing keep all segments of the police department informed. This can often be a monumental task in itself. The constant commitment to training clearly demonstrates the department's determination to implement this change. The next undertaking involves a series of critical thinking-type seminars to further enhance community policing.

—*Louis DiRenzo, Camden Police Department*

I watched with a bit of caution the development of community policing. It seemed that, as the saying goes, "Where there is a will there is a way." Community policing provided the officers with a way if they had the will and cared. Many officers did not believe in the principles. It would take a lot of effort to convince those season veterans that community policing worked better than traditional policing. You would not be able to do away with reactive 911 calls, and police performance continued to be judged by how fast the officer arrived at the scene.

If the future chiefs did not remain entrenched to follow the overall mission, community policing was doomed to utter failure. The Mischief Night operation helped demonstrate that there was a place for community-based programs but not a cure-all for the replacement of traditional police responses. My career followed traditional lines. I saw the glimpse of pride in the eye of many police officers when a program yielded good results. The staff that sur-

Retired Detective Thomas Gorszynski, Camden Police Department

rounded Chief Pugh knew what they were doing. My concern, if any, will be with future generations of police officers who are expected to continue the excellent traditions of quality law enforcement already put in place.

—*Thomas Gorszynski, Detective, Retired, Planning and Development Unit*

I want to see community policing succeed. Its expensive because it takes more personnel to keep the various substations and mini stations manned. You cannot leave police radios and equipment exposed so in place of one 'house mouse,' as the officer who is assigned to desk duties is referred to, there may be four or more sitting in an office and unable to leave. Per shift per day, that's conservatively $125,000 in salaries wasted that are not on routine patrol. And when the officers are out because of injury, days off, or sickness the figure goes even higher. So there is a price to pay for being "closer to the community."

I've also found a lot of officers are confused about just what community policing is and what it is not. Many officers attempt to be assigned to community policing to "get out of work", so who really benefits? And costs . . . you need to multiply by four the cost of four copy machines, more phones, more repairs, more of everything is needed for every remote location you try to maintain. That's often overlooked. I never saw so many broken fax machines. And in the city, we process arrests centrally for controlled record keeping. So no time is saved by the substations. Getting the grass cut can turn into a major project.

Still, if the commitment is made, there seems to be a light at the end of the tunnel. But we will never be able to do away with answering the emergency 911 calls. We may, however, alleviate some of the nuisance calls so cops can get to where they are going much quicker. We'll see. I remain skeptical to some degree. No citizens expect a cop on every block. There are just not enough of these guys to go around.

—*Sergeant Raymond L. Garrison, Planning and Operations*

Others Talk about Camden

Camden has been very progressive with its efforts to implement the philosophy of community policing. As a neighboring municipality, we experienced improved interpersonal communications. As the program continued we participated in Mischief Night as well as award recognition programs. Both police departments utilized their already established Police Athletic Leagues to create a series of three-on-three basketball games. The interdepartment rivalry enhanced our relationships and built cohort-type

Lieutenant William Johnson

friendships that serve to eliminate a number of problems. Now we are looking for ways to share data through common computerized methods that permit a quick method for exchanging information. This would not have occurred if it was not for Chief Pugh's visions of cooperative networking.

—William Johnson, Police Lieutenant, Gloucester
City Police Department, New Jersey

I have watched with intensity the progress of Camden Police Department's implementation of community policing. They have organized a plan that demonstrated the propensity to succeed. The enthusiasm of the police administrators demonstrated clearly that community policing can work successfully if a systematic plan is put into place. CPD is a model of an open system for organizational management.

I had the opportunity to actually observe the various programs as part of a ride-along with the police chief in 1998. No matter what part of the city we traveled, the response was the same. Camden police and the community were trying to be partners against crime and the fear of crime.

—Gene Evans, Coordinator/Chair, Camden County
College, Blackwood, New Jersey:

Community policing seems to be a positive step. I was hoping to actually see more police riding and walking around but the old ways continued for quite a while. There were days on end when police were not to be found even with community policing programs. On other occasions police officers remained in my store for long periods (actually hours) and interfered with clerks and customers. The police department never seemed to be there when I needed them most, but managed to hide out all other times at the store too long.

The contacts did increase over time, and I became more involved in city government committees. That's when I began to understand the dynamics.

David Garrison, Merchant, Civic Leader

One-on-one contacts were most important. The community thing seems to work but I still have a constant fear that when I need a cop, they will not respond to my plea for help.

Through police classes and meetings I have learned to be more descriptive in my plea for help. Now, I can get a police officer at my store quicker than my neighboring businesses. In place of "I need a police officer" it has become "I need some help, the perpetrator is here now."

There needs to be more understanding. I was born and raised in the city. I have moved my residence here, and my place of business is here. I need to be involved.

My brother serves as a police sergeant and I have seen a distinct difference as time has gone by on tactics. The approach by the police is definitely changing.

But what happens if the police decide that there is a better method coming down the road and leave me and my business holding the community policing method alone? I fear that someday [the police] will return to a more reserved posture like earlier years.

—David Garrison, Camden City Merchant and Active Civic Leader

My business is located near the edge of Camden and we hardly ever see police officers patrolling the neighborhood. In fact, many officers don't even know that my block is part of Camden. We are broken into constantly. All in all, I see a little hope for progress. But I have volunteered too! I serve now as a special officer and I have trained dogs for search and rescue. So, in a way, I have more of an interest and knowledge of what's going on. But progress is slow. Being accepted by police officers is a long progress.

Training for specials has long lags. I ended up attending Gloucester County Police Academy for 26 weeks at night, losing business because Camden takes so long to put a class together. I guess it's because they were doing away with auxiliary police officers and the new duties were going to be different. Chief Pugh was great and Chief Hill too. I hope Chief Allenbach continues to help the specials and the businesses of Camden. I still feel that my store will be broken into at night but I am thankful for progress to date.

—Bruce Kanis, Owner, American Photo Transfer

SUMMARY

The chapter opened with a discussion about the focal point of Camden police's intervention for ten years which was referred to as Mischief Night. Camden's history and demographics were revealed along with a departmental profile. Their community policing philosophy was reviewed including their official decisions about decentralization and the outcomes that emerged from those decisions. The chiefs of police revealed their perspectives about policing and community policing. Mischief night's historical development, its impact, and the city's action including various outcomes were volunteered. Camden's plan for their problem oriented policing and partnership were clarified leading to a number of plans to resolve mischief night. Finally, a number of statements were presented by members of Camden's management team, officers, and community members.

CONCLUSION

Camden's plight can be summed with the idea that there were too many chiefs, too many officials, too much poverty, too much crime, too much officer and community resistance, and too little professional leadership. Camden worked hard towards a specific resolution seemingly ignoring all other issues. Police partnerships were linked with other justice agencies as opposed to community partnerships until the CPD realized that they must reach out to the community especially church leadership to bridge their inadequacies. They ignored the basic principles of what community policing is about—community participation which includes community decision making prerogatives. In Camden, their chiefs as directed by Camden's political power brokers made the decisions about police service including deployment, service priorities, promotions, disciplinary actions against officers, and community programs. Centralized authority has downfalls in the 21st century especially when officers and community members have little input with hands-on managers who are manipulated by politicians. How did Camden resolve the challenge of community policing? They didn't. Camden failed at those initiatives due largely to mistrust in police leadership by apparently everyone including police personnel, residents, and town hall. With that said, it is not clear that a community policing initiative is the best strategy for Camden. The hard working officers and residents of Camden clearly have other priorities that concern them that seemingly takes precedents over community policing strategies.

After ten years, their community policing strategy evolved into programs that are presently called POPP under the direction of the mayor as opposed to the police department. The focus of POPP's programs relates to providing alternative activities to children: Movie outings, skating activities, all-night parties at area schools cafeterias and pumpkin hunts. The department's role has returned to that of arrest, calls, and stops, but it is said that a CP oriented philosophy changed to an assisted role, helping the community accomplish their social goals through leadership of the office of the mayor and partnerships. It is unclear who those partnerships are with.

DO YOU KNOW?

1. The problems faced by Camden police officials were described as being influenced by city history, city demographics, and the reputation of the police. In what way might each of these components impact police strategies?

2. Elected officials, city managers, and police supervisors evaluated the productivity of an officer based on his or her number of response calls, response time, and arrest statistics. In what way might those measurements be inappropriate for the officers staffing the four new mini stations in Camden? How should their productivity be measured?

3. A critical decision was made concerning whether to implement community policing as a program and concentrate its efforts in one area or to adapt the philosophy of community policing city-wide and gradually decrease traditional programs. Which decision was made by police leadership in Camden and what was the outcome? Why would you make the same or a different decision?

4. Some decisions led patrol vehicles that often required repairs and the oldest two-way radios to be given to the community policing officers. Their steady tour of duty resulted in lost pay, and other officers felt that community officers worked "banking hours." How did this happen and how was it eventually resolved? What would you have done if you were in charge?

5. Some of Camden's difficulties in establishing police strategies were associated with a lack of managerial theory as practiced by private organizations. For instance, utilizing chief turnover as an example, demonstrate how this component influenced Camden's community policing implementation. Describe other examples.

6. Describe some of the early practices of the department in their attempts to control Mischief Night pranks. Given the limitations and unstable nature of police command in Camden, how would you have deployed your officers?

7. The combination of traditional policing methods and innovative programs with community involvement proved successful in resolving Mischief Night problems. Explain the strategies used by the department. What would you do differently if you were in charge?

8. One of the chiefs ordered his officers and asked officers from other agencies to wear Class A uniforms during Mischief Night altercations. What was his rationale? In what way do you agree or disagree with his perspective?

9. The Camden Police Department successfully demonstrated proactive policing designed for specific purpose. Those partnerships that were formed were partnerships between officers and other public personnel to solve a specific situation. Describe the partnership experiences referred to in this passage and explain in what way you agree or disagree with this conclusion.

10. In the comments made by community members, what indicators do you see suggesting that the trust relationship between the police department and the community members requires attention. How would you solve these issues?

CHAPTER ELEVEN

CONCLUSION

CHAPTER OUTLINE

This chapter begins by explaining the neglected areas of community policing, leading to some general impressions of the principal researcher. The question "Does community policing exist?" is answered, leading to components of community policing strategies and a recommendation concerning evaluation skills followed by a narrative concerning an operational definition grounded in nine common experiences of the agencies. Some cautions and general observations are reviewed prior to the closing statement.

NEGLECTED AREAS OF COMMUNITY POLICING

Within this study, it appeared that many groups were neglected by the community policing efforts and those areas might be targeted for future partnerships. They included specialty groups such as gangs, the elderly, the physically and mentally challenged, different culture groups, and non-English and/or limited English-speaking individuals. Clearly ignored groups were Spanish speaking residents and individuals from Asia.

For example, a refugee family is robbed at gunpoint, in their own neighborhood, by Asian gang members. They don't call the police for three reasons: fear of gang reprisals, language barriers, and a fear of the police (Powerful Partnerships, 1998). Unfortunately, there are many stories such as this one, and victim characteristics can be plugged in to match any of the individuals in the specialty groups just listed. For instance, one estimate is that 17 percent of the American population has a physical or mental disability and that one million people use wheelchairs. As police and specialized groups build communication and trust, the path to community policing partnerships can deliver quality police service to those individuals. Police agencies need to find ways to recruit those populations into community groups. Also in cities in this study with a large spanish presence such as Camden, Sacramento, and St. Petersburg, little grassroot outreach was made with individual culturally diverse populations.

IMPRESSIONS

With that said, it must be acknowledged that as the principal researcher waded through the data and considered his interactions with commanders, line officers, trainers, supporting agencies, local leadership, and community members, a general impression was developed that included the following concepts about community policing:

- It is time consuming.
- It is suspicious.
- It is a lot of rhetoric filled with political promises that are not expected to be kept.
- It leads to uncertainty about policies, regulations, objectives, and required input.
- Yet, general optimism about its potential exists.
- Many police officials and officers want it to work.

DOES COMMUNITY POLICING EXIST?

It has been advanced by some writers that there is an important distinction between the self-image of the police and their day-to-day reality of routine policing (Goldstein, 1987; Walker, 1984). The emphasis on crime control is and has been largely a matter of what the police say they are doing about crime, argues Walker. Those writers might imply that the police also manipulate community policing efforts in order to advance professional and political autonomy (Dantzker, 2000; Manning, 1997; Walker, 1984). The police, and rightfully so, have their critics some of whom suggest that an officer's authority is affected by a host of regulations of which civil statutes are one variety (McNamara, 1967; Stevens, 1999b, 1999g, 2000). And, even before the implementation of the due process revolution, punishment-centered police bureaucracies encouraged a lay-low-and-avoid-trouble mentality (Van Maanen, 1974). Therefore, it comes as no surprise that large polls report that a vast number of Americans have a low opinion of decisions made by the police (Bureau of Justice Statistics [BJS], 1999). Even when an agency engages in a justified critical response, community members reject that deployment and imply the police are reckless (Stevens, 1999a, 1999e, 1999f). Yet, the American public has a litigious nature and has brought civil suits against officers in record numbers, often influencing day-to-day, serve-and-protect decisions compounding occupational stress (Stevens, 1998e, 1999a, 2000). Yet, the BJS (1999) reports that we are more likely to be a victim of a violent crime today then at any other time in American history. So, regardless of how some individuals theoretically perceive the reliability of police self-imagery, in the real world, when someone is breaking into your home late at night, do you know who to call for help? Fact is, middle class America relies on police integrity to protect us and to defend our democratic existence.

However, it is in our best interest to acknowledge the reality that some law-abiding individuals see violence as an appropriate response due to lack of police protection, then it should also be clear that law enforcement, the threat of incarceration, and/or the threat of capital punishment are not deterrents of criminal activities for chronic offenders (Stevens, 1992a, 1992b, 1998c, 1999f). Even in domestic violence and aggravated assault situations, where evidence suggests that an arrest be mandated, many officers are reluctant to conduct such an arrest (Stevens, 1998b, 1998c). Their biggest reason: the courts protect criminals more than law abiding citizens. Last, after chronic officers are incarcerated, the gangs, drug trafficking, crimes, and violence continue (Stevens, 1997b, 1997c, 1997d). In fact, prison time for both male and female offenders seems to enhance the desire of offenders to commit greater crimes of violence than they had prior to their last conviction (Stevens, 1994, 1998a). Thus, to control chronic offenders, our justice system needs to change with the times.

Others advance the thought that community policing itself is a "pipedream"—more rhetoric or inflated promises than reality (Albritton, 1999; Riechers & Roberg, 1990). Those writers imply that community policing might be just barely realized until there are major changes within the organizational structure, management style, and personnel. Furthermore, even with those organizational changes, community policing might never become a reality, they argue. Therefore, one central question asked in this study about community policing is whether it is rhetoric or reality. The evidence from the nine agencies in this study gives one answer—yes, community policing exists. Is it needed to help control crime? Again, it appears from the surveys conducted by several of the agencies including Broken Arrow, Columbus, Fayetteville, Lansing, Sacramento, and St. Petersburg that community policing made a difference. Community members reported that crime was down, they felt safer, and they felt optimistic about the future because of the community policing efforts. Even in Camden where community policing failed, of the community members responding to this study, there was a feeling that they felt safer and that crime could be controlled.

This thought finds congruence with other writers who show, through an empirical study in West Palm Beach, Florida, some positive findings about citizens' perceptions of crime and police work through community policing efforts (Liou & Savage, 1999). Specifically, some respondents in their study felt crime was decreasing and others felt police work was improving. The positive perceptions of community policing are also evidenced in the analysis of citizens' perception of their neighborhood improvement and their relationship with police.

Yet, community policing is operationalized differently in each agency, as is to be expected since no one model is compatible with every department and community relationship.

However, major changes are not necessarily required prior to implementation since each agency is unique unto itself and each begins the community policing implementation process at a different starting point. Nonetheless, commonalities exist among the agencies that can be documented and measured. That common tread running through the agencies in this study largely consists, to varying degrees, of five components:

- Philosophy,
- Empowerment,

- Partnerships,
- Proactive solutions, and
- Evaluations.

Philosophy relates to the department-wide fundamental principle of an agency to conduct police business primarily as a proactive, preventive agency through community partnerships as opposed to a reactive, incident-driven agency.[1] Empowerment refers to authority within an organizational structure that is flattened. That is, the means including schedules, training, and responsibilities to solve community problems is vested in the lower ranks. Commanders take the role of facilitators who support those lower ranks and must strive to become a professional leader commanding through values instead of dictates. Partnerships are established to solve community problems between police and community members, businesses, and/or private and public agencies. Partnerships include recruiting, maintenance of those partnerships, and decision-making prerogatives of community members. Proactive solutions are products of those partnerships that are arrived at through identification, analysis (collect and consider information), recommendations, prioritization (rank order), and response (implement solutions).[2] Evaluation refers to objective standardized methods of assessing solution results, partnerships, empowerment issues, and philosophy compliance.

Therefore, agencies that can document all five components, to varying degrees, carried on business through a community policing design. Of the nine agencies, the ones that could not document community policing designs were Nashville and Camden. However, there were many agencies in the initial collecting stage of this work that reported having a community policing strategy in place at their agency. But, upon investigation, little evidence supported their claims (see Chapter 1, Appendix 2). However, there is the thought that a community policing philosophy may not be in the best interests of every agency due to a host of reasons some of which include their inability to implement it efficiently.

POLICE THEORY

If community policing is grounded in a normative sponsorship theory as advanced by Trojanowicz, it can mean that as various groups share common values, beliefs, and goals, the more likely it is that they will agree on common goals when they interact together for the purpose of improving their neighborhoods. There are two problems with this idea. First, the community does not always come together to solve neighborhood problems. Sometimes community members have other agendas and sometimes their agenda is a specific community problem. Other times they might have culturally diverse ideas about public order. Nonetheless, once their objectives are met, their participation dwindles. Second, the other concern relates to community contact by the

---

[1]Community policing isn't limited to a single squad or a specific section of the city.
[2]SARA is an excellent process. One technique added to that process is prioritizing the problems to be solved. (Scan, analyze, prioritize, respond, and assess—SAPRA.)

police, which may be for the sake of community contact, rather than a means to solve specific community problems. This thought is consistent with community policing officers who have been given the task of contacting the community for the sole purpose of contacting them (Tyson, 1997). Many police agencies are ineffective because they suffer from the "means over ends" syndrome, Tyson says. That is, they have been too concerned with the means of responding to citizen complaints and not concerned enough with the ends, which are the problems that lead to citizen complaints in the first place.

However, some of the most serious problems in understanding how far a community policing strategy has advanced is in political neutrality and a lack of expertise in measuring police performance. Political candor is beyond the scope of this text and as one can guess, a book in itself. But a strong recommendation that emerged from the findings of this study is that agencies require personnel who have mastered the craft of measuring police performance or hire out, if for no other reason than to support and validate outcomes of strategies such as community policing.[3]

In an attempt to add to the growing body of knowledge about community policing, and to test the predictive utility of this perspective as a philosophy, nine departments were examined. However, relying on an appropriate process to aid in this examination, largely only documented material (with an exception of the comments from the chiefs and/or principal contributors) was accepted as opposed to opinion. Herein is one advantage of sound evaluation strategies versus opinion and/or experience. Reliable evaluation contains methodological designs that can often produce dependable predictions while providing a body of knowledge that enlightens policy makers, hence, leading to informed decisions.

It can be argued that appropriate documentation is a breath closer to truth (than mere guesses or gut feelings) since the likelihood is greater through research to advance other evaluations and/or theories which could propose collaborative predictive values. Guesses, although often wrapped in experience, which of late have been referred to as a form of profiling, is what places many agencies and/or their personnel into harm's way. It is important to note, however, that while experience is a vital asset, once it is linked with sound evaluation skills, the prospect for success is greater. Evaluation can complement practical experience in many ways. However, evaluation skills without experience can give rise to spuriousness, invalid findings, and unreliable and in some cases unlawful recommendations. Evaluation in the public sector, particularly justice agency research, is far different than evaluation in the private sector recognizing litigation potential and, of more importance, issues of public trust.

Recalling many of the pains experienced by the agencies and their community members in this study, one issue is certain. If they had personnel with sound evaluation skills, the path to success would have been more certain and they would have known where they were when they arrived there. In addition, they could have supported their position or achievements more accurately

---

[3]CYA - Cover Your Ass!

(much to the satisfaction of advocates and opponents). Therefore, the strongest recommendation flowing from those findings is that police agencies should obtain the expertise of a trusted evaluator in order to have alternative recommendations that might bring them closer to the values of a democratic society without compromising public safety.

Of interest, without exception, each of the agencies in this study has major research universities in their backyards, many of which are leaders in community policing research. Many of the agencies solicited research help—or did they?[4] However, regardless of the answer, measuring public agencies should be conducted by an experienced evaluator.

AN OPERATIONAL DEFINITION: NINE EXPERIENCES

Since the work in this study examined and documented police activities of departments using community policing strategies, then the common elements used by those agencies can help shape a working definition of community policing. However, an operational definition was not initially developed but rather allowed to emerge from the data themselves. In this sense, it could be said that a grounded theory of discovery was used to help better understand the principles of community policing from the perspective of the agencies themselves rather than from a theoretical perspective (Glasser & Strauss, 1967).[5]

These components in this study were chosen because the police agencies collectively felt that they were important experiences for their agency. Ranking these components in their order of importance was not a primary goal for the agencies or for this work. These issues are consistent with the literature suggesting their significance to community policing strategies (Police Executive Research Forum, 1996; Skogan, et al., 1999; Wilson & Kelling, 1982). Because one goal of this work is to examine community policing through the experiences of American police departments, this interpretation can give rise to an operational definition. Yet, as expected, each agency had its own ideas about the elements and working strategy of each item in each category.

One perspective that has emerged in this work and confirmed in most of the literature is that there is a perfect community policing model compatible with every agency does not exist. Every jurisdiction is unique because of its own history, demographics, cultural and economic mix, region, tax base, management, civic leadership, public perception, and numerous other nuances. What worked well in one agency or in one neighborhood might not work as well in a similar agency or in another neighborhood even in the same city. With that said, it might prove helpful to review the perceptions of the agencies collectively to help draft, along with police experiences and the experiences of the community, a working definition toward community policing.

For the purpose of this exercise, all the data from the nine agencies were pooled. Agency names and other characteristics that could identify a police

---

[4]It was reported that Trojanowicz lent positive leadership in Lansing.

[5]For a closer look at how theory can emerge from the data rather than the other way around, see Stevens (1999e).

agency were deleted. From that huge pool of data, the writer asked four of the contributors to put the data into two categories based on whether they thought it was experienced and/or worked more often or it was less experienced and/or worked less often by police agencies moving toward a community policing initiative. The data from the contributors own department was not part of the data they individually reviewed. The next step in this process was to put the data (experienced/worked more often and experienced/worked less often) into a matrix consisting of nine task components:

- events motivating community policing agendas
- training
- measuring community policing performance
- organizational change
- philosophy
- recruiting community members
- maintaining community support
- decision-making community prerogatives, and
- changing community programs

What follows is hardly an exhaustive list, nor is this list intended to imply that if an item is missing that it is not worth pursuing or conversely, if an item is on the list that it must become part of every agency's community policing strategy. Caution is advised because these items are presented only to show how they fit within the framework of the agencies in this study. Additionally, the items are in no way intended to suggest that they are the best or the worst methods of conducting police business or operating community policing prerogatives. What the writer intended to do was to create a working study that provides a dialogue into the world of policing and community partnerships grounded in the agencies studied. This work should not be considered a final or an approved version of community policing strategies by any of the agencies in this study. Lastly, the writer edited the findings to fit within the framework of these pages and to keep the identity of the agencies confidential.

Task 1: Events Motivating Community Policing Strategies

Experienced/Worked More Often: Sometimes a specific or several city council officials promoted the hiring of a new chief who had community policing experience because city officials initially tried to establish community forums that provided information regarding what type of police service (and police department) the residents should have, but ultimately realized that they knew little about policing and less about community police agendas. Their motivation to establish community forums was probably centered in votes, power, and the well-being of the public they served. But they also learned that the community forum process was time consuming and stressful and eventually wanted someone with community experience to lead that endeavor. Therefore, what was experienced more often by police agencies that succeeded in building a foundation in community policing strategies was linked to the installation of a new police chief who provided the greatest stimulus toward a community policing philosophy. A variety of current events also pushed police agencies into community policing solutions such as riots, a catastrophic event (happening once or once a year), and/or an opportunity that had little to do with controlling crime and more to do with someone's personal agenda. Whatever propelled an agency toward community policing was of less significance than compared to a police agency's response including the serious efforts of line officers and community members some of whom followed policy mandates and others who resisted it. For example, crack cocaine hit a particular public housing complex in the mid 1980's which was already plagued with drugs, violence, and crime promoted intense police intervention. Some of the residents of the public complex cried out for help and police management responded with a community policing solution (or so officers and community members thought). The program was called "Thomas Park Patrol" (after the name of the complex), and a dedicated group of officers were tasked with working with residents to rebuild their trust in police policy (which often changed), to identify community problems (which were clouded with a lack of trust and respect for the police), and to work in partnership toward resolving those problems (most of those officers had little training or incentives to change their concepts about public housing). Yet, there was suspicion on the part of some community members that the Thomas Park Patrol was a rouge to make more arrests and on the other hand, a suspicion on the part of some officers that the department was getting soft on crime. Through sincere interaction on everyone's part, bridges were built over some of those gaps of distrust.

Experienced/Worked Less Often: Events that led to a less efficient community policing initiative were centered in the priorities of some or several city officials. That is, unlike the above scenario where officials encouraged police management leading to community policing activities, some departments experienced continual involvement on the part of city officials in police matters whose conduct demonstrated a lack of concern for the welfare of the department (which might well be an appropriate position for officials assuming their priorities are their constituents). However, alienation flowed from the relationship between city hall and the police department because of those political priorities (or at least that's the perception of many commanders). Then, too, some of those officials and inexperienced police leaders supported programs which were standardized items pulled from a shelf much like prepackaged goods in a store, rather than tailored to the specific audience or specific problem. Lastly, what also worked lest toward building a sound community policing initiative was programs used only in high crime neighborhoods since those programs became social class specific and used less often in neighborhoods that reported less crime. Those more crime communities felt singled out for more police intervention. And there were feelings from less crime community areas that they were abandoned but paying for the intervention in other communities.

Task 2: Training

Experienced/Worked More Often: One strategy that seemed to work to the advantage of a police agency that tried to advance community policing initiatives was to train officers, supervisors, and commanders before the execution of a community policing strategy. Prior to community policing initiatives, most police training focused on firearms qualifications and shooting scenarios. Those training programs were balanced by providing a variety of required and elective training courses to the officers. Officers and community members were encouraged to seek outside training (by qualified instructors and institutions) too, and were provided with resources to do so.

Also, agencies provided free community policing training to law enforcement officers, community residents, city employees, social service agencies, and private sector representatives. The core courses consisted of community policing prerogatives, problem solving, SARA, and police-community partnerships. Training initially consisted of a forty-hour community policing school and a forty-hour multicultural diversity course, sponsored by the department.

The focus for educational programs changed from an internal in-service approach to educating agency personnel to an external outward focus on educating and reaching the community with information that was designed to prepare them to handle day-to-day threats to their personal welfare and standards of living. Weekly cable television shows written, produced (sometimes with the aid of business contributions), and directed by a police agency and community groups became commonplace and distance learning programs helped further quality of life issues that led to law-abiding behavior.

Experienced/Worked Less Often:

- Student specific community policing training.
- Police academy community policing certification programs (since all models must be different to accommodate departmental and community nuances and links).

Task 3: Measuring Community Policing Performance

Experienced/Worked More Often: Those agencies that were serious about establishing community policing initiatives measured community policing performance primarily by two factors: first, citizen perception of the quality of police services as they related to addressing their crime and safety concerns; second, the extent to which officers embraced and practiced the tenets of community policing and problem-solving. Departments tracked problem-solving initiatives, complaints for rudeness/inappropriate conduct, and performed regular performance evaluations on their officers to determine their level of activity, community involvement, and the attitudes they exhibited to the public. Primarily, community feedback and response to various programs was centered in surveys conducted by volunteers, consultants, police personnel, and via email from Internet web sites.

Police managers attended a large number of community meetings and community forums. Additionally, line officers and managers attentively listened to community members at those meetings, and discussed what they heard with community members enrolled at citizen police academies and training courses, and those who attended civic meetings such as the local chamber of commerce meeting. Largely, attentive listening skills and clarification of what they heard helped toward a stronger customer service approach consistent with resident safety and quality of life issues.

Another method of evaluation was when other organizations in the community emulated an agency's effort. For example, one police agency had a local crime stopper program that was operated by a crime stopper council. As that program gained success, other organizations such as the local community college started their own crime stopper program and asked for assistance from the council. Finally, opening an agency to outside evaluation of their philosophy and their community policing efforts was the most helpful tool available for a department especially if a department had less support from civic leaders than desired. Once an evaluation was completed, civic leaders seemed to support the agency with more energy than before the evaluation regardless of the results of the assessment.

Experienced/Worked Less Often: An agency that lacked an assessment component went through the initial motions of establishing a community policing initiative, but it seemed that their planing, implementation, and execution of community policing practices lacked an output similar to police agencies that exercised assessment of police performance. Part of that output related to the ability of the agency to make changes among their personnel and their community members. Furthermore, those agencies continued to measure, revere, and publicize arrest rates, response time, service call assistance, and dollar amounts of confiscated property and contraband. The problem that arose with that method of measurement glorified an account, as an example, of when a police agency closed one crack house and arrested one crack dealer and informed everyone that the entire block was impacted. But it had not impacted the entire community as a whole. (Yet, if the people living on the block were encouraged to continue their participation with the police, and their message was spread to other blocks within the community). Lastly, those agencies that became careless with the identities of successful citizens involved with community programs such as a Citizen Police Advisory Council were targeted by politicians who turned those councils into election committees.

Task 4: Organizational Change

Experienced/Worked More Often: Prior to a national interest in community policing strategies, many police executives instituted organizational change to meet policing challenges. One organizational change made by many executives was to primarily decentralize their patrol division through mini stations or districts throughout the jurisdiction. Command, too, was decentralized at the mini-station level enhancing police service. As community policing initiatives were considered by executives, the utility of mini-stations appeared to be an efficient level for problem-solving strategies especially since most of officers involved with community policing were from the ranks of the patrol officers. Many of those mini-stations or precincts had a gym and meeting rooms for citizen meetings, and provided them free of charge for community events including community policing initiatives. It was at that level, through the office of the chief, that information about organizational changes and community policing potentials was disseminated and input encouraged. That two way communication effort was an important link to gathering information and personnel compliance. Community policing functions were adopted more smoothly than anticipated at the precinct level, and for those agencies that had not decentralized, community policing endeavors offered an excellent opportunity to do so.

Furthermore, some of the police agencies that had city hall support were encouraged by city officials including mayors. For instance, in one progressive city where the police department had planned a community policing initiative, the mayor encouraged the department through the statement of : "Decentralization of the police department is not being done as an end in itself; it is being done to help foster open and honest communication between the police officers and the citizens they serve. This open communication leads to the identification and solving of problems which in turn makes our city a better place to live and work."

To more effectively operate a decentralized agency while accommodating a drain of manpower to successfully initiate a community policing strategy, police executives of some agencies developed and implemented an alternate response policy for handling routine police calls for service, including a no-report system, offense report officer program (light-duty officers who handle calls for service over the telephone), and limited accident investigations to those involving injury/criminal charges/government vehicles and so on. This alternate response policy enabled a large number of officers to be unplugged from patrol and reassigned to community policing details.

Crime investigation units were also decentralized in some of the commands and often answered to the same captain who also commanded patrol and property crime investigators for that district. The property investigators worked on randomly assigned cases and on areas and problems with the goal of preventing as well as anticipating future trends. However, some investigative functions remained centralized such as juvenile and narcotics. In time it was hoped that staffing levels would allow an agency to further decentralize all centralized functions since this perspective is computable with and required of a community policing philosophy.

Experienced/Worked Less Often: Strategies that seemed to work less often in the best interests of implementation of community policing endeavors were those agencies that had not decentralized and where their executives had not instructed agency personnel about a department-wide reorganization. Those executives had not asked for input from personnel. One guess might be that those executives possessed unprofessional managerial skills, and/or they were primarily a hands-on-manager, and/or city hall had not given those executives permission to move forward on community policing issues. It's odd that when these agencies eventually decentralized, their quasi-military chain of command stayed intact with little room for change among the hierarchy. Another outcome that seemed to mirror those agencies was that their mini-stations were located largely in strip malls or in out-of-the-way centers whereby citizens who volunteered to staff them were never clear what they had to do there or who was in charge.

Task 5: Philosophy

Experienced/Worked More Often: Those police agencies that established community policing prerogatives with a sense of integrity developed and implemented a community policing philosophy more often than other agencies who simply established a program and referred to it as a community police program. One community policing plan to follow started with the approval of policy makers to change the organizational structure and other police agencies to better understand their options. At the same time, police managers reached out to the personnel and to the community to get their input about the changes. Managers linked personnel and community input to a plan to change agency mission, philosophy, and expectations that was best performed after researching the available information on community policing across the country. A model of the developed plan was discussed among personnel and community members alike. Most community policing initiatives were piloted in a specific section of the city and/or were designed to deal with a specific problem. Few officials thought that it would or should become city-wide/department-wide until they reviewed the results, which were often slow in coming, producing impatience and frustration for all concerned (but both outcomes were anticipated as a result of an appropriate literature search).

Optimally, community policing was described as community members, social and public agencies, business and civic leaders working within an association to mutually identify problems or issues, prioritizing those problems, developing a response or strategy toward resolving those problems, and finally, resolving those problems that lead to crime which ultimately influence quality of life issues for residents who lived in the area and for workers.

For example, living conditions, relationship expectations, and pure selfishness can lead to crimes of domestic violence. As domestic violence became an issue through partnership disclosures and confirmation through police records, it became a priority for the community, strategies were recommended, police action taken. In collaboration with local domestic violence services, the police agency developed and received a grant to fund domestic violence councilors and volunteers to accompany police officers in domestic violence calls.

Arrest became a secondary priority to professional intervention which helped bridge the gap between family violence and deterrence.

Experienced/Worked Less Often:

- Police programs as shown on a departmental brochure lacked a method of contacting an individual officer or community member connected with those programs.
- Community committee meetings that met at some indecisive site to accomplish some undisclosed list of objectives, and/or met to largely bash police performance.
- City officials and community leaders who held a vendetta with the police.
- Other committee meetings where members were primarily informed about the limitations and problems of the department.
- The community member proposals were usually related to the programs in place and not to the problems of the community.

Task 6: Recruiting Community Members

Experienced/Worked More Often: What worked most often in an effective drive to recruit community members was for police management and community trained officers to persuade civic leaders from churches, business, and public entities (i.e., schools, social services, neighborhood organizations) to become organizers in an effort to recruit local residents and local workers who frequented their establishments to conduct a block-by-block effort to increase membership. City organizational directors were called upon to help recruit citizens through the news media, fliers in water bills, and brochures in tax bills. Civic leaders, organizational directors, and their recruits were asked to establish meetings times, bylaws (including election process and methods of change) and responsibilities, and to elect their leaders from the ranks of the recruits. Establishing group rules or standards that governed the behavior and expectations of the community member leaders and its members was a vital link to the success of the community group. Also, understanding the limits of the community group's power, their authority and their relationship with the police, and their responsibilities were key components of successful community groups. Those limits, authority, and responsibilities meant more to their sense of ownership and investment especially when explained initially by the top police executives such as the chief of police or district commanders and reinforced during the life cycle of the group. The next task was to survey neighborhoods to identify problems, prioritize them, recommend solutions, and in concert with the police, establish a game plan to act on those recommendations. Of course, positive, realistic action was at the core of all serious community movements, and its process was collaborative and consensual. Both short-term and long-term objectives had to be prioritized, and community meeting participates had to recognize that both time and patience were required to accomplish those objectives. That is, they had to make a commitment to a sustained effort. Police agencies provided training of group trainers who in turn trained other community members. The agencies and the community members solicited commercial support from businesses to fund operation such as the Citizens on Patrol program and Mentor Youth Programs. Qualified officers who participated in school safety committees, school based partnership problem solving projects including the instruction of life skill courses at schools, churches, and committee meetings provided strong partnerships with the community. (Note: one observation of all the agencies examined was that all of them relied on only sworn officers to advance community policing strategies. Nothing says that community policing efforts must be in the hands of only sworn officers.) Measuring community policing efforts were a continual activity of community policing endeavors and results were publicly explained for best results.

Experienced/Worked Less Often: Misconceptions held by police leadership about the community member recruitment process decreased the potential of an agency to establish a progressive community policing initiative. For some reason that may have sounded logical at the time, a few agencies recruited community members from a sampling of 911 callers and victims of crime lists. This tactic produced a "big brother" effect resulting in the loss of any trust that had been established between the community and the police prior to the call to recruit them. Also, some agencies thought that if they informed community members of crime trends and policing projects through news releases that no other action was necessary. Unfortunately, those agencies failed to realize that many individuals don't read newspapers and that those who do are often specific-section readers indicating that "crime columns" might not be part of their reading agenda. Furthermore, agencies that encouraged patrol officers to build relationships with justice agencies, organizations, businesses, and citizens of the community frankly were not within their job descriptions nor were they trained or paid for such tasks. The agencies that were under the impression that those relationships placed the burden of solving neighborhood problems equally among all involved parties were mistaken since many officers resisted going outside their job descriptions and expectations in the first place. Police executives who held the perspective that problem-solving just happened by bringing community members and police officers together were usually surprised. Problem-solving does not happen by chance. Furthermore, managing environmental issues such as trash and abandoned car removal was not necessarily seen as a demonstration to the typical resident in poorer neighborhoods that the police agency was in earnest about quality of life issues especially if those community members were afraid to venture outside their homes. Partnerships that depended on police action to solve problems were positioned to failure since a community partnership meant that the community too held a responsibility to help in solving problems and compliance with laws and group regulation (it was reported in some districts that community member leaders demonstrated criminal activity thinking they were above the law). Individuals in citizen groups often stayed involved as long as they felt threatened and needed the police to solve a particular problem. Once that specific problem was solved, their participation dwindled. Politicians utilized committee groups and community policing equipment as devices to enhance their voting records or to turn public opinion.

Task 7: Maintaining Community Support

Experienced/Worked More Often: What worked most often in police agencies that took community policing seriously consisted among other things of maintaining community support. One of the best methods of continuing community support was to institutionalize the problem-solving process in all facets of the agency and in the community. In this sense, institutionalization or what can be described as making the problem-solving process a standard procedure, and the officers and community members routinely utilized those processes. The officers and community members put those procedures to practical use, and realized the fruits of their efforts. Successful community meetings were those attended by individuals (officers and residents) who perceived the police as unlimited in their problem-solving abilities and saw their own role in the community organization as that of influencing the decision-making process. Leadership rotated to each committee member over an agreed on time table.

Opportunities for problem-solving and community maintenance for the agency and/or the community organizations was also obtained from political support from the city manager/mayor, other city departments, city council members, public organizations such as welfare and social work agencies. Police agencies and/or community organizations that solicited city hall and other departmental and organizational help generally experienced great returns. The rationale accepted by police and community organizations that show positive results understood that the police was not the answer to crime alone. Crime was a community issue. Problem-solving was accomplished through city departments such as inspections, zoning, garbage, public works, and so on. When city officials or other department heads demonstrated cooperation with problem-solving efforts, residents experienced fewer problems and felt a sense of ownership in the community.

Also, citizens who used mobile substations to communicate with officers and supervisors instead of having to visit the station downtown felt a greater sense of ownership with their community. They learned the names of the officers, their pager numbers, and received photos of them as if they were baseball cards. Mobile substations visited schools, churches, and shopping centers as part of permanent assignment. Officers regularly made contact with local businesses in their beats to ensure regular communication and to obtain emergency contact information for local merchants.

Experienced/Worked Less Often: The fastest way agencies in this study lost community support was when the agency took the position that police matters were under the secrecy of police who held a "professional autonomy."

Task 8: Decision-Making Community Prerogatives

Experienced/Worked More Often: Agencies that made a serious attempt to implement community policing initiatives empowered community groups (and line officers) with decision-making prerogatives. City administration, schools, businesses, religion, and neighborhood citizen committees elected (in two cases were appointed) representatives to sit on police committees and/or boards such as cadet advisory boards and police disciplinary boards. These positions were not as mere observers but as active voting members. These representatives had input in such areas as where a police cadet was assigned in the police organization, reviewed cadet performance, assignments, and in some cases reviewed dossiers of the training officers who familiarized those newly sworn officers with the streets. In addition, they had input at police disciplinary committees after an internal affairs investigation and such committees as a board of police commissioners, which reviewed new policies, procedures, budget, deployment, and promotional processes. And one police agency actually performed police service through the means of a contract with the representatives of a community. Community members made most of the decisions about deployment and service priorities. The agencies that allowed community decision-making influences rationalized that in a democratic society it was expected that the community had the biggest hand in those processes, and that police executives held the task of that of a facilitator leading community members (and line officers) to appropriate and legal decisions.

Experienced/Worked Less Often: In agencies where decision-making processes and ultimately community policing initiatives were more rhetoric than reality, community members were told what the problems were in the people themselves and what problems would be solved by the police and what problems the community had to solve. The police agency used the community meeting to explain police policy and the law. Community Watch Patrols were examples of programs operated to empower the police not the community since it operated on incident driven agenda. Community members became watch dogs of crime and when a crime happened, they called police dispatch. When that program was one of the few programs in the community, there was question by community members about its integrity concerning proactive prevention measures.

Task 9: Changing Community Programs

Experienced/Worked More Often: The majority of changes in community policing programs involved growth. As the police department structure grew and changed, the department had additional resources (many did not) to utilize for additional community policing programs. Since the inception of the community policing philosophy in the U.S., most agencies implemented a number of programs and assignments directly for the community in an effort to provide additional exposure and networking with the public. Agencies kept up with change and many utilized measuring methods of police performance to aid them in implementation of those changes.

Occasionally, there was an opposite position. For example, when one agency in this study deemphasized their Citizens on Patrol program for a while due to a group of citizens who were in conflict with a resident in their neighborhood, mediation suggested that this was an isolated incident and the program was resumed. The largest change in the way departments had performed as a whole was that they became public in their orientation and many of them strived to solve the problems they were faced with rather than trying to remedy the particular situation (and make it go away. For instance, the answer one agency had to prevent juvenile crime was "to wait." That is to wait until the juvenile offender was old enough to become an adult). Furthermore, agencies became more aware of resources such as grants through community policing initiatives, and there was a push toward obtaining funding to further police services in their communities.

An example of a specific program change included the experiences of one agency that noticed their juvenile crime levels and drug crime levels in particular were not decreasing, but were in fact increasing. The agency came to the conclusion that some of their most problematical juveniles were well known to the agency or came from dysfunctional families. Therefore, the chief made a very controversial decision to replace DARE programs in the schools with the Family Intervention Team (FIT), a program he hoped would make more of a long-term impact on the community. The success of FIT required proving a negative reaction. That is, the children the agency focused on do nothing that would show up as a statistic. Because of the age of the clients at the time of agency intervention, measurement would not come quickly. Accordingly, it might be said that a change from a traditional perspective of law enforcement to a proactive perspective takes a long time.

Experienced/Worked Less Often: Of those agencies that changed community policing programs, those that had difficulty in succeeding were the ones that demonstrated a weakness of balance. That is, those agencies focused on the short term objective usually linked to traditional perspectives such as high visibility patrols. Some agencies looked primarily at long term objectives creating anxiety for community members since they, police executives, and police policy makers became impatient with too few results to show that progress was met. Short term objectives and long term objectives were balanced in the serious agencies.

GENERAL OBSERVATIONS

The new police chief in Broken Arrow brought independently operated programs in the city such as Citizens on Patrol and Seniors and Lawmen under centralized control, thereby bringing a city-wide perspective to police services of the agency. Another result produced by her decisions was that fewer individuals opposed her community policing initiatives as contrasted with Camden and to a lesser extent St. Petersburg, where the chiefs were constantly negatively bombarded by departmental members and outsiders producing an inability to unify the department to advance, oddly enough, to a decentralized departmental strategy. Each agency in this study reported manpower shortages, budgetary restrictions, and increases in calls for service and accountability. But only one agency designed a method to add more officers, a larger budget, advanced technological methods to handle calls for service resulting in fewer demands for departmental accountability through police service contracts with new housing neighborhoods—Precinct 4 in Harris County. Maybe there are some lessons there for everyone? Public agencies competing for private contracts.

Nonetheless, departmental burdens visited on each agency by resistant personnel and unyielding civic and community leaders seemed to be experienced by all of the agencies in this study to some degree or another, producing a harder task for police leaders trying to implement new initiatives. However, those burdens were more disasters and in some cases continue to plague the police departments in Camden, Fayetteville, Nashville, and St. Petersburg. It is despairingly doubtful that Camden and Nashville will reach St. Petersburg and Fayetteville's level of quality police service in the near future. One reason fostering that belief is that the officers in St. Petersburg and Fayetteville demonstrate more compliance with change than Camden and Nashville officers as evidenced by police disciplinary accounts.

One reason for those differences in officer resistance could relate to the idea that St. Petersburg and Fayetteville officers are disciplined for minor infractions less often than officers in Nashville and Camden. In fact, there appears to be a link between the treatment of officers by police executives and their resistance levels to change. Research should be conducted to determine if there are any strong links between police policy concerning officer treatment and their resistance levels to change and/or new strategies or regulations. Disciplinary reports in Camden are too vague to make any decisions.[6]

---

[6]Oddly enough support for this perspective comes from inmate populations. That is, when comparing similar level prisons containing similar level offenders, prisons that reported the fewest restrictions had fewer disciplinary problems. Inmates who had been subjected to less volatile prison environments indicated further that they were less likely to reoffend on release. Strict enforcement of custody rules caused more disciplinary problems than it resolved. Also, more authoritative supervision produced more disciplinary actions than a less supervised close inmate–custodian environment. In a sense, violence begets violence, and more supervision with problem populations translated to more, not less, disciplinary activity. See Stevens (1997c, 1997d) for more details. Last, do not read between the lines, since there is no intent in my thoughts that officers should be exempt from laws, but I might suggest that they should be subjected to similar laws as other individuals in similar jobs. When one group of individuals or in this case, workers are differentiated on the basis of their employer, do serious questions arise and do some of those questions include sound managerial practice?

Furthermore, Nashville, St. Petersburg, and Camden reported a huge lack of both trust and support by the community and civic leaders, but that lack of trust by some members of the community was also documented in Fayetteville and Columbus, and it surfaced in Lansing too. Yet, Fayetteville, Columbia, and Lansing were able to isolate (sometimes) that lack of trust and advance a new police strategy that changed or is changing the way they conduct police business. But it became evident that the agencies were conducting business differently among community groups, too. That is, with some community groups there were a lot of hands-on relationships with community members; with other groups, the community policing officers met with group members individually in addition to group meetings. In Camden, for example, the religious leaders met with police alone and in small groups. That technique seemed to work well for the Camden PD relative to their specific event problem-solving task. While other departments made little distinction between group techniques, there appears nonetheless to be something to the idea of group techniques that might bring a community policing initiative closer to its objectives. Therefore, despite Camden's being slowest to adapt a community policing prerogative, learning from their approach is helpful.

Continuing along that line of reasoning, maybe Camden's belief that it takes two to three decades to change a traditionally centered department to a community-centered department has merit. After all, most chiefs stay less time in their jobs than the required transitional time necessary, and that's when things get out of control. Yet, even those departments who claimed fewer "uprisings" from officer resistance and civic and community leader interference during a transitional period had their problems, such as Columbus. That is, when Columbus was experiencing a transition, they were not "officially" aware that change wouldn't happen over night. Everyone concerned with community policing initiatives in Columbus became frustrated and angered that the results were not as forthcoming as expected. It was learned, after the fact, that there is always a "neutral period" when little happens despite the fact that a major change is under way. Once that idea became known, individuals were reported as being more relaxed and allowed the program to flow. Could police researchers as opposed to generic researchers have spared them from that experience? But, as Sacramento reported, they are currently moving beyond the sphere of most community policing initiatives by partnering with justice agencies, leading this researcher to wonder if a community policing philosophy will come full circle and neglect community members by partnering with those organizations who can help make more stops and more arrests?

Through all of the above discussion, Harris County, although a different type of agency than the others in that their top executive is elected and doesn't rely on officials for his job, developed a competitive police package where community members made an actual contract with a group to provide specific police services within specific limitations might be suggested that chief of police become an elected position? Fortunately, that's not my prerogative. But Harris County has created a community police strategy that is farther advanced than any other partnership arrangement studied and one that seems to have many advantages. One reason for this observation is that officer resistance and both civic and community leadership seem to represent, along with a lack of sound research practices, the primary obstacles or supports to quality police service such as proactive problem-solving strategies in all of the accounts presented by the eight of the nine agencies. Furthermore, it seems that a lot of the officer resistance is fueled by outsiders and unpolished police managers (who are supported by outsiders) more than from professional insiders, implying that city hall may be more political than practical when it comes to providing the public with quality police service. What can be seen as successful police service therefore relies heavily on departments with sound evaluation assistance and positive links to city hall. Dealing with community leadership might be less problematic if civic leaders were more supportive toward police practices. With all the evidence from this study, one single statement that might address policing would be that police managers control their agencies less often than politicians. Therefore, my best recommendation would be that police managers obtain managerial skills and, obtain information from many sources including practical assessment of police performance to help make informed decisions.

In Closing

Recognizing the importance of professional intervention to solve specific quality of life issues, as opposed to the typical police response of temporarily fixing a problem through an arrest, is vital to crime control efficiency. While police agencies need to control the root causes of crime, the problem is that if real crime is ignored, it will escalate both in frequency and in intensity. Because crime is a response in most cases to living conditions, relationship expectations, and pure selfishness, most of those issues are not police business. Therefore, finding the balance between professional intervention for the purposes of prevention, crime escalation, and police responsibility is the community policing task. Yet, officers, virtually at every rank, cannot make decisions about professional intervention if policy, regulations, and employment expectations dictate otherwise. The traditional, incident-driven police organization (and policing as an institution) must alter policy, regulations, and expectations to fit within a contemporary framework of policing strategies in the twenty-first century. Just as community policing models are different in different jurisdictions and within those jurisdictions, so to are community group techniques.

Primarily, police leadership must become a facilitator toward community needs, utilizing community resources such as expertise in collaboration with the police through a partnership to achieve a safe community. Community policing as a strategy helps people govern themselves.

Do You Know?

1. One of the reasons cited as to why some individuals do not contact the people when victimized was fear of the police. Under what conditions

might people fear the police? How can community policing initiatives help solve a fear of policing?

2. Some writers believe that community policing practices are inflated promises more often than reality. Can you explain why they might think that?

3. Can you explain why there is a different operationalized definition for each department and that no one model of community policing is compatible with every police agency?

4. Identify and describe the common threads of community policing initiatives running through each police agency experience.

5. Identify and describe the components of community policing strategies.

6. Identify the strongest recommendation made by the author concerning information and explain the rationale supporting his perspective.

7. Identify and describe the nine similar experiences that arose during the transitional experiences of the agencies in this study as they tried to move from a reactive to a proactive agency.

8. What were the primary obstacles that weakened community policing ventures? In what way might those obstacles stand in the way of quality police service?

9. What were the researchers' primary recommendations concerning community policing initiatives? In what way do you agree or disagree with those recommendations?

REFERENCES

Albritton, J. S. (1999). Simply inflated promises. In James Sewell and Steven Eggers (Eds.), *Controversial issues.* Needham Heights, MA: Allyn & Bacon.

Barrett, B. (1998, December 27). Taking aim at LAPD. *Daily News,* p. xx.

Bayley, D. H. (1998). *What works in policing.* New York: Oxford Press.

Bowers, W. J., & Hirsch, J. H. (1987). The impact of foot patrol staffing on crime and disorder in Boston: An unmet promise. *American Journal of Police, 6,* 17–44.

Bureau of Justice Assistance. (1994). *Understanding community policing: A framework for action.* Washington DC: U.S. Department of Justice, U.S. Government Printing Office (NCJ 148457).

Bureau of Justice Statistics. (1999). *Sourcebook of criminal justice statistics of 1998.* Washington, DC: U.S. Department of Justice, U.S. Government Printing Office [On-line]. Available: http://www.albany.edu/sourcebook/1995/pdf/ t232.pdf.

Cardarelli, A. P., McDevitt, J., & Baum, K. (1998). The rhetoric and reality of community policing in small and medium sized cities and towns. *Policing: An International Journal of Police Strategies & Management, 21*(3), 397–415.

Carter, D. L., & Radelet, L. A. (1999). *The police and the community.* Upper Saddle River, NJ: Prentice-Hall.

Champion, D. J., & Rush, G. E. (1997). *Policing in the community.* Upper Saddle River, NJ: Prentice-Hall.

Community Oriented Policing Services (COPS). (1999). Vice President Gore announces $12 million to help communities add 170 officers to America's streets. [On-line]. Available: http://www.usdoj.gov/cops/news_info/press_releases/default.htm

Community Policing Consortium. (2000). *Community police partnerships for COP.* [On-line]. Available: http://www.communitypolicing.org/about2.html

Community Policing Pages (CPP). (2000). Dedicated to continuing the work of Robert C. Trojanowicz. [On-line]. Available: http://www.concentric.net/ ~dwoods/horror.htm

Currie, E. (1999). Reflections on crime and criminology at the millenium. *Western Criminology Review 2*(1). [On-line]. Available: http://wcr.sonoma.edu/ v2n1/ currie.html

Dantzker, M. L. (2000). *Understanding today's police.* Upper Saddle River, NJ: Prentice-Hall.

DeLeon-Granados, W. (1999). *Travels through crime and place: Community building as crime control.* Boston, MA: Northeastern University Press.

273

DuBois, J., & Hartnett, S. M. (2002). Making the community side of community policing work: What needs to be done. In D. J. Stevens (Ed.), *Policing and community partnerships*. Upper Saddle River, NJ: Prentice-Hall.

Eck, J. E., & Rosenbaum, D. P. (1994). The new police order: Effectiveness, equity, and efficiency in community policing. In D. P. Rosenbaum (Ed.), *The challenge of community policing: Testing the promises* (pp. 3–23). London: Sage.

Frost, L. (1998, October). Protecting our environment. *Law & Order, 46*(10), 143–146.

Glasser, B., & Strauss, A. (1967). *The discovery of the grounded theory.* Strategies for Qualitative Research, Chicago: Aldine.

Goldstein, H. (1979). Improving policing: A problem oriented approach. *Crime & Delinquency, 25,* 236–258.

Goldstein, H. (1987). Toward community-oriented policing: Potential, basic requirements and threshold questions. *Crime & Delinquency, 33*(1), 6–30.

Goldstein, H. (1990). *Problem-oriented policing.* New York: McGraw Hill.

Green, J. R., Bergman, W. T., & McLaughlin, E. J. (1994). Implementing community policing: Cultural and structural change in police organizations. In D. P. Rosebaum (Ed.), *The challenge of community policing: Testing the promises* (pp. 92–109). Newbury Park, CA: Sage.

Howard, G., & Tweedy, E. M. (1980). Police civil liability—supervisory liability. (NCJ 67438). [On-line]. Available: http://excalib1.aspensys.com/scripts/rwisapi.dll/@abstracts.env.

Klockars, C. B. (1985). *The idea of police.* Beverly Hills, CA: Sage Publications.

Klockars, C. B. (1988). The rhetoric of community policing. In J. R. Greene and S. D. Mastrofski (Eds.), *Community policing: Rhetoric or reality?* New York: Praeger.

Kraska, P. B., & Kappeler, V. E. (1997). Militarizing American police: The rise and normalization of paramilitary units. *Social Problems, 44,* 1–18.

Liability Reporter. (1999). [On-line]. Available: http://aele.org/.

Liou, K. T., & Savage, E. (1999). Citizen perception of community policing impact. *Journal of Public Administration and Management* [On-line]. Available: http://www.pamij.com/liou1.html.

Maguire, E. R. (1997). Structural change in large municipal police organization during the community policing era. *Justice Quarterly, 14,* 547–576.

Manning, P. K. (1997). *Police work: The social organization of policing.* Prospect Heights, IL: Waveland Press.

Masterson, M., & Stevens, D. J. (2002). The value of measuring community policing performance in Madison, Wisconsin. In D. J. Stevens (Ed.) *Policing and community partnerships.* Upper Saddle River, NJ: Prentice-Hall.

Mastrofski, S. (1983). The police and non-crime services. In G. Whitaker and C. D. Phillips (Eds.), *Evaluating performance of criminal justice agencies.* Beverly Hills, CA: Sage Publications.

McNamara, J. H. (1967). Uncertainties in police work: The relevance of police recruits' background and training. In D. J. Bordua (Ed.), *The police: Six sociological essays* (pp. 163–252). New York: John Wiley & Sons.

Moore, M. H. (1994). Research synthesis and policy implications. In D. P. Rosenbaum (Ed.), *The challenge of community policing; Testing the promises* (pp. 285–299). London: Sage.

Moore, M. H., & Trojanowicz, R. (2000). Policing and the fear of crime. In W. M. Oliver (Ed.) *Community policing: Classical readings* (pp. 83–95). Upper Saddle River, NJ: Prentice-Hall.

Nowicki, D. E. (1998). Mixed messages. In G. Alpert and A. Piquero (Eds.), *Community policing* (pp. 265–274). Prospect Heights, IL: Waveland Press.

Oliver, W. M. (2000). *Community policing: Classical readings.* Upper Saddle River, NJ: Prentice-Hall.

Parks, R. B., Mastrofski, S. D., Dejong, C., & Gray, M. K. (1999). How officers spend their time with the community. *Justice Quarterly, 16*(3), 483–517.

Pate, A. M. (1989). Community oriented policing in Baltimore. In D. J. Kenney (Ed.), *Police and policing: Contemporary issues.* New York: Praeger.

Peak, K. J., & Glensor, R. W. (1999). *Community policing and problem solving: Strategies and practices.* Upper Saddle River, NJ: Prentice-Hall.

Police Executive Research Forum. (1996). *Themes and variations in community policing: Case studies in community policing.* Washington DC: Police Foundation.

Powerful Partnerships. (1998). *Twenty crime prevention strategies that work for refugees, law enforcement, and communities.* Washington DC: National Crime Prevention Council [On-line]. Available: http://www.weprevent.org.

Riechers, L. M., & Roberg, R. R. (1990). Community policing: A critical review of underlying assumptions. *Journal of Police Science and Administration, 17*(2), 105–114.

Skogan, W. G. (1990). *Disorder and decline: Crime and the spiral of decay in American neighborhoods.* New York: The Free Press.

Skogan, W. G., & Hartnett, S. M. (1997). *Community policing, Chicago style.* New York: Oxford University Press.

Skogan, W. G., Hartnett, S. M., DuBois, J., Comey, J. T., Kaiser, M. & Lovig, J. H. (1999). *On the beat: Police and community problem solving.* Boulder, CO: Westview Press.

Stevens, D. J. (1992a). Examining inmate attitudes: Do prisons deter crime? *The State of Corrections—American Correctional Association: 1991,* 272–279.

Stevens, D. J. (1992b). Research note: The death sentence and inmate attitudes. *Crime & Delinquency, 38.*

Stevens, D. J. (1994). The depth of imprisonment and prisonization: Levels of security and prisoners' anticipation of future violence. *Howard Journal of Criminal Justice, 33*(2), 137–157.

Stevens, D. J. (1997a). Influences of early childhood experiences on subsequent criminology violent behaviour. *Studies on Crime and Crime Prevention, 6*(1), 34–50.

Stevens, D. J. (1997b). Origins of prison gangs in North Carolina. *Journal of Gang Research, 4*(4), 23–35.

Stevens, D. J. (1997c). Prison regime and drugs. *Howard Journal of Criminal Justice, 36*(1), 14–27.

Stevens, D. J. (1997d). Violence begets violence. *Corrections Compendium. The National Journal for Corrections, 22*(12), 1–3.

Stevens, D. J. (1998a). The impact of time-served and regime on prisoners' anticipation of crime: Female prisonization effects. *Howard Journal of Criminal Justice, 37*(2), 188–205.

Stevens, D. J. (1998b). Incarcerated women, crime, and drug addiction. *The Criminologist, 22*(1), 3–14.

Stevens, D. J. (1998c). Mandatory arrest, spouse abuse, & accelerated rates of victimization: Attitudes of victims and officers. *The Criminologist.*

Stevens, D. J. (1998d). Urban communities and homicide: Why American blacks resort to murder. *Police and Society, 8,* 253–267.

Stevens, D. J. (1998e). What do law enforcement officers think about their work? *Law Enforcement Journal, 5*(1), 60–62.

Stevens, D. J. (1998f). *Inside the mind of a serial rapist.* Bethesda, MD: Austin & Winfield.

Stevens, D. J. (1999a). American police resolutions. *Police Journal, LXXII*(2), 140–150.

Stevens, D. J. (1999b). Corruption among narcotic officers: A study of innocence and integrity. *Journal of Police and Criminal Psychology, 14*(2), 1–11.

Stevens, D. J. (1999c, December) College educated officers. *Law and Order, 47*(12), 37–41.

Stevens, D. J. (1999d, September). Police officer stress. *Law and Order, 47*(9), 77–82.

Stevens, D. J. (1999f, March). Police tactical units and community response. *Law and Order, 47*(3), 48–52.

Stevens, D. J. (1999g). Stress and the American police officer. *Police Journal, LXXII*(3).

Stevens, D. J. (2000a). Civil liability and arrest decision. *Police Journal, LXXIV,* 235–259.

Stevens, D. J. (2002). Community policing and police leadership. In Dennis J. Stevens (Ed.), *Policing and community partnerships.* (pp. 185–210). Upper Saddle River, NJ: Prentice-Hall.

Taylor, R. W., Fritsch, E. J., & Caeti, T. J. (1998, May/June). Core challenges facing community policing: The emperor still has no clothes. *ACJS Today, XVII*(1).

Tyson, G. (1997). Community policing in North Carolina. Unpublished research. Available at the North Carolina Justice Academy, Salemburg, NC.

Van Maanen, J. (1974). Working the street. In Herbert Jacob (Ed.), *The potential for reform of criminal justice.* Thousand Oaks, CA: Sage Publications.

Walker, S. (1984). Broken windows and fractured history: The use and misuse of history in recent police analysis. *Justice Quarterly, 1*(1), 75–90.

Wilson, J. Q., & Kelling, G. L. (1982, March). The police and neighborhood safety. *The Atlantic Monthly,* pp. 29–38.

Worrall, J. L., & Marenin, O. (1998). Emerging liability issues in the implementation of adoption of community oriented policing. *Policing, 21*(1), 121–136 [Online]. Available: http://excalib1.aspensys.com/.

Wycoff, M. A., & Skogan, W. G. (1998). Community policing in Madison: An analysis of implementation and impact. In David H. Bayley (ed.), *What works in policing* (pp. 158–173). New York: Oxford University Press.

Index

Abandoned vehicles, 75
Accessibility, 69
Administrative agents of change, 187
Agency resources, 73–74
Agents of change, 186–187
Alarm monitoring ordinance, 190
Alert Neighbors programs, 37
Analysis, 15. *See also* Data collection
Animal control services, 38
Are You OK?, 190
Arrest record, 146
Assessment, 15
    Broken Arrow Police Department,
      51–53
    Columbus Division of Police, 103,
      106–107, 110–114
    Fayetteville Police Department,
      199–200
    Harris County Precinct 4 Constable's
      Office, 161
    Lansing Police Department, 131
    St. Petersburg Police Department,
      211–213, 217
Attorney, 196–197
Automobiles, abandoned and junk, 75
Auto Theft Action Camp, 190

Bike patrols, 78, 151, 158
Block organizing, 207
Broken Arrow Police Department,
    26–27, 59
    background information, 37
    citizen survey summary, 39, 42–45
    city name, 36
    commitments, 29–31, 36

community-based programs, 31
community members' comments,
    57–59
crime statistics, 39
example of success, 54–55
implementation plan, 53
initiatives, 45–53
jurisdiction demographics, 23
leadership, 27–29
plan, 33–34
police officer comments, 56–57
programs, 37–38
rationale, 27
reshaping programs, 32
resistance to change, 35–36
schedule, 34–35
skills practice, 54
training, 53–54
Web site, 20
Broken Arrow Police Reserves, 38
Burglary follow-up, 87
Buy/bust operations, 83–84

Camden Police Department, 228–229,
    249–250
    comments, 245–249
    current status, 240
    decentralization, 233
    Hill, William, 237–238
    history and demographics, 230–231
    implementation, 232–237
    jurisdiction demographics, 23
    Mischief Night, 238–240, 241–245
    problem-oriented policing and
      partnerships, 240–245

problems, 229
profile, 231–232
Web site, 20
Canine unit, 157
Career Criminal/Liaison Unit, 98–99
Cars, abandoned and junk, 75
Change
  agents of, 186
  Broken Arrow Police Department,
    35–36
  Columbus Division of Police, 101–103
  organizational, 261–263
Child Development Community Policing
    Program (CDCPP), 81–82
Child safety programs, 38
Citizen commentary. *See* Commentary
Citizen expectations, 72–73
Citizen recruitment, 264–266
Citizen representation
  Broken Arrow Police Department,
    45–47, 49–50
  Columbus Division of Police, 105, 106
  Lansing Police Department, 129–130
  Metropolitan-Nashville Police
    Department, 69
  St. Petersburg Police Department,
    220–221
Citizens on Patrol, 38
Citizens Police Academy (CPA), 38, 150
Citizens United to Track Truants
    (CUTT), 132–139
Citizen survey
  Broken Arrow Police Department, 39,
    42–45
  Lansing Police Department, 142–144
Citizens Volunteer Auxiliary, 190
Civilian firearms training, 190
Client perspective, 13
Code Enforcement Team, 190
Collaborative strategies, Broken Arrow
    Police Department, 48–49
Columbus Division of Police, 91–92,
    114–115
  crime reports, 120
  evaluation, 110–114
  initiatives, 105–107

Jackson, James G., 109–110
jurisdiction demographics, 23
MAPP, 94–97
MAPPSTAT Crime Strategy Meetings,
    103–105
obstacles encountered by, 92–94
organizational structure, 116–117
program highlights, 118
Strategic Response Bureau, 97–103
training, 107–109
uniform crime index offenses, 119
Web site, 20
Commentary
  Broken Arrow Police Department,
    57–59
  Camden Police Department, 245–249
  Fayetteville Police Department,
    200–202
  Harris County Precinct 4 Constable's
    Office, 162–164
  Lansing Police Department, 140–141
  St. Petersburg Police Department,
    222, 223–225
Commitments
  Broken Arrow Police Department,
    29–31, 36
  Sacramento Police Department,
    174–176, 177–178
Communication, 69
Community-based programs, 31
Community cleanups, 76–77
Community involvement. *See* Citizen
    representation
Community liaison section, 98
Community meetings, 68, 79–80
Community oversight, 215–216
Community policing, 1–2, 271
  aims and issues emphasized, 2–3
  and community support, 266
  decision-making, 267
  defined, 7–8
  events motivating, 258–259
  existence of, 253–255
  limitations, 5–6
  motivators for, 9–11
  neglected areas of, 252

objectives of, 15–16
obstacles, 3–5
operational definition, 257–268
organizational change, 261–263
performance measures, 260–261
perspectives, 12–14
philosophy, 263–264
problems of, 16–17
and problem solving, 14–15
programs, 267–268
rationale and philosophy, 8–9
recruiting community members,
    264–266
theory, 255–257
training, 260
Web sites, 19–20
See also specific case studies
Community policing case studies, 271
agencies represented, 6
commitments, 24–25
data collection, 6–7
expectations, 17
general observations, 268–271
impressions, 253
jurisdiction demographics, 23
text format, 17
Web sites, 20
See also specific case studies
Community Policing Consortium, 19
Community Policing Pages, 19
Community Policing Television (CPTV),
    190–191
Community relations, 191
Community resources, 73–74
Community revitalization perspective,
    12
Community services, 124–125
Community support, 67–68, 266
Community Watch coordinator, 191
Community Watch Council, 191
Contract deputy program, 152–154
Crime analysis, 38, 191
CRIMELINE, 38
Crime prevention
    Broken Arrow Police Department, 38
    Fayetteville Police Department, 191

Harris County Precinct 4 Constable's
    Office, 151
Crime rates
    Metropolitan-Nashville Police
        Department, 62–63
    Sacramento Police Department,
        178–179
Crime reports, 105, 120
Crime response, 155–156
Crime statistics
    Broken Arrow Police Department, 39
    Fayetteville Police Department, 198
Crimestoppers, 191
Crime-targeted strategies, Broken Arrow
        Police Department, 47–48
Criminal Information Unit, 99
Cultural agents of change, 186
Culture, community-oriented policing
        as, 173
Curfew, 80
Customer perspective, 13

DARE, 151
Data collection, 6–7
Debris cleanups, 76–77
Decentralization
    Camden Police Department, 233
    Columbus Division of Police, 107
    Fayetteville Police Department, 200
    Lansing Police Department, 131
    St. Petersburg Police Department, 220
Decision-making process, 267
    Broken Arrow Police Department, 47–49
    Columbus Division of Police, 105–106
    Lansing Police Department, 130
Demographics
    Camden Police Department, 230–231
    Harris County Precinct 4, 148
    jurisdiction, 23
Department attorney, 196–197
Deployment, 12, 47
Divisions, Sacramento Police
        Department, 168–170
Domestic violence units, 37, 151, 157
Drug prevention, 38
Drug stings, 84

Effectiveness-based community policing model, 16
Efficiency-based community policing model, 15
Enforcement section, 98
Enforcement strategies
  Metropolitan-Nashville Police Department, 82–87
  Texas, 154
Environmental issues, 74–78
Equity-based community policing model, 15
Evaluation. *See* Assessment

False Alarm Responses, 199
Family Intervention Team (FIT), 191
Fayetteville Police Athletic League Judo Program, 191
Fayetteville Police Department, 182–183, 202–203
  commentary, 200–202
  crime statistics, 198
  department attorney, 196–197
  description, 184
  Hansen, Ronald, 193–196
  historical events, 184, 186–188
  initiatives, 198–200
  jurisdiction demographics, 23
  organizational chart, 185
  profile, 183
  programs, 188–193
  training, 197–198
  Web site, 20
Federal Bureau of Investigation (FBI), 19
Feedback
  Broken Arrow Police Department, 47–49
  Columbus Division of Police, 105–106
  Metropolitan-Nashville Police Department, 69
Firearms training, civilian, 190
Focus groups, 104
Funding
  Broken Arrow Police Department, 50–51

Columbus Division of Police, 106
  Fayetteville Police Department, 198–199
  Lansing Police Department, 130
  St. Petersburg Police Department, 223–225

Gang intervention, 191
Gang prevention, 38
Generalists, 172–173
Governmental agencies, 67, 73–74
GREAT, 151
Grove View Terrace Substation, 191

Hansen, Ronald, 193–196
Harris County Precinct 4 Constable's Office, 147, 164–165
  assessment, 161
  bike patrol, 158
  canine unit, 157
  commentary, 162–164
  contract deputy program, 152–154
  crime response, 155–156
  demographics, 148
  domestic violence unit, 157
  functions of, 147–148
  Hickman, Ron, 160
  hiring-out practices, 151–152
  historical events, 149
  jurisdiction demographics, 23
  mission statement, 148–149
  Moore, Dick, 158–159
  mounted patrol, 156
  profile, 155
  programs, 150–151
  rationale, 149–150
  Texas law enforcement, 154
  training, 160–161
  Web site, 20
Hickman, Ron, 160
Hill, William, 237–238
Hiring-out practices, 151–152
Historical events
  Broken Arrow Police Department, 51
  Camden Police Department, 230–231
  Columbus Division of Police, 106

and community policing, 258–259
Fayetteville Police Department, 184, 186–188, 199
Harris County Precinct 4 Constable's Office, 149
Lansing Police Department, 130
St. Petersburg Police Department, 207–210
Homeless Project Program, 191

Implementation
Broken Arrow Police Department, 53
Camden Police Department, 232–237, 242–245
Columbus Division of Police, 100–101
Metropolitan-Nashville Police Department, 70
St. Petersburg Police Department, 209–210
Information Program, 104
Initiatives
Broken Arrow Police Department, 45–53
Columbus Division of Police, 105–107
Fayetteville Police Department, 198–200
Lansing Police Department, 129–131
Metropolitan-Nashville Police Department, 70
St. Petersburg Police Department, 219–220
Internal mobilization, 172
Investigative section, 98–99

Jackson, James G., 109–110
Junior public safety program, 151
Junk vehicles, 75
Jurisdiction demographics, 23
Juvenile Restitution Program, 191
Juvenile strategies, 78–82

K-9's, 191

Lansing Police Department, 121–122, 144–145
arrest record, 146

citizen survey, 142–144
community officer activities, 131
community president commentary, 140–141
community services, 124–125
initiatives, 129–131
jurisdiction demographics, 23
North Precinct, 125–127
observations and departmental influences, 122–124
and parole officers, 141–142
South Precinct, 127–129
strategies, 132–139
training, 132
Web site, 20
Law enforcement strategies. *See* Enforcement strategies
Leadership, 27–29
Legitimacy, 13–14

MAPP (Mission Aligned Policing Philosophy), 94–97
MAPPSTAT Crime Strategy Meetings, 103–105
Media, 205–207
Meetings. *See* Community meetings
Mentor programs, Lansing Police Department, 136–139
Metropolitan-Nashville Police Department, 61–62, 88–89
communication, 69
community meetings, 68
community member expectations, 72–73
community policing guide, 66
community support, 67–68
crime rates and experiences, 62–63
departmental objectives, 63–64
enforcement strategies, 82–87
environmental issues, 74–78
and governmental agencies, 67
implementation, 70
jurisdiction demographics, 23
juvenile strategies, 78–82
mission statement, 65
philosophy, 66–67

plan, 64–65
project significance, 64
rationale, 66
relationship building, 70–72
resources, 73–74
success stories, 87–88
Web site, 20
Milazzo, Carl, 196–197
Mischief Night, 238–240, 241–245
Mission Aligned Policing Philosophy.
    See MAPP
Mission statement
    Harris County Precinct 4 Constable's
        Office, 148–149
    Metropolitan-Nashville Police
        Department, 65
    Sacramento Police Department, 167
Mobile One, 192
Mobile Two, 192
Moore, Dick, 158–159
Mounted Patrol
    Fayetteville Police Department, 192
    Harris County Precinct 4 Constable's
        Office, 156

Nashville. *See* Metropolitan-Nashville
    Police Department
National Criminal Justice Reference
    Service, 20
National Night Out, 38
Neighborhood Improvement Team, 192
Neighborhood meetings. *See*
    Community meetings
Neighborhood Notifier, 77–78
Neighborhood organizations, 126–127,
    128
Neighborhood-oriented community
    policing, 15
Neighborhood Watch, 128, 135–136
Neighborhood Youth Activity (NYA), 127

Officer Blue, 192
Officer Friendly, 192
Opportunity, 174
Organizational change, 261–263
Oversight, 215–216

Parole hearing objection committee,
    86–87
Parole officers, 141–142
Partnerships
    Camden Police Department, 240–245
    Sacramento Police Department,
        177–178
    St. Petersburg Police Department, 216
Performance measures, 260–261
Philosophy
    community policing, 8–9, 263–264
    Metropolitan-Nashville Police
        Department, 66–67
Planning
    Broken Arrow Police Department,
        33–34, 53
    Metropolitan-Nashville Police
        Department, 64–65
Police Band "Roll'RZ," 192
Police Executive Research Forum
    (PERF), 19
Police officer commentary. *See*
    Commentary
Police Reserve Program, 192
Police resources, 73–74
Police Surgeon Program, 192
Policing theory, 255–257
Political agents of change, 186
Press, 205–207
Problem identification. *See* SARA;
    Screening
Problem-oriented policing, 15
    Camden Police Department, 240–245
    Fayetteville Police Department, 193
    St. Petersburg Police Department, 210
Problem solving, 12–13, 14–15. *See also*
    specific case studies
Profile
    Camden Police Department, 231–232
    Fayetteville Police Department, 183
    Harris County Precinct 4 Constable's
        Office, 155
    Sacramento Police Department, 167
Programs
    Broken Arrow Police Department,
        31–32, 37–38

changing, 267–268
Fayetteville Police Department,
    188–193
Harris County Precinct 4 Constable's
    Office, 150–151
Lansing Police Department, 128–129
Sacramento Police Department, 171
    See also specific programs
Prostitution operations, 84
Prostitution stings, 84–85
Pugh, George D., 234–237

"Quality of life" laws, 86

Rape Aggression Defense (RAD), 151
Rationale
    Broken Arrow Police Department, 27
    community policing, 8–9
    Harris County Precinct 4 Constable's
        Office, 149–150
    Metropolitan-Nashville Police
        Department, 66
Recruiting, 264–266
Reengineering report, 104–105
Reengineering teams, 104
Relationship building, 70–72
Repeat Offenders Program, 192
Reports
    Columbus Division of Police, 104–105
    Metropolitan-Nashville Police
        Department, 69
    St. Petersburg Police Department, 205
Representation. *See* Citizen
    representation
Resources, 73–74
Response, 15. *See also* Crime response
Retreats, 213–214, 217–218
Reverse drug stings, 84
Reverse prostitution stings, 84–85
Roadblocks, 85

Sacramento Police Department,
    166–167, 179
    community-oriented policing, 171–177
    crime rates, 178–179
    divisions, 168–170

jurisdiction demographics, 23
    mission statement, 167
    partnerships, 177–178
    profile, 167
    programs, 171
    uniform crime report, 180
    Web site, 20
St. Petersburg Police Department,
    204–205, 225–226
    assessment, 211–213, 217
    block organizing, 207
    commentary, 222, 223–225
    community involvement, 220–221
    community oversight, 215–216
    current status, 218–219
    decentralization, 220
    funding, 223–225
    historical events, 207–210
    implementation, 209–210
    initiatives, 219–220
    jurisdiction demographics, 23
    and media, 205–207
    national recognition, 210–211
    partnerships, 216
    problem-oriented policing, 210
    reorganization, 214–215
    reports, 205
    retreats, 213–214, 217–218
    training, 221–222
    Web site, 20
Santa Fe Substation, 192
SARA, 15
Saturation patrols, 85
Schedules, 34–35
Screening, 15. *See also* SARA
Senior citizens, crime prevention for, 38
Sex offenders, registered information
    on, 38
Skateboarding, 55
Specialists, 172–173
Sting operations, 84–85
Strategic goals, 176–177
Strategic-oriented community policing,
    14
Strategic Response Bureau (SRB),
    97–103

Subsidies. *See* Funding
Support. *See* Community support

Technical agents of change, 186
Texas law enforcement, 154
Tobacco prevention, 38
Trading Card Program, 192
Traffic calming and enforcement
    requests, 38
Training, 260
    Broken Arrow Police Department,
        53–54
    Columbus Division of Police, 107–109
    Fayetteville Police Department,
        197–198
    Harris County Precinct 4 Constable's
        Office, 160–161
    Lansing Police Department, 132
    Sacramento Police Department,
        173–174
    St. Petersburg Police Department,
        221–222

Trash cleanups, 76–77
Truancy, 80, 132–135
Trust, 33–34

Undercover operations
    buy/bust, 83–84
    prostitution, 84
Uniform crime index offenses, 119
Uniform crime report, 180

Vacation Watch Program, 151
Vehicles, abandoned and junk, 75
Victim assistance, 151, 192
Violent Crime Task Force, 193

Watch orders, 38
Web sites, 19–20
"We Care Bear" Program, 193
Wilson, Gilbert "Whip," 239–240

Zone Investigator Unit, 98